CILIN II:
A SOLO SAILING
ODYSSEY

EDGAR D. WHITCOMB

Former Governor of Indiana

authorHOUSE®

AuthorHouse™
1663 Liberty Drive
Bloomington, IN 47403
www.authorhouse.com
Phone: 1-800-839-8640

First published by AuthorHouse 11/14/2011

ISBN: 978-1-4567-6806-5 (e)
ISBN: 978-1-4567-6807-2 (dj)
ISBN: 978-1-4567-6808-9 (sc)

Library of Congress Control Number: 2011907093

Printed in the United States of America

ACKNOWLEDGEMENTS

THE COMPILATION OF THIS BOOK WAS A team effort. Thanking them in no way shows the gratitude I feel for their immeasurable help in guiding me through my journey but acknowledging their efforts here shows my deepest admiration for their efforts.

Dr. Rosemary Messick, Dr. Frank Sandage, and Chuck Poehlein provided counsel and guidance in preparation for the manuscript. Hank Williams provided me with a Trimble Galaxy INMARSAT-C satellite radio that tabulated daily position reports, and kept me steering the CILIN II in the right direction throughout my journey. Mrs. Judy Van Osdol sacrificed her lunch hour to type the daily position reports and Mr. Sidney H. Showalter tabulated segments of the cruise. Mary Evelyn Gayer committed many hours typing the first drafts of this manuscript, and Stephanie Thompson and Deborah Seibert who assisted in the final draft of the manuscript.

This book has been quite an adventure. I am eternally grateful to all those men and women, who in the course of my journey, gave me aid and who sheltered me from the storm; including the selfless men and women aboard the helicopter and the fishermen who pulled me from the coral reefs.

Thank you all for your hopes and prayers for my safe journey while circumnavigating the globe and for all the help you provided me while writing of my solo sailing odyssey.

— Edgar D. Whitcomb

Contents

FOREWORD

AT A TIME IN HIS LIFE WHEN most of us kick back in the easy chair and avoid as much responsibility as possible, Edgar Whitcomb set out on an adventure that would take him around the world and last for six years.

It would be a test of courage and endurance few of us ever experience. His courage had been tested before – in WWII – much of which he documented in his book, *Escape from Corregidor*. But this would be different – a seat-of-the-pants adventure for which he was ill prepared.

What prompted this man, at 71, to sail solo not only the Pacific but the Atlantic Ocean with no previous sailing experience, knowing full well that perils of weather, piracy, injury or health could end not only his adventure but his life at any point along the way?

In 1986 Edgar was at a crossroads of his life. He needed a new direction and at that time he decided that life on a sailboat would be the greatest thing a person could do. He thought thoroughly about it, he dreamed about it, and a chance reading of a poem gave the impetus he needed to make up his mind.

Finally, he set out on his journey, not knowing how far it would take him, but at each port of call he decided to keep going. He would eventually circumnavigate the globe – most of it alone.

The great naturalist, John Muir, said "The man who does not commune with nature is in danger of losing his soul." Edgar's will was tested to the limit on that journey and there is no doubt his soul found rejuvenation and a new purpose and peace from communing with the sea.

In the years since that epic journey, it has been his crowning achievement to affect, in a positive way, the lives of all who have come to know him.

— Chuck Poehlein

My Odyssey Begins

THE WHITCOMB ODYSSEY MAY HAVE BEGUN IN May, 1633 when Puritan John Whitcomb boarded a sailboat in Weymouth Harbor, England to sail to America. It continued 356 years later when I boarded a sailboat in Gibraltar to sail to America.

Our circumstances were remarkably different in many ways. John was in his forties and sailing on a very large sailboat. His wife, Frances Cogan, 11-year old Catherine, 9-year old John, 7-year old Jonathan, 6-year old Robert, 4-year old James and 2-year old Johanne, together with 15 other families, accompanied him.

The miseries and suffering of these families in their effort to find a new life for themselves in America can only be left to speculation at this late date. One thing known for certain is that 2-year old Johanne, their baby daughter, died during the trip.

When I sailed, I was 71 years of age and alone on a 30-foot sailboat, and starting a new adventure of my own volition.

Life in colonial Lancaster, Massachusetts, where they settled, was austere and hazardous in finding food and reasonable shelter from the elements, together with attacks by savage Indians that took the life of another family member.

After some 30 years of the primitive life, eight of which were spent living on Lot No. 33 in Lancaster, it was written that John Whitcomb met the inevitable hour. He died at the age of 74 and was laid to rest with the other forefathers of the hamlet in the old burial ground. Today no fragment of even a battered stone marks his resting place. But the heritage of that ancient Puritan is in the lives of his thousands of descendants who, over the years, have spread to the ends of the earth to become farmers, factory workers, bankers, lawyers, teachers and even a space scientist.

One of the thousands of descendants of immigrant John was James Whitcomb, who served as the eighth governor of the State of Indiana. Hoosier Poet Laureate James Whitcomb Riley was named after him. As a direct descendant of immigrant John Whitcomb, I also served as governor of Indiana from 1969 to 1973.

I was born on November 6, 1917 in Hayden, a town of 225 people in south-central Indiana. The town was comprised of a school (first through twelfth grades), two general stores, three blacksmith shops, a Methodist church and a Baptist church. U.S. Highway 50 traversed the town and the B&O Railroad bordered the south side of town. More important to us in the early days was Six Mile Creek that passed a quarter of a mile east where we spent many hours swimming and fishing in the summertime.

Growing up in such a community offered many opportunities for recreation in the school and church. There were basketball and baseball games, class plays and because of the size of the school, I was able to participate in all of the activities. I also played trumpet in our five-piece orchestra.

During my sophomore year, at the age of 15, I started thinking about what I wanted to do in my life. One thing I knew for certain was that I did not want to grow up and get tied down in Hayden without seeing some of the important places in history. It had happened to my father and his father before him. Both had gotten married and settled down without ever having the opportunity to travel and see important places in history.

In the year of 1933, the country was in the throes of the great depression. My father's employment was in an automobile factory in New Castle, 80 miles from Hayden. I saw him only on weekends. But all four of my grandparents lived nearby and provided good company for me.

In those days there were no field trips in Hayden for school children to visit Chicago, New York or Washington, D.C. as in later years. If I traveled to those places, I knew I would have to hitchhike or ride freight trains. I thought about it over and over and saved $20.00 from working for neighboring farmers. First, I would go to Chicago to visit the World's Fair and stay with my aunt. She would be surprised at my arrival because I had no intention of letting her know of my future plans.

In order to make my trip, it was necessary that I leave home without telling my parents. They would not have given me permission. So on a Sunday morning in June, 1933, under the pretense of going to Sunday School, I walked past the church to the highway a quarter of a mile away where I had hidden a small travel bag with toilet articles and extra under garments.

While waiting for a ride, I looked back across the fields to my old hometown of Hayden. Looking back across the B&O Railroad track was the cemetery where a large stone marked the grave of my great grandfather, Albert Whitcomb. In 1834 at the age of seven years, he had traveled with his family in a convoy of 40 wagons from Steuben County, New York to settle in Indiana. Then there was the two-story brick school building where I would be enrolling for my junior year when I returned.

Soon Sunday school would be in session. As I viewed the peacefulness of the village, I realized that life would be exciting for me in the days ahead, but I had no idea how exciting they would be.

As I stood there in the morning sun, I suddenly had some second thoughts about making my trip. Was I doing the right thing? Would I get in trouble? I did not know anyone else who had made such a trip.

Life at home had been pleasant and we were a very happy family with my loving mother and father, two sisters and a younger brother. I did not have any good reason for leaving home other than a desire to see those important places in history.

My thoughts of home were suddenly interrupted when a Model A Ford driven by a middle-aged man stopped to give me a ride. We visited and he was surprised to learn that I intended to catch a freight train to Chicago. He was glad to let me off at the Pennsylvania Railroad tracks in Seymour.

I waited for more than an hour until I heard the whistle of an approaching train, which caused my heart to beat a little faster. Soon I would be on my way. It was an exciting moment when the train stopped and I climbed aboard a boxcar.

It was nightfall when I finally reached Chicago. There I found an elevated train that took me near the address of my aunt. She was, of course, surprised and glad to see me and welcomed me with open arms. The next day I mailed a one cent post card to my mother telling her of my whereabouts, a practice I exercised every day when possible for the duration of my trip.

After a week in Chicago, viewing the wonders of the 1933 World's Fair, I said goodbye to my aunt without telling her of my intentions to travel to the eastern part of the country. I rode the South Shore electric train to Hammond, Indiana where I boarded a freight train headed east.

I climbed to the top of a boxcar as the train picked up speed. It was mid-afternoon with clear, warm weather as we plowed across the open countryside of northern Indiana but in the evening the weather became chilly as the sun dipped below the horizon. Then it became very cold and dark with no moon to be seen in the sky.

I felt I needed to get a place out of the cold wind but to move from one boxcar to another in the black of night was a problem. There was nothing to do but crawl to the end of the car, stand up and jump to the next car. I did it successfully several times. Had the freight train passed under a low bridge as I jumped from car to car in the black of night, this story would not have been written.

My gamble paid off with dividends. I came upon an unbelievable situation. I found a car with warm air coming out from under the catwalk. I stretched my body along it and felt the warmth of air emitting from below. I concluded that I was on a car loaded with turkeys or chickens. Whatever the source of the heat, it provided warmth for my body throughout the night.

When the train stopped for a long time at dawn, I learned that I was on the outskirts of Fort Wayne, Indiana. Near the track was a wooded area known as The Jungle, where a number of hobos congregated, waiting for the next train. It was good news that there was a bakery within walking distance where I could buy a sack of day-old donuts for a nickel and a quart of milk for ten cents. They would be my favorite rations for days to come.

After several days riding freight trains and hitchhiking, I finally reached Boston and stood at the harbor where my immigrant ancestor, John Whitcomb, had first landed in America with his family exactly 300 years earlier. It was difficult for me to imagine the wooded forest and muddy harbor that greeted those immigrants of so many years ago.

I found the Old North Church and Beacon Hill, and then hitchhiked on to the south to see the famous Plymouth Rock before proceeding on to New York. On Long Island, I visited Roosevelt Field where Charles A. Lindberg had taken off to be the first person to fly solo across the Atlantic Ocean. It occurred to me that he had made his famous flight just six years before my visit there.

My odyssey took me on to Washington, D.C. where I toured the White House. At 15 years of age and in my wildest dream, I could not have imagined that 40 years later I would be a guest of the President of the United States on many occasions. After the White House tour, I walked to the Washington Monument and climbed to the top as was possible at that time.

It was mid-July in 1933 and my trip had been a great success. I had seen all the things I wanted to see, Boston Bay where the famous Boston Tea Party had taken place, the Old North Church, New York City, Roosevelt Field where Lindberg had taken off for his trip across the Atlantic, the White House and the Washington Monument. As I departed Washington, D.C., it occurred to me that school in Hayden would not be starting for more than a month. I was sure that I would have time to hitchhike to Florida and be back in time to start my junior year. It was an easy decision, so I headed south.

Traffic was very light on the highways in the state of Virginia and I made very slow progress hitchhiking. In the evening I found a railroad station and decided to wait for a freight train. Luck was with me because it was not long before I heard the whistle of a train approaching the station and headed south. When it stopped, I was surprised to find a number of young men in one of the boxcars. I was happy they welcomed me and learned that they were from Maine and that they were also headed for Florida. After traveling alone for so many days, it was good to have company.

Out the open door of the boxcar we could see the countryside of Virginia as darkness closed in but with the darkness came the cold air again. There was no relief from it as I had found on my first night out of Chicago when I got comfort from warm air from a carload of chickens.

Throughout the night the rattling of the wheels on the rails provided a rhapsody to be punctuated from time to time by the forlorn sound of the train's whistle. From time to time, the train stopped in small towns along the way. At such times, new passengers climbed into our car or departed. Most of them were African-Americans coming aboard for a short ride.

After a very long, miserable night, the train came to a stop and everyone aboard jumped off and starting running across the open fields as if the train were about to explode. I followed suit. I had no idea why we were running and was unable to ask anyone. I noticed that when the African-Americans came to a cottage occupied by African-Americans, they stopped and mingled with the people.

At last, I reached a highway and held up my thumb to the first car. I was in luck. It stopped, but my luck was short lived. Out jumped the Sheriff. He grabbed me and pushed me into the car. It was then that I noticed that the other occupants of the car were some of my friends from Maine who, like me, had been on their way to Florida.

After a short ride, we passed a road sign that told us we were entering Hamlet, North Carolina. At the City Hall, we were ushered to the courtroom where we were told that we were being charged with riding a train without a ticket and if found guilty would be sentenced to 30 days in the North Carolina chain gang. I had never heard of such a thing.

There were about six of us standing in a line and each one pleaded guilty to the charge except me. I remembered that my grandfather Whitcomb, who was a Justice of the Peace back home, had said that many people plead guilty when they could avoid prosecution by pleading not guilty. I did not understand what he had meant but I thought I would give it a try.

The Judge was taken aback by my reply of "Not guilty". Then he asked a lot of questions about the names and address of my parents. "But why won't you plead guilty?' he asked.

Tears welled up in my eyes as I replied, "Because if I have to serve 30 days, I won't get back home in time to get back to school."

Then things got back to normal in the courtroom. The six of us were herded to a jail cell in the basement to spend the night before being taken to the chain gang. I had seen them working along the roads while being supervised by armed guards and dogs. That was not for me but I did not know what to do.

It was a long, long night in the jail cell as I wondered what the morrow might bring. Then in the morning a jailor appeared in front of our cell.

"Which one of you is Whitcomb?" he shouted.

I wondered why I was being singled out as I stepped to the door. Then I got the good news. I had no way of knowing that during the night the court officials had telegraphed my mother in Hayden, Indiana and notified her that I was in jail and could be released by the payment of a fine of six dollars. She had promptly telegraphed the six dollars and I was told that I was free to go. The jailer released me and sent me on my way with the admonition that I not travel by freight train. With that, I hitchhiked back home to enroll in my junior year of high school.

Upon reaching home, I was very apprehensive about how I might be received. Though I had written numerous postcards to tell of my travels, I had received not one word from home. My concern was short lived. The moment I opened the front door, my dear mother greeted me with open arms saying, "That was a long trip to Sunday School."

I found the old hometown just as I had left it and was back in school in the fall, playing basketball, playing trumpet in the school orchestra and enjoying life as if I had never left home. The following summer, I made another trip by hitchhiking and freight train to California, but that is another story.

During the years after high school I attended Indiana University and served as navigator on a bomber in World War II.

Subsequently I was married and raised a family of four daughters and one son. I practiced law and served as State Senator, Secretary of State and Governor of Indiana.

Life had been good to me and I had done almost everything I wanted to do until after 31 years of a wonderful married life, our marriage fell apart. I found myself alone with no purpose in life. I was devastated and did not know what to do or where to go. After that I returned to Hayden to live alone in the house where I was born. It was the same house where I had lived with my Mother, Father, and brother and sisters 53 years earlier when I had left home to see important places in history.

By this time, my own children were grown and living their own lives and their mother had taken up residence in California. I was growing old and needed something interesting to fill my time. It was not going to be found in Hayden, Indiana where the most exciting events of the day were the school buses converging upon our little school at about 8:00 o'clock in the morning and the arrival of the U.S. Mail just before noon at our one-room post office a block from my home.

One thing came to mind. For many years I harbored a dream that I might one day sail among the Greek Islands and view the ruins of that great civilization of antiquity. But time had passed me by. I was 68 years old and I had very little experience in sailing except at the Lake Monroe Sailing Club in Indiana. Carl Jackson, Dean of Libraries at Indiana University and a member of the Club had recently sailed solo across the Atlantic Ocean from Marblehead, Massachusetts to England. I asked him what kind of boat he would recommend for solo sailing in the Mediterranean Sea. His recommendation was that I buy a 30-foot boat with adequate headroom in the cabin and with unobstructed passageways on either side of the deck from stern to the bow. He also recommended that I should employ a professional surveyor to examine the boat. That all sounded reasonable enough if I should really go sailing among the islands. I mulled the matter over and over in my mind. Should I or should I not try sailing alone among the Greek Islands? Then one day, while thumbing through an old sailing magazine, I came upon a poem that struck my eye. As I read it over and over, it seemed as if it were written just for me. It read as follows:

On an ancient wall in China where a brooding Buddha blinks
Deeply graven is this message, "It is later than you think."
The clock of life is wound but once and no man has the power

To tell just when the hands will stop, at late or early hour.
Now is all the time you own, the past a golden link.
Go cruising now, my brother. It is later than you think.

(Author unknown)

The poem inspired me as it has surely inspired other people over the years. I thought about it long and hard. I even memorized the poem. In due time, I finally made up my mind. I would go.

A few days later, my 28-year-old daughter, Shelley, came to Hayden for a visit. I was a bit timid about breaking the news to her about my plan until she gave me the shock of my life. Without hesitation, she volunteered that she would like to go with me on such a trip.

Shelley was an Indiana University graduate and an excellent swimmer. I knew we would enjoy a wonderful summer of sailing and viewing ancient Greece and learning about Greek history and mythology.

WE VISIT THE GREEK ISLANDS

IN THE SPRING OF 1986, SHELLEY AND I flew from New York to Athens to sail the islands and learn about Greek history and mythology. Before starting our search for a sailboat, I happened to call up a longtime friend who had worked in state government with me in Indiana a number of years before.

My friend was Dr. Vasilos Basil Kafaris, a highly educated man who had enjoyed a meteoric rise in the business world since returning to his native Greece. In 1986 he held the office of President of the Agricultural Bank of Greece, one of the largest banking institutions of the country.

I told my friend of our intention to sail among the Greek Islands and learn about Greek history and mythology. His response was, "Athens has a lot to offer but if you are interested in history and mythology, you should take a trip to Delphi."

"Delphi," I repeated. "I have never heard of it."

"You will", he stated, and with that he arranged transportation together with a driver and guide to take us on one of the most interesting trips of our lives. It was an exciting 86-mile ride from Athens through the mountains to the west to find a treasure trove of ancient Greek history and mythology unlike anything I could ever have imagined. We were overwhelmed and very grateful by the generosity of Dr. Kafaris.

11

At Delphi we learned that Zeus, the greatest of all gods, had determined that Delphi was the center of the world by releasing two eagles, one from the east and one from the west and causing them to fly toward the center. The point where they met was determined to be the center of the earth. That was Delphi. That was enough to make it a very important place, but there was much more to the story.

Ancient Greeks considered that since it was the center of the earth, it was also the closest point to heaven. The Oracle of Delphi was able to communicate with heaven through the spirit of Apollo to obtain information and advice on personal matters as well as affairs of state. Over the years, governments throughout the Greek world sought the Oracle's advice. As reward for the good advice, great treasures were heaped upon the Oracle. So great that ornate treasury buildings were constructed to house gold, silver and jewels being brought to Delphi.

In addition to the treasury buildings there was a temple to Apollo, an ancient theater and some of the finest statues and art in all of Greece. There was far too much to learn and see in one day. We realized that we would need more time to thoroughly explore the wonders of Delphi.

Back in Athens, we climbed the Acropolis to view the Parthenon, which crowns the city with its columns and demonstrated why, with all of its wonders, Athens once was proclaimed to be the most beautiful city in the world.

There was much for Shelley and me to learn about Greek history and mythology. First, we decided to learn all we could about Homer, the great poet who was credited with writing the Iliad and the Odyssey. What we learned was incredible.

First, we learned that there is no solid agreement on the date of Homer's birth. Estimates range from1150 B.C. to 685 B.C. Some scholars even question whether there was ever a Homer. Also, there is no agreement about the place of his birth. That honor is claimed by seven different cities including Smyrna, Chios, Colophon, Salamis, Rhodes, Argos and Athens.

It is generally agreed that Homer was blind and went from place to place reciting his poems. He left nothing in writing. It was said that his poems were repeated and handed down from generation to generation. They may have been put to writing in 150 B.C. in Athens. Out of the speculation and confusion came two of the western world's greatest epic poems, the *Iliad* and the *Odyssey*.

Having learned of the various theories about Homer, we turned to Greek history for a better understanding of Greek mythology. But the more we learned about Greek history, the more we came to realize that Greek history and mythology are so intertwined that it is sometimes difficult to determine what is history and what is myth.

Some scholars questioned whether there had ever been a Trojan war. Homer's Iliad was a thrilling story of how the Greeks had gained access to the city of Troy by parking a huge wooden horse outside the gate of Troy and then withdrawing their ships as if they were departing in defeat. The Trojans moved the wooden horse inside the gate but while they slept that night, Greek soldiers came out of the horse and, with the help from the returning ships, defeated the Trojans. The Trojan War of some ten years in length was dated as 1194 to 1184 B.C.

Many years later a German businessman by the name of Heinrich Schliemann became enamored with the poetry of Homer and set out to prove that there had been a Trojan war as described in the Iliad. He had previously been engaged in the import business and was reputed to have mastered many different languages including English, Dutch, Russian, French, Italian, Spanish and Portuguese. He was ambitious and determined to gain great wealth. In pursuit of that wealth, he followed his brother to the California gold rush in 1850 where he prospered.

Upon the death of his brother he returned to Europe where in 1852 he married a Russian lady by the name of Katherina Lyshena. It turned out to be a very unhappy marriage with her refusing to live with Heinrich. Years later, he returned to America and obtained a divorce in 1869 from Katherina in Indianapolis, Indiana.

Subsequently, Heinrich wrote to a friend in Greece requesting that he find him a Greek wife. Specifications with the request were that she should be young, poor, good-looking, well educated and familiar with the works of Homer. The friend complied with the request and Schliemann wasted no time in traveling to Greece where he was introduced to Sophia Engastromenos. Heinrich and Sophia were married three months later in September 1869. But that is not the end of the story.

Thirty-year-old Heinrich and eighteen-year-old Sophia became the Bonnie and Clyde of the archeological world in the latter part of the nineteenth century as they went about Greece and Turkey, plundering archeological sites and hiding the treasure they uncovered in different locations in Greece. All the while, he was being guided by passages from the Iliad and the Odyssey.

Heinrich, with untold wealth, hired crews of laborers to excavate at Troy, Ithaca, and Mycenae. In the process, his workers crashed through layer after layer of artifacts that may never be recovered. He kept no records of the date of his discoveries nor did he follow recognized archeological procedures of the day.

The treasures Schliemann uncovered were awesome, including gold earrings, necklaces, pots of gold and silver and two diadems. He established a museum in Athens to display some of his treasure, but in his old age he took a major portion of it to his homeland where it was placed on display in a Berlin museum. During World War II, when the Russians overran Berlin, the treasure disappeared. It was not until 1992 that the Russian government admitted that the Schliemann Treasure was securely housed in the Pitkin Museum in Moscow.

We knew that there was much more Greek history but the time had come for us to start looking for a sailboat that would suit our purposes. We traveled from Athens to the nearby port of Piraeus, where we looked at boats in several shipyards but found nothing that appealed to us. One boat broker in Piraeus provided us with a computer printout of boats in his inventory. Upon examining the list, I found that 24 of the 48 boats listed were located on the island of Rhodes, 257 kilometers east of Athens. The remaining 24 boats were scattered throughout various islands. We decided to take an overnight ferryboat to Rhodes to continue our search.

In Rhodes we visited the Camper Nicholson Boat Broker at 48 Americus Avenue. From there a salesman took us to the Commercial Harbor, a short distance away, where we started our search. It did not take long because the third sailboat we looked at seemed to be just what we were looking for. It was 30 feet long, with adequate headroom and unobstructed passage on both sides of the deck from stern to bow.

The boat bore the name, "CILIN II", but we never learned what the name stood for because we never communicated directly with the boat owner. All negotiations were through the Camper Nicholson Agency. We were told it was bad luck to change a boat's name, so CILIN II she remained for the ten years I owned her. With the bad luck we suffered with her in those years, I often wondered what my luck would have been had I changed her name.

CILIN II had a new 37-foot mast and rigging which raised a question in my mind whether the previous owner had been dismasted and that was the reason she was for sale. We learned that the previous owner, Paolo Rocco of Milan, Italy, had spent his summer vacations for the past nine years sailing the seas. The large number of courtesy flags aboard suggested that CILIN II had visited many ports during those years.

According to the salesman, the asking price for the boat had been $15,000 U.S. A prospective purchaser had offered $10,000, which the owner rejected. The owner then made a counter-offer of $13,000. The prospective purchaser passed it up and the broker gave us the benefit of the bargaining. So we became the proud owners of CILIN II for $13,000.

The purchase agreement provided that the seller would provide a title free and clear of any encumbrances. It was registered in Italy and it took the Italian government a year to provide me with a free and clear title, during which time I sailed CILIN II under an Italian flag. In the meantime, I had only a bill of sale to show my ownership.

We found CILIN II to be completely equipped and seaworthy except for the necessity of sanding and scraping the hull below the waterline to apply two coats of anti-foul paint, to prevent the growth of algae and barnacles. It was hard to believe our good fortune in finding such a fine boat for that price. She was an Arpage, designed by Michael Dufour, S.A. of LaRochelle, France in 1970 with a 24 hp Volvo diesel engine. Her dimensions were 30 feet long (just as Carl Jackson had recommended) and her beam was 10 feet.

The hull above the waterline was an unblemished, glossy white. Her previous owner had surely taken good care of her, and I thought many times that if I had to outfit a boat to go to sea, I never would have thought of all of the equipment that was aboard when I bought her.

Items included with the boat were:

Six-man inflatable lifeboat
Six and one-half foot inflatable dinghy

Two and one-half horsepower Yamaha engine
Walker Trailing Log
Pylorus
Whisker Pole
Depth finder
VHF radio
Spare tiller and rudder
Stereo radio with tape player

The navigator's table contained three sets of dividers, three triangles and a set of parallel rulers.

The galley was furnished with an adequate supply of cooking utensils, including stainless steel pots and pans, settings of silverware, plates, drinking glasses, and cups and saucers for six people.

In the anchor well on the foredeck were a Plow, Danforth and a Fisherman anchor. In the V-berth at the bow were two jib sails, a spare mainsail and a colorful spinnaker sail. In addition, there was a 12-foot sailboard complete with sail. We would become intimately acquainted with this equipment in the years ahead.

I had never sailed a boat with so much equipment before, but on June 28, 1986 I was eager to get acquainted with the boat and the mysteries of the sea.

During the time Shelley and I were getting the boat in shape, we lived aboard "on the hard" (in boat storage on land) in the Commercial Harbor area at Rhodes. After a few days of hard work, we were ready to go to sea.

I knew nothing about reefing the sails or the operation of the 24 hp Volvo diesel engine, so we employed an Italian skipper to instruct us on our first trip at sea to Marmaris, Turkey, 28 miles to the north of Rhodes. The Italian lad took until 2:00 p.m. to take care of formalities with the Greek officials at Rhodes.

We learned that a Transit Log was required with details about the boat and its equipment. We also needed to provide a crew list with the names of passengers and crew together with the passport numbers and a myriad of details for clearing with the port captain, immigration, customs and medical officer. Then we were ready to sail. We quickly learned that the Aegean Sea kicks up at mid-afternoon with brisk winds and a choppy sea. I wondered how Shelley was taking it and if she were as nervous as I was during our first trip of about six hours.

We anchored in the crowded port at Marmaris, Turkey without incident and set out on the process of clearing in to the port with the officials. The various offices were located in different places along the shore. One was on the waterfront but others were down a side street and another up a flight of stairs on the backside of a building. It was like a scavenger hunt as we sought out one office and then another to display our Transit Log and crew list and answer the officials' questions. Fortunately, all transactions were in the English language but not always easy to understand.

With officials satisfied, we set out to explore our exotic environment of Marmaris for a couple of days before heading back to Rhodes. The trip was uneventful but enjoyable. At Rhodes we moored in Mandraki Marina adjacent to the Commercial Harbor. I suffered a weak feeling when our Italian skipper parted and left me in charge. Mandraki Marina was a bustling place with yachts from around the world crowded two and three deep along the quay. When a boat next to the quay needed to move out, it was necessary for boats in front of it to make way; consequently there was an epidemic of tangled anchor rodes.

It was an exciting and nervous moment on July 6, 1986 when Shelley and I pulled anchor and headed out of the crowded marina and into the Aegean Sea alone. Our destination was the ancient city of Lindos, 23 miles south along the east coast of Rhodes. I was so unsure of my ability to handle the boat that we traveled the entire distance on the 24 hp Volvo engine without ever raising the sails.

We entered Palestra Bay at Lindos and anchored CILIN II without incident and were pleased that our first trip had been successful. The Village of Lindos had far exceeded our expectations. We learned that there was an Acropolis high on the hill above the bay, which we visited. We also learned that the bay was ideal for swimming and for wind surfing, so we launched our 12-foot sailboard and enjoyed our first experience at wind surfing. We had many spills and it was sometimes necessary for neighboring boaters to tow us back to our boat with their dinghy because we were unable to control the direction we were sailing.

Lindos and Rhodes were a paradise for exploring the wonders of the Greek Islands. This was what it was all about. I looked forward to spending the summer doing just what we had done at Rhodes and Lindos, exploring ancient structures, swimming, wind surfing and feasting on Greek food.

After a wonderful week at Lindos we pulled anchor and headed back to Rhodes, fully satisfied with our first venture at sea. This time I raised the mainsail and jib and enjoyed the wonderful feeling of being carried along by the wind for the first time on CILIN II.

At last we were approaching Mandraki Marina and wondering how I would manage to anchor amongst all of those boats. I circled one time and glided into an anchorage like an old professional. No one watching could have imagined my nervousness at that time.

When we were securely anchored and the boat was at rest, Shelley gave me a surprise that I was not prepared for. It was shocking news that she wanted no more sailing. Why? I wondered why she would give up the opportunity to enjoy the kind of experiences we had enjoyed for the past two weeks. I suspected that she had been more nervous while we were sailing than I had realized. Maybe she felt that sailing with her father at the helm was an unsafe way to travel, or maybe she had already satisfied her curiosity about life at sea. It was hard for me to argue that point and it was a very sad day for me. We were up at 5:00 the next morning for the walk from the marina to the Olympia Airlines office for Shelley to catch her bus to the airport and her plane to New York and home.

After she left, I sat on the deck surrounded by other boats with dozens of people milling around, boats leaving and boats arriving, and felt very sad and very much alone. I had so much looked forward to the summer with Shelley. She had been great company, but now I would be sailing alone. In my dreams of sailing the Greek Islands, I had never dreamed it would be this way.

TO PANORMITIS

FOR A TIME IT SEEMED THAT EVERYTHING dated from July 14, 1986. That was the date Shelley left me and I found myself alone as the captain of a boat without a crew. Now there would be no one to hold the tiller while I prepared food and did things about the boat and no one to talk to.

There were plenty of things to do as I prepared to go to sea. Other boats had people to help put things together. I had to do it myself. There were dozens of yachts at anchor next to the pier and yachts were arriving and departing all of the time. One problem I faced was that it seemed there was an epidemic of anchor lines being caught up by other anchors. CILIN II had been moored for five days between two large charter yachts and I was so sure the anchor would be fouled that I enlisted the captains from each boat to assist me in casting off. My worries were all in vain. The engine was started, my mooring lines to neighboring yachts were released and the anchor weighed without any problem. CILIN II was on the way amidst applause from neighboring sailors.

As CILIN II moved out of the harbor, I noticed the monument of a deer perched high on columns on each side of the entrance to the harbor like sentinels saluting arriving and departing yachts. They offered a silent farewell to CILIN II as she departed Mandraki Marina, headed for the tiny island of Simi 28 miles to the northwest. As CILIN II motored into the Aegean Sea, she left in her wake one of the most interesting islands she would visit on her tour of the Greek Islands. A 105-foot bronze monument had once stood on a promontory overlooking Mandraki Harbor and was recognized as one of the seven wonders of the ancient world. The original had stood for 56 years but was destroyed by an earthquake in 224 B.C.

As I left, I thought about the fantastic history of this one island. The island had suffered many wars until 1309 when the Knights of St. John, at the instigation of the Pope, changed the island of Rhodes into a great fortress to protect the crusaders on their journey to regain the Holy Land from the Turks. The Turks, however, invaded Rhodes with 200,000 men and eliminated the Knights of St. John as an operating force, leaving their magnificent fortification dating from 1500 A.D. as a major attraction for generations of European tourists.

With the wind out of the northwest, the direction I had to travel, I decided to leave the sails down and go on the engine. I looked back to see the resort city of Rhodes with its crystal white buildings and crowded beaches fade in the distance across the water. I had begun my own sea odyssey there. To the starboard in the distance were the rugged mountains along the coast of Turkey. I was on my way. It was an exhilarating yet chastising feeling.

After about three hours, the wind picked up and the waves became more turbulent, as was normal in the Aegean Sea in the early afternoons. Later the wind became more violent and CILIN II was bouncing around on a choppy sea. I felt there was nothing to worry about. I had faith in the boat though I had not encountered such rough weather before.

In the late afternoon, when the waves calmed, I suddenly realized that in the excitement of setting out on my first trip alone, I had neglected to eat any lunch. Then I wondered how I could manage to get some food. There was nothing prepared for lunch and I could not leave the tiller. I had read of sailors lashing the tiller so the boat would hold a heading. That was not for me. I tried it but could not make it work. Finally, hunger took over my better judgment. I dropped the tiller, dashed into the cabin, grabbed a loaf of bread, and dashed back to retrieve the tiller. The problem had been solved and lunch on the first day of sailing was composed of half a loaf of bread. Then the matter of quenching my dry throat. The problems was solved in the same way as before, with a dash into the cabin and back, I quickly found that sailing alone is not as enjoyable or as convenient as when there is someone to hold the tiller when needed.

Evening was coming on with the sun sinking low in the western sky, but I was not near my destination. The island of Simi was visible in the distance. Then there was a small island to the port. With the two islands for reference points, it became apparent that CILIN II was making very little progress. The current and the wind were too much for the little 24 hp. engine. From my chart, I could find no indication of a cove where the boat could be anchored for the night. The thought of being caught at sea in the dark on my first solo sailing adventure was beyond anything I had ever expected. The situation was becoming desperate.

As I scanned the distant horizon across the sea, I thought I saw an object in the water far ahead of me. Could it be a big rock? I watched it for a long time before I could tell it was moving. It was a small boat and it was moving in my direction. Maybe I could get some help. After a long time it became apparent that it was a small fishing boat being powered by an outboard engine. I could see that there were two men aboard as it drew nearer.

When the boat was within earshot, I shouted, "Do you speak English?" It was good news when one answered back, "A little."

I told them that I needed to find a place to anchor for the night. Then they engaged in a long conversation between themselves in their native tongue that I assumed was Greek. While talking they waved their arms, pointing to different locations along the shore of the little island to the south, which I later learned was the Isle of Seskli. I got the impression that they were talking about a safe place to anchor. Then I thought they were saying something about a beautiful cove. Beauty was not what I was looking for. I was looking for security, a place where the boat would be safe for the night.

Finally, after their long discussion, one of the fishermen beckoned for me to follow them and I felt good that there was someone who would locate a secure anchorage for the night. Until that moment, I was uncertain what would happen or where I would be when darkness spread across the sea.

We proceeded to the south across the channel between the two islands. As we approached the small island, we passed a number of boulders in the sea along the shore until my guide pointed to a cove where I could anchor. Being uncertain about the depth of the water, I sailed back and forth in front of the cove a couple of times. The thought crossed my mind that the fishermen might be guiding me into shallow waters so that they could plunder my boat, a thought I later regretted.

Finally, I decided I had no other good options, so I headed into the cove. When I glanced back at the fishing boat, I could see one of the fishermen waving his arms frantically. He was warning that the course I was taking would take me into a shallow, rocky area. He then led me to a spot where I could anchor safely in 15 feet of water.

It was then late in the evening. The trip I had thought would take six hours had taken nine, yet the destination was still several miles away. Across the cove in the twilight I could see the fisherman setting their nets for the night. In my gratitude for their kind assistance, I pumped up the dinghy and paddled over to present them with a bottle of Italian wine left on the boat by the previous owner.

The generous assistance by those two fishermen was the first of many I received as I sailed the seas, but not all helpers had been so kind. The cove was well protected from the wind and the waves. It was a quiet and restful place, and after an exciting day of sailing, I climbed into the bunk for a good night's sleep, with no thought of anything to eat.

I awoke the next morning at dawn to find the fishing boat was nowhere to be seen and I was alone in a beautiful, peaceful cove. After a breakfast of coffee, a fresh peach and a couple of slices of bread with orange marmalade, I pulled up the anchor and headed for Panormitis on the southern end of the island of Simi. This time I raised the main sail, attached the hanks on the jib and headed out.

The sea chart showed a large bay on the southwest side of the isle of Simi, but as I sailed along, I saw no sign of it. Then I came to realize the big difference between navigating an aircraft, as I had done for years in the Air Force, and navigating a surface craft on the water. I knew that I was very near the bay but where was it? If I were in an aircraft, it would have been easy to see, yet the entrance to the bay was nowhere in sight. At long last I spotted it. It was a fairly narrow entrance into a fine, big bay.

Upon passing through the entrance, a beautiful picture spread out before my eyes. It was the Greek Monastery of Panormitis with many white buildings and a big tourist boat tied up at the dock with hundreds of tourists milling about the place. I anchored in about 18 feet of water in the vicinity of several yachts in the northern section of the bay and felt very comfortable after my first solo trip at sea. There was no customs office or other bureaucratic problems. It was a very relaxing situation.

After a short rest, I pumped up the inflatable dinghy and paddled over to the dock to see what was going on. It turned out that a big tourist cruise ship had arrived from the Island of Rhodes for a visit to the monastery. It was an exceedingly colorful place with some 200 candles hanging from the ceiling, all illuminated by electric lights.

The priest was conducting services in which he waved a baton emitting smoke. Sometimes he disappeared into a separate room for a moment. I learned that it was all a well-orchestrated program for the tourists from Rhodes. As a cruise ship entered the bay, the church bells chimed for a long time, heralding their arrival. Upon reaching the dock, there were soft drinks for sale to the thirsty passengers and in the monastery was a box to receive drachmas for those who purchased candles. After the services, the visitors were invited to tour a small museum with a nominal entrance fee of one drachma.

The cruise ship departed and I was back on CILIN II before I heard the church bells chime as yet another flotilla of tourists sailed into the bay. I concluded that the monastery was surely the most prosperous in all of Greece.

The bay was a very restful place, away from the wind and waves of the sea. On the second day something happened which would change my whole attitude about sailing the seas. A German lad from a nearby yacht came for a visit. He observed a stainless steel rack on the stern of CILIN II.

"Where is the rest of it?" he asked.

"Where is the rest of what?" was my reply.

"The other parts to your self-steering device?" he answered.

I had to admit that I did not know what he was talking about. Then he climbed aboard, rummaged through some of the items in the storage bin and came out with an aluminum piece about three and a half feet long and six inches wide. He attached it to the mount on the stern and threaded some lines through pulleys.

"This is your self-steering device. It is an automatic pilot and it is all complete," he announced. "It is mechanical and uses no electricity."

It was a surprise to me because I had not known that such a thing existed. It was not until I was back out on the sea again that I understood the real significance of the device. When it was engaged and properly tuned, it took over the guidance of the boat and allowed me to eat, read and sleep for long hours at a time. It was really better than having an extra crew-member because it did not eat or talk back. Admittedly, I addressed some very abusive language to it when the winds were light and its performance was erratic.

I never knew the German fellow's name. I wish I did because he introduced me to something I had never known about before that time. It is the usual case that knowledge and wisdom are passed from the old to the young, but here I was most grateful the process was reversed.

The following day I departed Panormitis and headed for the city of Simi on the northern end of the Isle of Symi. I was beside myself with joy at the new device, which made sailing such a pleasure. I was so delighted that I sailed almost to the Turkish mainland before turning to enter a long channel to Simi. Darkness came too quickly so that I could see nothing whatsoever before me. It was rank foolishness to proceed, but proceed I did until the lights of the city came into view. I vowed that I would never do that again. I should have hove to or anchored, if possible, and waited for daylight.

During the following days I made my way along the southern coast of Turkey until I reached a new Turkish marina known as Kemer.

KEMER TO CYPRUS

PUTTING THE BOAT UP AT THE END of the sailing season and preparing for departure to the U.S. provides a time for sailors to visit unlike any other time of the sailing season. During the sailing season, everyone is on the go but at the end of the season things come to a stop. It is a time to renew acquaintances with old friends and make new acquaintances. At Kemer I met Russell and Marge Handy. Russ was a retired TWA pilot from Kansas City. He and Marge owned a condo in Antibes, France and sailed the Greek Islands year after year in their yacht, NOHRA'S ARK. Then there was Ted Norman from Weybridge, Surrey, England who was reputed to have been the youngest squadron leader in the RAF during World War II. There were also Dr. Jim Casey and his wife, Shirley, from Oxnard, California and a number of other very interesting people.

It was a congenial group and typical of the dozens of people I would meet as I sailed the seas. As we visited, I noticed that there was a lot of talk of the wonders of the excavations at Ephesus. I had passed it by, but with all of the talk about it, I decided to go see it for myself. It was a thirty-five cent minivan ride for the 55 miles to Antalya. A guide took me to the main bus station, purchased a ticket and escorted me to my reserved seat on the bus.

The bus ride was an experience. The bus was full as it headed out across the high plains of Turkey on the eight-hour ride to Izmer. A bouquet of fresh flowers graced the bus dashboard and Turkish music blared from the speakers as we rolled along over a fine macadam highway.

Every hour of the way, a driver's assistant offered a complimentary bottle of cold drinking water and provided rose water to freshen our hands and face. The music continued incessantly.

At a rest stop, I stepped to the counter of an ice cream parlor. In ports while sailing along the coast, I had ordinarily been able to get a three-dip cone for 100 lire (about 16 cents in American money). I held up three fingers, laid down a 100 lire note and was delivered three, three dip cones. I learned that the inflated prices in resorts along the coast did not prevail at the inland ice cream parlors. I stood in the hot sun looking for someone with whom I could share my dripping ice cream. Seeing no help in sight, I slurped away at the cones until it became necessary to chuck the dripping remainder into a nearby trash can and get back on the bus.

It was dusk when the bus rolled into the busy Turkish city of Izmer. There I was able to find lodging in a hotel occupied by American military personnel. It was a real treat to enjoy my first steak dinner in months and more of a treat to find that I would be sleeping in a king-sized bed. It was the first time I had slept anywhere other than on CILIN II for weeks. To my surprise, it did not turn out to be the restful night that I had anticipated. I dreamed that CILIN II was drifting away from her mooring. Time and again I would get in the dinghy and return her to the mooring. I pitched and tossed in the oversized bed until at dawn I felt that I had very little rest.

The streets of Izmer were interesting and I was curious to see the city but had no time. Instead I boarded a minivan for the 50-mile trip to Ephesus. From the bus stop, the place was not like I expected it to be. I walked a long distance between temporary stands where merchants were hawking a variety of souvenirs for tourists. Then I came upon the scene of Ephesus. It was awe-inspiring. I observed a huge amphitheater more than 2000 years old. It had been excavated and repaired and now was being used for public programs, including school commencement exercises.

There were also the ruins of a library building, a women's gymnasium and many other buildings. In a modern interpretative center, I learned that water had been piped to third floor apartments more than 200 years ago. There was also a street of white marble with marble columns along the side. The original extent of the road was unknown at the time of my visit. I overheard a guide say that if they continued excavating at the present rate, it would take 75 years to uncover the city. It had been a magnificent seaport but silt and sand had filled in the shore until now it was only a couple of miles from the Mediterranean Sea.

There was a story that the apostle John had warned the residents of the city that unless they changed their sinful ways, their city would one day be rubble. And rubble it was. In that rubble is the history of a remarkable civilization which archeologists may be unraveling for generations yet to come.

After spending much of the day seeing all I could see and learning all I could learn about the magnificence of Ephesus, I made my way back to Kemer to prepare to sail to Antalya, Turkey. The 18-mile sailing trip along the coast from the Kemer marina to Antalya was delightful with a calm sea and a fair breeze from the port beam. The process of clearing out had been simple because all of the necessary offices were in one building. The marina was a model established by the Turkish government in an effort to promote tourism. Clearing out was so simple that I asked, "Are these the signatures I need on my transit log?"

"You are cleared out and ready to go," was the response of one of the officials. I am sure that I would have asked more questions if I could have foreseen the difficulties I would be facing at the next port.

The sun was bright and sailing was like a dream. I adjusted the automatic steering so that I could make a cup of coffee and enjoy the view of a high mountain range along the coast. Up ahead, the coastline appeared to turn at a 90° angle to the east. I knew that the picturesque marina of Antalya was nestled in that corner of the coast. There were many yachts moored in the marina, but there was little problem in finding a vacant slip.

It was good news that all of the port officials were located in the near vicinity. Clearing in would be easy. Everything went fine until I reached the customs office. There the officer in charge pretended that he could not understand English. He examined my transit log and through an interpreter let me know that I was in trouble. I did not have the signature of the medical officer at Kemer. I was to be fined $400 in U.S. money.

"But I asked if I had all of the necessary signatures and was told that I had them all," I pleaded.

A little fellow standing next to me who had been acting as interpreter whispered to me, "Come out in the hall. I can get you out of this for $200."

"We are going to take care of it right here. I am not going out in the hall to talk to you," I answered.

Again the customs officer spoke up. The interpreter told me that the official said that I might have a bad disease. "I don't have any disease and the officials at Kemer told me that I had all of the signatures I needed on the transit log," I insisted. "I will go to jail before I pay $400," I added. I might not have been so brave had I known the terrible reputation of Turkish jails. Going to a Turkish jail could have been a disaster of the worst kind.

I then offered to take a minibus back to Kemer to get the signature of the medical officer. "But he won't let you go," was the response of the interpreter.

The argument went on for a long time until I thought I had made my point. I was able to leave the office, but the interpreter followed me down the stairs, insisting that he could take care of my problem for much less than $400.

"I do not need your help," I replied.

I immediately went to a nearby post office and placed a telephone call to the Kemer marina. "The customs officer here wants to fine me $400 because I did not get the medical officer's signature on my port clearance from Kemer," I explained.

The response was a surprise to me. "We do not have a medical officer here and he knows it." Kemer was only 18 miles down the coast. He could have picked up the phone and called Kemer. The interpreter tagged along with me back to the boat. When I finally got rid of him, I felt that my troubles were over, so I set out to explore the city of Antalya.

I climbed the steep hill from the port to find a city with wide streets and modern buildings. After traveling a short distance I came upon the Sultan's Market with row upon row of narrow passages lined with shops of all kinds, including shoes, dresses, electronics, jewelry and almost anything imaginable. There was one section with marble work, another with galvanized metal and another with oriental rugs.

I stopped at a knife shop and explained to the proprietor by sign language that I wanted to buy a stainless steel, serrated knife for slicing bread. It needed to have a blunt point for safety on the boat. In a little while, he produced a fine knife exactly to my specifications that was to serve me for years on the boat.

At another stand, the operator observed that the umbrella I was carrying had lost the cap from the top, leaving a sharp point exposed. He quickly provided a new cap with threads that fit my umbrella exactly. The price was nominal and I thought that it would be hard to think of any item of merchandise that would not be available in the Sultan's Market.

In the afternoon I struck up a conversation with a young man on the street. He spoke to me in perfect English and told me he had recently graduated from medical school in Turkey. We visited and he and his 15-year old nephew offered to take me to the Antalya Museum of Ancient History. There I saw artifacts dating back 5000 years. In our conversations, I learned that they were Muslim. The 15-year old boy had never heard of the Holy Bible. The uncle explained it to his nephew and then told me that Muslims accepted the Old and New Testaments, but to them Jesus was just another prophet.

He also told me that in days gone by, when Turkish families had guests come to their homes, they would serve tea, but after the television show "Dallas" became popular in Turkey, those who could afford it served whiskey to their guests.

In traveling about the city, I saw pictures of American personalities on display in store windows and on shop walls. It soon became apparent that the most popular pictures were of Marilyn Monroe and Elvis Presley. It was the same in Greece and Israel.

The trip around the city had so occupied my thoughts that I forgot about my problems back at the customs office. It was dark by the time I returned to the marina. The place took on a festive atmosphere with many bars and cafes displaying colorful, subdued lights and people crowded about the area. There were many people eating and drinking in open-air restaurants as others promenaded along the walkway in front of the boats along the shore.

The following day I talked to other sailors along the dock and learned that the customs officer was trying to shake down many of them. They reasoned that his monthly pay was the equivalent of two hundred dollars in U.S. money. That was a reasonable salary in Turkey, where prices were low compared to the U.S. His problem was that he saw so many "rich people" sailing in expensive yachts and he wanted to share in the wealth. He was a crook.

When I went back to clear out of the port, I found that my troubles were not over. The customs officer still wanted a $400 fine even though I reminded him that there was no medical officer at the Kemer Marina. The same interpreter was there. We argued until he became convinced that I had no intention of paying him $400. To save face, he finally agreed to allow me to take my transit log to the commercial harbor ten miles away to get it signed by the medical officer there. The taxi ride cost 5000 lire, but that was cheap compared to the $400 being demanded.

The medical officer at the commercial harbor was a genial fellow who was glad to put signature on the transit log for a small fee. He was not a doctor but merely a political appointee. He did not examine me or ask any questions about my health. The suggestion that unless I had medical officer's signature I might be importing some terrible disease was pure nonsense.

With my transit log in order, I was able to clear the port of Antalya and continued sailing on the way to Alanya at 8:20 in the morning of September 25, 1986.

The weather was clear and bright as I sailed eastward along the Turkish coast. By late afternoon I could see a giant, ancient, amphitheater ahead. It looked like a good place to stop for the night. I wanted to go ashore and visit the site but it did not appear that the anchor was holding well. With only about ten feet of water, I put on the facemask and went to the bottom to plant the anchor. There I found the bottom to be shale and of questionable holding. There was only one other yacht in the vicinity so I paddled my dinghy over to ask the captain what he thought of the location as a place to anchor. He seemed annoyed that I would bother him. He had an 80-pound anchor and he was satisfied with the holding. My plow anchor was 18 pounds and I did not feel good about it.

As I lay on the bunk, I could see the multi-colored lights and hear the blare of music from a nightclub off the port beam. The wind was from the south where there was a line of rocks protruding from the water. I took comfort in knowing that if the anchor dragged, I would be blown away from the rocks and toward the shore half a mile away.

When I awoke that night, I could see no lights off the port beam nor was there music blaring into the night. Up on deck I could see that the lights were still aglow, but the wind had shifted 180°. The lights were off the starboard beam. CILIN II had turned around. If the anchor slipped, I would be blown into the rocks. It was 3:30 a.m. when I pulled anchor, gave the rocks a wide berth and sailed on into the night. As I left the anchorage, I noticed that the other yacht was nowhere to be seen. The gruff captain had learned that the shale bottom did not provide good holding even for his 80 pound anchor.

After sailing a few hours through the gray of dawn, I was able to make out the outline of a promontory. That was my next destination because I knew that on the other side was Alanya, Turkey. I felt good that I was so close, but as the morning wore on, I had the feeling that CILIN II was suspended in space. Several hours passed and we seemed no closer than we had been before. It was mid-afternoon before I could make out small boats motoring up to the promontory and then disappearing as if they had entered a cave. Upon drawing nearer, I was sure that was the case. Cruising boats were taking passengers into caves at the base of the promontory.

Upon finally anchoring at Alanya, I was delighted to see the Kohl's, a couple from the Netherlands. We had met and gotten acquainted at Antalya. We visited and took a hike to the top of the promontory to view the ruins of a castle that dated back to the time of the Crusades to the Holy Land in 1100.

Shops in the city sold Turkish rugs, jewelry, furs, leather goods and a variety of items of interest to tourists. I purchased a couple of small rugs for my daughters and a gold necklace for my son, John. The shopkeeper's first question was, "Sprecken Deutsch?" It was second language for that part of Turkey. With a manpower shortage in Germany after World War II, many Turks found employment in German industries. They worked a few years and then drove back to Turkey in a new Mercedes automobile. Most taxicabs in Antalya were German-made Mercedes.

From Alanya, Turkey, the next stop would be the island of Cyprus. It was 100 miles and I had never sailed that far alone. Mr. Kohl and I agreed that we would put in to a little cape on the northwest corner of the island. I set out in the middle of the afternoon. He would come later. Sailing was fine in the early evening, but at night the sea became very rough. I could see lights from shore but did not see any ships. I wondered if the weather might be so bad that fishing boats would not venture out from harbor. I slept in the cockpit, waking up frequently to observe the condition of the sea and the weather. By dawn the sea calmed and the winds were not so strong. At daybreak I could make out the outline of the mountain of Cyprus. I felt foolish that I had worried about any navigational problems. It would have been difficult to miss the island.

I headed for the northwest tip of the island where I was to rendezvous with Mr. Kohl. Then toward noon, a big black cloud to the southwest appeared to be coming in my direction, moving fast. Then heavy wind and rain. Then there was a noise that I had never heard before. Large hailstones splashed in the water all around CILIN II, then pelted the boat with a resounding clatter. The hailstorm lasted for several minutes and the sea became very rough. With the wind from the southwest and a very rough sea, I was sure it would be unsafe to try to approach the cape to meet with Mr. Kohl. I headed south toward Paphos on the southwest end of the island. I was determined that unless the storm subsided, I would sail on past Paphos and remain in the open sea until the weather calmed.

I was about half way along the west shore of Cyprus when the storm subsided. I had been using a Walker Trailing Log to measure my distance traveled. It is a cord about an eighth of an inch in diameter and about 100 feet long. One end is attached to a small torpedo shaped object with fins, which drags in the water. The other end is attached to a counter to tell how many miles the boat has traveled. At the end of a trip, the cord needs to be pulled in while the boat is moving and before reaching port.

As the cord is pulled in, the end that was attached to the counter must be fed back into the water so that the kinks can be straightened out of the line. Then the cord can be pulled in and wound up for storage. It is a cumbersome thing but well worthwhile because of its accuracy when no other navigational devices are available for measuring distance traveled. Modern navigational equipment has made the Walker Trailing Log an obsolete relic, but at the time it was the best thing I had to measure distance traveled.

I was pulling the cord in to bundle it for storage when I was startled to hear the whine of a police siren. I could not believe it. I had been so intent on retrieving the cord that I had not noticed the approach of a Greek patrol boat. The driver was agitated that CILIN II was displaying a Turkish flag high on a starboard shroud. By his hand signals I could tell that he wanted the flag removed immediately. I was in Greek waters flying a Turkish flag but I could not safely abandon the cord that was being wound in. I continued pulling in the cord, much to the agitation of the driver of the patrol boat. Then I grabbed a knife, put it in my teeth like a pirate from days of old, climbed up the mast and removed the offensive Turkish flag. I then put up a Greek flag. My assailant then saluted the flag and sailed away.

By the time I sailed into Paphos harbor, the sea had calmed and the wind was light. The approach into the harbor was easy, but I was surprised to see it so un-crowded. I circled a couple of times and found an ideal place to anchor. Very soon, after the anchor was fixed, I was advised that I was in a reserved area. The harbor was kept clear for the arrival of the KARINA II the next day, along with the Governor. I would have to move to the other side of the harbor.

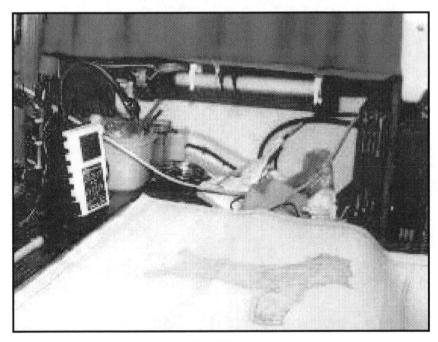

Sea Chart

I fired up the engine and started to the other side of the harbor when the engine stopped dead. In the excitement of the moment, I had foolishly failed to up the anchor and the propeller had hit the anchor chain. The chain was over the propeller shaft so that I could not move. I saw a couple of soldiers standing on shore talking. I asked one if he would go in the water and release the chain for $10. He was happy to do it and I was happy to pay him.

I moored on the other side of the bay next to a British yacht. It displayed a colorful array of pennants strung from the bow to the top of the mast and then to the stern. I learned that there was to be a celebration the next day honoring the arrival of the Governor. In addition, the KARINA II would be making a stop on its tour of the Greek Islands. KARINA II was a replica of a Greek boat that had been brought up from the bottom of the sea where it had been lodged for 1500 years. The replica had recently returned from a parade of tall ships at the New York Statue of Liberty. It was a matter of one-upmanship for the Greeks over the Turks because the Turks held the original KARINA in the Turkish section of Cyprus while the Greeks paraded the replica, named KARINA II, about the Greek Islands and to New York City.

It was apparent that CILIN II would have a front row seat for the arrival of KARINA II. I had collected a number of courtesy flags from various countries but I had no inclination to go to the trouble of making a display. It was not our show. The captain of the British boat next to me prevailed upon me to help him as he hung out even more flags. He asked me to feed rope onto the pulley of his power winch as it pulled him to the top of his mast. I fed rope on to the pulley as he went higher and higher. Then I called to him, "What if I get you up there and can't get you back down?"

He chuckled at that and continued his work until it was time for me to let him back down. Then it happened. I had allowed the rope in the winch to get crisscrossed so that I could not let him back down. Try as I might, there seemed to be no way to untangle the rope. I was embarrassed. It was no longer funny. There sat my new friend in his boatswain chair, helpless to move. Another British sailor on a nearby boat saw our predicament and offered to give a hand. He may have been in such a situation before because he knew exactly how to solve the problem. He climbed aboard, took hold of the rope and called, "Pull yourself up so I can get some slack."

The captain at the top of the mast shimmied up the mast a couple of feet, thus providing slack in the rope at the winch. Then our rescuer used the slack to untangle the rope around the winch. It was easy. Why did I not think of it? Anyway, we were all relieved as the captain was slowly lowered to the deck.

The marina shore was crowded with people the next day waiting for the arrival of the Governor and KARINA II. A number of yachts, wind surfers and a couple of patrol boats left the marina to meet and escort the KARINA II into the harbor. Then at last we saw a brown, rectangular sail of the replica of the ancient KARINA II as she approached the marina entrance. Due to the direction of the wind, the sail was quickly lowered and brawny men manning the old-fashioned looking oars brought her in to her mooring.

I had seen the arrival of the Governor and the KARINA II, so I set out to see the city of Paphos.

Paphos to Larnaca

My departure from Paphos on October 3, 1986 was much less eventful than my arrival had been. The weather was fine for sailing as I passed many large ships along the way. At one point, a large transport came so close that I was concerned about being run over, as I was on a starboard tack and could not turn away. The boat's pilot either did not see me or he was trying to see how close he could come to me. In either event, I suffered some anxious moments as he passed me by, leaving me rocking wildly in his wake.

I observed an airfield that I took to be British, and considered going into shore but since I did not have good sea charts of the area, I passed it by. It was a mistake because it was completely dark when I reached the harbor at Lemasol. Although I searched for a long time, sailing through large ships anchored near the port, I was unable to find the entrance. At last I called on the VHF radio, "This is CILIN II, a sailboat. I need help in finding the entrance to the harbor."

There was no response, though I repeated my message a number of times. Then at last I anchored and found that CILIN II was in about 15 feet of water. The wise thing would have been to put out an anchor light and remain there until dawn. I did not always do the wise thing. I weighed the anchor and set out to sea headed for Larnaca to the east.

CILIN II passed several large ships at anchor. Then I saw a red light to my starboard. I thought nothing of it for a moment until I realized that it was another small boat on a collision course with CILIN II. I made an abrupt turn to port and narrowly averted a collision in the dark.

We sailed on through the night and were farther out to sea than was necessary. We had sailed past Larnaca and it was necessary to sail back to the northwest for what seemed like a long distance. As we grew nearer, I could see buildings that gave the appearance of skyscrapers. By that time I had sailed all day and all night. There appeared to be a huge parking lot in front of the buildings. It was marked off in sections for buses and for large trucks and it seemed that CILIN II was traveling to a lower level toward the big parking lot. This hallucination lasted for a long time and until I came close to the shore. There were no skyscrapers and there was no parking lot. At last I could see a large number of masts of sailboats, but the entrance to the marina was not readily visible. In sailing eastward along the coast, I finally spotted it and made an easy approach into the large marina.

Weary as I was after sailing for 24 hours, it was again necessary to clear in with the port officials before resting from the long trip. Fortunately, the formalities were all handled at one location. In short order I was back on board CILIN II and in the bunk for a good sleep.

Larnaca was a well-organized marina with friendly personnel and excellent facilities. It has been a favorite spot for circumnavigators coming through the Suez Canal to stop for repairs and provisions before heading into the Mediterranean Sea. It has also been a convenient place for sailboat captains in the eastern Mediterranean to store their boats during the winter season. In the early spring it becomes a beehive of activity with sailors repairing their boats. Painting, electrical repairs, carpentry work and plumbing chores are all necessary before starting a new sailing season.

CILIN II was moored at the first open slip I found upon entering the marina. In my early days of sailing, I did not use the VHF radio to announce my arrival or to get instructions from the dock master about where to moor the boat. I was so timid about my ability to bring the boat in that I did not want anyone to know I was coming until CILIN II was safely inside the marina.

After securing CILIN II in a vacant slip and clearing with the officials, I was ordered to move to a slip on the west side of the marina.

Help in casting off the lines was available in the person of Barbara Walker. It was a surprise seeing her and her husband Bob again. They were aboard the first American yacht I had encountered when I sailed into Marmaris, Turkey. It had been a thrill to see a big American flag on a beautiful yacht with the name of SNAP DECISION HOUSTON, TEXAS, painted across the stern.

Lockheed Aircraft Company had hired Bob Walker on a $27,000,000 project to install airport landing facilities in Saudi Arabia. The terms of the contract had come into dispute. Lockheed suspended the operation and Bob and Barbara Walker went sailing on a yacht in the Mediterranean Sea. I met them in a number of different ports as I sailed. A visit with them came to be like a visit back home.

On the west wall of the marina I moored next to a 30-foot yacht named TINKER BELL, occupied by Jennings and Tamar Braun from Tel Aviv, Israel. We became friends immediately and since Tel Aviv was to be my next destination, I wanted to learn all I could about the place.

LARNACA TO TEL AVIV

ON CYPRUS, I SPENT TWO WEEKS IN the city of Larnaca, sightseeing and getting acquainted with the place. I learned that relations between the Turks and Greeks were not good. In fact, there had been a shooting war between the two countries in 1974, about 12 years before my arrival. I traveled to Nicosia, the capital city, and there I met a Swedish Air Force Captain, Stefan Helsing, whose duty with the United Nations peacekeeping forces was coming to an end. He told me that he was a sailor and owned his own boat back home and he volunteered to sail to Tel Aviv with me.

I was glad to have company for the trip considering that it would be about 180 miles, much farther than I had ever sailed alone before. Captain Helsing came aboard a couple of days before departure and volunteered to purchase provisions for the trip. Later he came with a couple of loaves of bread, a dozen cans of tuna, several packages of crunchy crackers and much more.

We filled our fuel and water tanks, and after the captain checked the weather forecast at the RAF station, we departed Larnaca on Saturday morning, October 18, 1986. It was a clear day. After a short time we enjoyed a good breeze from the west that carried us along at a good speed. Toward the middle of the afternoon, the wind grew stronger and waves grew heavier. Finally, the waves started breaking over the starboard so that whichever one of us was at the tiller would be drenched with cold salt water.

I was totally unprepared for such conditions. My search for foul weather gear produced only an old plastic raincoat with but one sleeve. That was the one that would give the best protection from the water coming over the boat. We took turns wearing the coat when it was our turn at the helm.

In the course of the evening, a big, black, threatening cloud gathered in the sky back toward Cyprus. The sea was growing rougher and the Captain suggested that we should turn back. To me it seemed foolish to turn back toward the cloud, so we forged ahead. I did not know it at the time but the thing that was bothering the Captain was that he was feeling ill. It was almost midnight when he gave up all together and retired to the bunk in the cabin where he remained until dawn. Our progress was slow because of the direction of the wind.

At midday on the second day, catastrophe of the worst order struck CILIN II. Many disastrous things can happen to a small sailboat on the high seas but few things can equal the distress in finding there is no way to make hot coffee. The bottled gas under the two-burner gas stove hissed and refused to ignite. What to do? Tired and weary, what I wanted more than anything in the world was a hot cup of black coffee. Panic gave way to a faint hope when I remembered a small blue canister stacked with the junk in the compartment behind the galley. I jerked up the cushion and board covering the compartment and sorted through the junk for the canister. It was attached to a little mount that made it possible to heat water, a cup at a time, for coffee. The mission was saved. On to Tel Aviv!

Captain Helsing managed the tiller through the afternoon and night to make up for his absence the night before. It was near 4:00 a.m. as we approached within five miles of Tel Aviv. I had carefully studied the sea chart, owned by my friend Jennings Braun, until I felt that I knew the coast very well. In the dark of the early morning I was frantically searching through a publication known as "Reeds Radio Manual." It provided the frequencies and location of radio stations in the Mediterranean. What was more important to me was that it showed drawings of some of the major ports. When I found Tel Aviv, all it said was "All vessels must check in with the Israeli Navy upon entering

Israeli waters." We were in Israeli waters and we had not checked in with anyone. We learned later that Israel was at war with three of its neighboring countries. They did not want any terrorist sneaking in at night in an attempt to blow up their facilities.

While I was pondering our situation, a very bright light flooded CILIN II. Behind the light was a ship that looked as big as the Queen Mary. I stepped out into the cockpit. Then a voice over a bullhorn, "Identify your vessel!"

I shouted, "This is CILIN II. I am Captain Whitcomb, An American. We are headed for Tel Aviv."

"Why did you not call on the radio when you entered Israeli waters?"

I thought about that and could think of no sensible answer. Before I could realize what I was saying, I blurted out, "We did not want to bother anybody." I realized after the words left my lips that I could have said nothing more foolish.

A series of questions followed about who we were, where had we been, and what did we have aboard the boat and on and on. Finally the light on the big patrol boat went out; the boat pulled away for a distance and stood still in the water. Then it circled back toward us with the big light turned on again and with more questions. It was a relief when they finally sailed away from us. Then the problem of how we were going to find our way into the Tel Aviv Marina. The shoreline in the distance was a blur in the early morning light; so I called on the VHF radio.

"Israeli Navy. Israeli Navy. This is CILIN II, a sailboat."

A clear female voice came back, "CILIN II. This is Israeli Navy. Go ahead."

"Israeli Navy, I am trying to locate the Tel Aviv marina."

The answer came back quickly. "Take a heading of 86 degrees. You are five miles out."

This told me that the Navy knew our exact location from the radar. As we drew closer to land, we could see a long wall and a large number of sailboat masts. It was the Tel Aviv marina. We sailed past the north end of the breakwater, made an abrupt turn to starboard, then a turn to the port to moor the boat near the marina office.

After clearing in and moving to our assigned slip, Captain Helsing gathered his belongings and headed to shore in hopes of getting a military flight back to his outfit in Cyprus. I slept.

Though I arrived in Tel Aviv in late October, I decided to remain there until Christmas to attend the annual nativity program in Bethlehem. Time went fast as I lived on my boat in the marina with about 500 other boats moored in the slips all around me. It was easy and inexpensive living. Cost for mooring the boat at that time was $5.00 per day. Along the shore nearby were modern hotels including Holiday Inn, Marriott, Sheraton and Ramada Inn, where the cost for one night was about $100 for a single room.

There were other advantages to living on the boat. The hatch remained open at all times. It had been unnecessary to lock the boat at any of the marinas in Greece, Turkey or Israel. Advantages of boat life in addition to the low costs were that I had my books, writing paper, clothes and food available at all times. I purchased a new Peugeot bicycle for $123 with a small basket on the back over the rear wheel. Many loads of groceries were transported over the months from the supermarket, a mere three blocks away to CILIN II. The marina was located at the very heart of the city. It was all very convenient.

I was alarmed one day to find that $3,000 in U.S. one hundred dollar bills was missing from its hiding place on the boat. It was no surprise since the boat was left wide open during times I was away. I was distressed and concerned, but I did not tell anyone, even the Braun's. In trying to determine how the loss occurred, I recalled that at one time three well-dressed men had been walking along the quay. They had stopped and one had asked if they might look at my boat. It was not an unusual request. Many people are interested in various types of boats and the configuration of the interior. I stepped out onto the quay to make room for the three of them in the boat. After the loss of my money, I decided that the three men were members of the Israeli secret police. They were checking the place out. It seemed reasonable to me that the army intelligence force might be interested in a solo sailor spending so long a time alone and traveling about the countryside. I considered that one of them might have come back at another time during my absence to search the boat and had found the $3,000. They had taken it and there was no way I could get it back. I was not without funds because I was able to draw more money on my Visa credit card at the bank.

I suffered in silence over the loss for days until one day, while digging deep into a compartment behind the bunk, I came upon a tidy little package all wrapped up where I had hidden it weeks before. It was my $3,000.

Tel Aviv

Tel Aviv was the gateway to the Holy Land. From childhood, I had learned smatterings of Biblical history and my visit to Israel served to remind me how little I actually knew of it. I learned that guided bus tours reached out from the city each day to various points of interest in the little country of Israel. The buses were modern, air-conditioned vehicles. The highways were excellent and the tour guides were well informed and articulate.

More important to me were the many tours with friends, Jennings and Tamar Braun. They sailed TINKERBELL back to Tel Aviv from Cyprus a few days after my arrival. From that moment for the next few months we were together many times, touring the country in their automobile, attending movies and musicals or enjoying the delicious picnic lunches from the basket Tamar brought from the TINKERBELL from time to time. Automobile tours took us to Bethlehem, Jerusalem, Haifa, Caesarea and Megiddo.

Getting acquainted with the Braun's gave me a window on Israeli life. I learned that the Braun's were parents of two children, a boy and girl. They had left Israel to return to the United States after they had completed their college education and fulfilled their military obligations. Girls, as well as boys, are required to serve in their military forces. Girls are required to serve two years but men must remain in the reserve service until age 35. Soldiers were stationed wherever there were crowds of people, at the theaters and at the entrance of public buildings. Packages and handbags were examined at the entrance to department stores and other public buildings. It was not unusual to see girls in the uniform riding public transportation toting an automatic rifle.

NATIVITY

I HAD REMAINED IN ISRAEL FOR A long time for two reasons. I wanted to learn all I could about the Holy Land and I wanted to witness the nativity celebration at Christmas. We had arrived in Tel Aviv on October 20 and Christmas was more than two months away. It was well worth the wait. A week before Christmas, I made a bus trip to familiarize myself with the route to Bethlehem. I found that in order to reach Bethlehem it was necessary to take the bus 50 miles to Jerusalem and then transfer to another bus for the ten mile ride to Bethlehem. It was easy, and while in Bethlehem I even rented a hotel room for the night of the celebration to avoid trying to find my way back to the boat in the midnight crowd.

That was all well and good until December 24 when I took the bus to Jerusalem. There was no bus to Bethlehem. Israeli soldiers took over from there. They took us by bus to a camp in the country where we waited in a tent while the passengers were required to pass through a metal detector gate before proceeding to Bethlehem. Upon arriving at Bethlehem, we were required to pass through a second metal detector before we were finally allowed to proceed to the celebration. It was said that several hundred visitors from various parts of the world were later denied access to the nativity ceremony because of a bomb scare.

The main portion of the celebration was performed in the Church of the Nativity that was erected over the site of the manger where Jesus was born. To view the manger it is necessary to walk down a flight of stairs to a room. There, the manger in no way resembles the traditional manger as depicted in nativity scenes in America.

It is said that Helen, the mother of the Roman emperor of Constantinople, traveled to Palestine 600 years after the birth of Christ and determined the location of events in the life of Jesus based upon what she could learn from local people. The story takes something from the veracity of the various locations of the various sites.

For example, the site of the crucifixion, on a hillside, is obliterated by a building that was constructed over the site. The building has been damaged by wars and reconstructed several times over the years. Cynics will tell you that you may be taken to any one of three different fields where the shepherds observed the star of Bethlehem, depending upon which tour service you employ. So it goes, but the trip to the Holy Land was very rewarding. The knowledge that you are in the area where Jesus was born, lived, taught and was crucified is enough.

The American Ambassador gave me a card to present to the Mayor of Bethlehem with the assurance that I would be invited to attend the ceremonies inside the Church of the Nativity. I did not present the card for the reason that I wanted to remain outside where a major program was presented on a large platform next to the church by representative groups from China, Japan, South Africa, the U.S. and many other countries. The South Africa Chorale group and the National Chorale from Washington, D.C. were outstanding. They performed on the platform, one after another, throughout the evening.

The grand processional of several hundred Catholic priests was very impressive. Dressed in black cassocks with lace and knee length surplice, they formed up in a military type column for their entry into the Church of the Nativity.

Midst it all, thousands of people milled about the area. Not to be overlooked were the young people, backpacker types drinking beer, being rowdy, and throwing their beer cans on the ground.

It was well after midnight when the crowds began to wane. I walked to my hotel room that was less than a city block from the church and the milling crowd and enjoyed a good night of rest.

CHRISTMAS DAY IN BETHLEHEM

CHRISTMAS DAY WAS PEACEFUL IN BETHLEHEM. THE crowd of people was gone, leaving the village in the hills as quiet as if they had never been there. I walked along the empty streets until I came to a marketplace higher up the hill from where the celebration had taken place. There were shops with meat, fruit, vegetables and various items useful in the home. People in the marketplace were carrying on their activities seemingly oblivious to the celebration that had taken place at the Church of the Nativity the night before.

I talked to no one. I just walked and thought. I wondered if there might have been a market at that location when Jesus was in Bethlehem. As I looked across the countryside at the rocky hills, it seemed hard to conceive of people going to war and dying over land that was so unproductive. After I had seen all there was to see, I wandered back to the bus station for the ride to Tel Aviv and the boat.

I had seen the Holy Land and visited the most sacred place in the world. I was ready to sail on.

Tel Aviv to Larnaca, Cyprus

AFTER A VERY MEMORABLE VISIT TO THE Holy Land, I headed CILIN II back to Larnaca, Cyprus, a 180-mile trip. It would be my longest trip solo to date. It would be one of the first times in my sailing career cruising the Mediterranean Sea that I would be returning to a familiar marina. On previous trips to unfamiliar marinas and harbors it had been necessary to spend hours studying the cruising guides to make sure the course was safe.

For the Mediterranean Sea there are about five major cruising guides. In the eastern part of the sea, I was most concerned with "The Greek Water Pilot" and "The Turkey Water Pilot." They contained pictures of each marina and harbor, depth soundings and the nature of the sea floor at anchorages telling whether it was sand, mud, shale or whatever. They also showed the location of obstructions to navigation such as sunken ships, shallow waters and underwater rocks. In addition, the cruising guide would give a thumbnail sketch of history and points of interest in the area.

The cruising guide was an invaluable tool for navigating unfamiliar waters, but this was my first trip where I would not need it. I had previously spent two weeks at Larnaca and knew the marina well.

The sky was clear and the wind was very favorable as CILIN II nosed out of the big marina at Tel Aviv. About 20 hours out, unexpectedly a new problem arose. I became very ill. Heavy on my mind was the question that had been asked by friends and relatives about my solo sailing. "What if you get sick at sea?" That question did not bother me because I felt that it would never happen to me. It did. I became painfully aware of it when my joints ached and that was accompanied by a fever and sore throat.

There was nothing to do but set the sails and the automatic pilot on a heading of 340° and climb into the bunk. I was well out to sea and at least another full day's sailing to my destination. I slept soundly as the boat moved along with a good breeze.

Some time later a strange sound crept into my semi-conscious mind. It was a "click-clack" sound at about two second intervals. What was it? Where was I? I rose up and looked out at the dark sea. It was dark in every direction.

Then I realized that the wind had stopped blowing. CILIN II was sitting dead in the water, motionless, except for the swinging of the boom with a "click-clack" sound as the boat rolled with the gentle swells of the sea.

There was nothing to do but to return to the bunk and wait for the wind to come up again. At some time in the night the wind did come up, so I set the sails and the automatic pilot and returned to the bunk. When I awoke again, it was broad daylight and the Sat-Nav told me that I was 40 miles from my destination. If the winds held up, I would reach the marina before dark.

This time I did not need to study the cruising guide as I approached my destination. It was all very familiar to me. I found an open slip, moored CILIN II and though I was still very sick, it was necessary to go to the office to clear in before returning to the bunk. The following morning I visited a doctor's office and then spent the next three days aboard CILIN II recuperating. Then I knew the answer to the question about what you would do if you get sick while sailing alone. The answer was that you sail on.

CRETE

THE NEXT LEG OF MY JOURNEY TOWARD Gibraltar was to be to the island of Crete. First I would sail to the tiny island of Sesklia to spend the night, then on to Crete. The winds were good and it was an easy trip of 24 miles from Rhodes. At the island I found what appeared to be a new dock. The place was isolated with only a young boy present. As I approached, I asked him by sign language if there was sufficient depth for me to moor at the dock. He smiled and indicated that it was okay. By this time it was late afternoon. He disappeared and I secured my mooring lines and settled in for a good night's sleep with plans for heading out early the next morning.

I was awakened after a couple of hours by a thumping of the keel on rocks and quickly realized that the water next to the dock was too shallow for my four and one half feet draft. I must move or possibly suffer structural damage to the hull. In the dark, I was unable to see any other place to moor the boat, so I quickly released the mooring lines and set out to sea in the direction of Crete. CILIN II was making good progress, so I set up the automatic steering device and prepared a meal of spaghetti and meatballs. After that I settled in for a long night of sailing. The wind was good but there were dark broken clouds in the sky.

We were making good progress when I noticed some water on the deck in the fore part of the cabin. That was unusual and it caused me some alarm. I could not imagine that the bouncing on the rocks had damaged the hull; but where was the water coming from? I quickly pumped the bilge and for a time there was no more water, but after a few minutes, water was again flowing across the deck in the cabin.

This was serious. The idea that the boat was taking on water and might sink at sea was terrorizing. Again I pumped the bilge but again there was more water. The only thing I could think to do was to turn back in hopes of reaching the harbor at Rhodes before the boat sank. At the time, I was 25 to 30 miles from the nearest island.

I ran to the tiller, released the self-steering device and turned the boat 180°, heading back to Rhodes. I glanced up at the stars to get oriented when suddenly the boom slapped across just over my head so violently that it shook the entire boat. In my agitation about water in the boat I had not given a thought that the sail would jibe. Later I learned that the aluminum boom suffered a deep dent as it banged against the shroud. From that time on, it was a constant warning to me about the danger of letting the wind get behind the sails when it is blowing strong. It made me a little weak to contemplate what would have happened to me had I been standing a little taller in the cockpit. It could well have been the end of my sailing career.

When I gained my composure, I again set the self-steering device to guide the boat while I went into the cabin to see how much water had accumulated. I again pumped out the bilge and waited, but to my great surprise and delight, there was no more water coming in. It was incredible! I could not believe it.

I would sail on back to Rhodes and see what had caused the problem. It might be necessary to haul the boat out of the water to assess the damage to the hull. That would be expensive and cause a delay in my traveling. Dawn was breaking as I finally approached the familiar Mandraki Harbor in Rhodes. This time I again anchored outside and east of the Yacht harbor where I had anchored before. It was much better than working my way into the basin where hundreds of yachts were moored, but here I would have to throw out my anchor and then paddle to shore with a couple of mooring lines to secure the boat.

It was particularly arduous this time because I was very weary from being awake so long and from having undergone the trauma of thinking that the boat was going to sink in the middle of the sea. First I pumped up the inflatable cushion that provided a seat in the dinghy and then suffered mild shock when it bounced off the deck and went adrift in the sea. I could not swim after it because I was not sure I could get back on the boat, even if I could capture it and bring it back.

I hurriedly pumped up the six-foot long inflatable dinghy with the foot pump, attached the oars and dropped it over the side. All the while the rubber cushion was drifting farther across the water toward a commercial dock where a giant ocean-going transport ship was preparing to cast off. I rowed frantically toward the inflatable cushion in hopes that I could retrieve it just as the ship moved out from the dock. I wondered how fast the ship could move and soon found out as it turned and headed directly toward me. I lopped the cushion into the dinghy and with it for a seat I was able to get out of the way of the oncoming ship.

When I climbed back aboard CILIN II, I was delighted to see that there was no more water in the bilge. Whatever had caused the problem had stopped and I was safely at anchor back in Mandraki Harbor after a frightful night at sea. It was necessary to paddle ashore first to secure a 75 foot long mooring line, and then do it again with the second line. Then instead of going ashore, I slept.

In the late afternoon I paddled ashore and walked along the long line of yachts crowded in the Marina. There were so many yachts that it was necessary for them to line up two and three deep from the quay. It would be necessary for the boats, other than the one closest to the quay in his line, to move whenever a boat closer to shore wanted to leave the harbor. In addition to this inconvenience, tangled anchor rodes were frequent occurrences.

The marina at Rhodes was one of the most popular in the Mediterranean for yachters from Europe and other parts of the world, and for good reason. The weather through the summer months and into fall was ideal for sailing and accommodations were excellent.

Since I had cleared out of the harbor the day before and planned to depart the following morning, I decided to by-pass the formalities of checking in and then clearing out again, but this time instead of going to Crete, I would head west to the Isle of Symi and then west from there. There was no more water coming into the boat and I felt safe in assuming that whatever had caused the problem had gone away. It was good to know that I would not have the expense connected with hauling the boat out of the water and the delay it would cause.

I thought the sail to Symi would be easy. I had done it two times before and considered that it would be easy. After retrieving the mooring lines and pulling the anchor, I was on the way. I had sailed about an hour when my heart sank. There was water running across the deck in the cabin again. Without hesitation, I turned 180° and headed back to the harbor. I found a place where I could anchor along the shore. There I did what I should have done much earlier.

I examined the area from which the water was flowing, and much to my surprise, I found that a hose from a through hull seacock to the commode had pulled loose. No water came into the boat when it was sitting flat in the water, but when the boat was on a starboard tack, the seacock was below the waterline. With the hose disconnected, the water was spilling out onto the deck. I could not believe that the problem was that simple, and I felt foolish for not having sought out the cause for the problem earlier.

Then I pulled the anchor and headed out again for the Isle of Symi.

WESTWARD FROM THE GREEK ISLANDS

NAVPAKTOS WAS AS PICTURESQUE AS ANYTHING YOU could imagine, with its tiny ancient port, Venetian water fountains fed by mountain springs and the ruins of the ancient castle strewn over the hillside. It would be my last stop on the Greek mainland. The tour of the Greek Islands reviewing the historic ruins of antiquity was over. I had visited 15 islands and sopped up more ancient history than I ever expected and the experience was far more gratifying than I had imagined. Not only had I learned much about Greek history, I had become immersed in the study of the various layers of civilization which had molded the history of the Mediterranean Sea since before the time of Homer. There had been the Phoenicians, Persians, Greeks, Romans, Venetians and Turks. Each had strutted on the stage of power for a while, left their mark on history, and departed. Only a scholar of history could put them in the proper perspective. My thumbnail sketch whetted my appetite to know more about archeology and history and what had gone before. I caught myself wondering what I would do with all that knowledge at my age of 70 years. I would not teach it and I would never know enough to write about it. That had already been done by better scholars than me. The one thing I knew for certain was that traveling through the Greek Islands had been exceedingly rewarding to me.

My plan upon leaving the mainland of Greece was to sail westward. By this time I felt that I had endured enough storms in the Aegean Sea that I could sail across the Atlantic Ocean alone; so on June 14, 1988 I headed west across the Ionian Sea. My destination was the island of Cephalonia, a distance of 60 nautical miles. The wind died down in the afternoon and it became apparent that I would not reach the island before dark by sailing so I fired up the Volvo engine to increase my speed. At last darkness closed in, leaving me three miles from shore. Not wanting to approach a strange harbor in the dark of night, I turned off the engine with the intention of spending the night at sea.

When I cut the engine there was a wild noise like I had never heard before. At first it was a very loud, undulating roar that finally wound down to a clicking sound. Having never experienced anything like that before, I had no idea what had happened. I opened the hatch to the engine and with the aid of a flashlight, saw that the propeller shaft had pulled loose from the engine. The sound had been that of the propeller blades striking against the rudder as it whirled to a stop.

CILIN II at Illini, Greece

What was I to do there in the dark and three miles from shore? It was clear to me that I should make an effort to secure the propeller and propeller shaft before they came loose and fell to the bottom of the sea. First, I lowered the sails, and then put on the safety harness to go over the side and under the boat with a short piece of rope to tie the propeller shaft in place. With that accomplished, I pulled myself back up on the deck. At that time I had not mastered the business of heaving to, so I spent the entire night at sea sailing back and forth between the island and the mainland. I learned much later that I could have reattached the propeller shaft to the engine myself. I did not know what else to do. At daybreak I decided to sail back to the Greek mainland and find a port where I could get the shaft repaired.

The wind was good in the morning as I sailed back to the east. Then at about 11:00 a.m. the wind died down completely, leaving the boat dead in the water. At that point I was alarmed to see water coming into the bilge through the propeller shaft hole. Unless I could control it, the boat would surely sink. The situation was desperate and it was then that I decided to call for help. It was a surprise and great relief when the Greek Coast Guard responded to my plea on the VHF.

After about an hour I saw a ship coming in my direction. It was a long, long wait until she finally drew alongside and threw a line that I attached to the bow. We were off, but where we were going I did not know. Suddenly I realized that we were being towed much too fast. I motioned for the captain to slow down. He did slow down for a while and then resumed his speed. That happened repeatedly during the trip.

I had assumed that it was a Greek Coast Guard ship that had me in tow, but after a while a much smaller vessel sailed alongside displaying Greek Coast Guard markings and the flags from a number of countries. I assumed that the flags represented countries of yachts previously assisted. The captain waved cheerfully and passed us by. What I did not understand at the time was that it was a commercial fishing boat that was towing me. The captain had heard my call for help and had raced to me ahead of the Greek Coast Guard vessel in order to collect a huge fee for saving me.

At last we reached a port that I later learned was Illini, Greece, where I was escorted to the port Captain's office. There I learned that I had been towed for 13 miles by a Greek fishing boat. I was greeted like a hero from the sea. People could not have been nicer to me until I was notified by the fishing boat captain that his charge for towing me was $1500. I was shocked. The port Captain, customs officer, immigration officer and all seemed to be one happy family, happy to be extracting a large amount of money from a solo sailor in distress. I thought of the Italian Mafia, but this was Greece. The port captain suggested that I could probably recover my loss from my insurance company.

"But I have no insurance. Lloyds of London canceled it when I crossed the 34° meridian on the way to Israel," I explained.

My audience was unmoved by my explanation and continued to insist that I should call on my insurance company. The phone rang and I was much surprised to learn that the call was for me. It was a lawyer who seemed to know all about my case.

"I will represent you and file a claim against your insurance company to recover your loss," he explained. "The bill for my services will be included and your boat will be impounded until our claim is satisfied."

The idea of having CILIN II impounded in a foreign port while an ambulance-chasing lawyer pursued a worthless insurance claim struck terror in my heart.

"Listen," I said. "You are a lawyer. I am a lawyer, too. I don't want to have anything to do with you." With that I slammed down the receiver, fully expecting to hear more from him, but he never approached me again.

A big tent was set up on the shore where a banquet was in progress for something unrelated to my situation. The Coast Guard Commander from the local district appeared, resplendent in his white uniform, and I was invited into the tent for a meal, being treated like a hero from the sea. The people were all very friendly and the delicious fish dinner was much appreciated since I had not eaten for more than 24 hours. Uzo, the renowned Greek wine, was offered, but I declined.

After the meal and outside the tent a young boy said, "You are famous. You are on the radio and TV." That was exactly what I did not want. I do not know what their reaction would have been had they known that their "turkey" was a former governor of a state which they had never heard of, and I was not interested in finding out what they would think about that. What I wanted more than anything else was to get back on the boat and get some rest.

It had been a long and exciting 36 hours since I had last slept, but gradually the reality of my dilemma began to sink in. With dismay I learned that before I could get any rest, it would be necessary to travel seven miles to the bank in the nearest town to draw $1,500 on my VISA card to pay for my rescue.

It was an expensive lesson but I was learning the ways of the sea. Much later I learned that when a sailor is in distress and calls for help, he should not expect a friendly neighbor to come and give him a helping hand. I came to believe that when a boat is in distress and in danger of being lost, the owner may be charged an amount equal to the value of the boat upon being rescued. This was my first, but not my last, experience at being rescued. Others would be even more expensive.

When we arrived back at the port of Illini, the crowd had dissipated, the big tent was gone and everything was quiet except for the waves lapping upon the shore. I bade my rescuer and the port captain goodbye and climbed aboard CILIN II and slept. At dawn the following morning I sailed away before there was any activity around the port, and headed for Catania, Sicily, 330 nautical miles across the Ionian Sea.

Greece to Catania, Sicily

It would have been easy to sail to the southern tip of Italy, but I had received reports of much pilfering of equipment from boats in southern Italian ports. Other sailors had said that anything left unattended on deck was likely to be stolen. This included dinghies, engines, life rafts and even dinghy engines. That report may have been unwarranted, but I did not feel good about stopping there.

It was a long but enjoyable sail across the Ionian Sea except that I discovered on the first day out that the blue warning light on the Volvo engine indicated that there was no oil pressure. I knew that to run the engine with no oil pressure could cause severe damage to the engine. So we went on with a dead engine.

The winds were favorable and the seas moderately calm as we sailed toward Sicily. At night the moon was bright and I noticed that schools of fish two to three feet long were swimming alongside the boat. It was the same, night after night during my voyage to Catania. Time and again the fish reflected the moonlight as their bodies turned in the water. I was not prepared with proper equipment for fishing but I found the prospect of a fresh fish dinner irresistible. At first I tried rigging a line of light fishing cord, but it quickly snapped. Then I tried the fishing spear, which I had never used before. The point was dull and simply bounced off the body of the fish as I shot at one after another. I missed the opportunity for a good fish dinner for the simple reason that I did not have the proper equipment. What I needed was a strong line and a lure. At no other place in my sailing experience did I have so many fish swimming alongside as if CILIN II were the mother ship for them. They came so close that I could almost reach down and grab them beside the boat.

It was a stroke of luck seven days later that my boat approached the big Catania Harbor during the daylight, since the engine was not working. It was also fortunate that the wind was very light. I managed to stay out of the way of large ships entering and leaving the harbor. My cruising guide showed me that there was a private club at the far north end of the harbor. I made my way gingerly in that direction and felt good at my success until I reached the club and was waved off. The guard was so emphatic in expressing his displeasure that I made a 180° turn and sailed back in the opposite direction. I could not explain to him that I had no engine. I believe he would have allowed me to moor, had I been able to explain it to him. The wind was so light that CILIN II was barely moving, but at least she was moving. The cruising guide showed another marina at the north end of another finger of the harbor. I successfully made the turn and, after a long time, barely made it to the mooring. I learned that it was a luxury marina that charged $16 per day. That was more than I had ever paid, but I was very glad to get back on dry land.

I found a couple of mechanics who agreed to repair the engine. They worked part of one day disconnecting wiring and exploring the problem. Then I became uneasy about having a couple of people I knew nothing about taking the engine apart. Finally I asked them to stop working on the engine, but to reconnect the wiring so that I could have lights and radio as long as the batteries held up. I paid them for their work and set out for the island of Malta.

CATANIA, SICILY TO MALTA

MY DECISION TO SAIL THE 90 MILES to Malta with a dead engine seemed reasonable enough at the time. I was highly suspicious of the situation in Catania. There was no reason for it because everyone I met was friendly. I could not shake the impression that the Mafia, a paralegal criminal brotherhood organization dating from the Middle Ages, was in control of everything worth controlling here. I wanted to get away from it.

The city of Catania gave the appearance of a once magnificent metropolis with interesting and ornate buildings. I tried to visualize how it might have been 50 years earlier, but in the latter part of the 20th century it gave the appearance of a decadent, crumbling city. Still, there were colorful parks being maintained by the populous in a bustling, once-beautiful city.

As I was preparing to depart, I came upon a yacht in another part of the harbor bearing an American flag. The crew was from San Francisco and I was glad to visit with them as the only Americans I had met in the city. It was bad news for me to learn that they had been moored along the wall in the harbor where there was no charge. I had been moored at a marina, paying $16 per day, and harassed early each morning to pay the moorage fee. The proprietor acted as if he thought I might depart without paying.

My new friends generously offered to tow me out of the harbor when they learned that I was sailing without an engine. At about two miles out I let them know that I could make it on my own from here.

They insisted on towing me further, but I foolishly declined their offer, a decision I was later to regret. After we waved goodbye, sailing became impossible for me. It was surely a combination of tricky winds and sea currents. CILIN II jibed repeatedly. Winds off 10,000-foot Mt. Etna, a mere 20 miles to the north, gave me a rough time. At night when the wind came up strong, I felt that my safest course was in a northeast direction just off the wind. In the dark of night I saw a big ship that appeared to be on a collision course with me. I altered course and was relieved when she finally passed me by. After the wind subsided, I finally got the boat on a southward heading, the direction I needed to sail in the first place.

Sailing south along the east coast of Sicily, I wanted very much to visit the ruins of the historic city of Syracuse, but without an engine I did not want to hazard entering and leaving the port.

It seemed a long trip to the southeastern tip of the island. In the morning of the next day out from Catania I saw many large ships passing Cape Passero to the south of me. When I reached what I took to be the Cape, I was passing between the mainland and an off shore island. Suddenly I noticed that the depth sounding was reading seven feet. I could not believe it. I had seen the big ships passing the tip of the island. There was surely something wrong with the depth finder. I watched with alarm as it read six, five and then four feet. With a four and a half foot draft, I was certain that the depth finder was faulty. Then the shocking sound of the keel scraping the bottom. I was dumbfounded until I realized that Cape Passero, with deep water, was to the east of the small island.

I pondered what to do next. I saw a number of young boys swimming along the shore. They paid no attention to me whatsoever until I beckoned to them. Then three of them swam out to the boat. By sign language I showed them that I was aground and needed help. Upon my urging, they gave me a hand. Fortunately the three of them were able to move the boat into what I thought was deep water. I thanked them, and being so happy to be afloat again, handed each of them a $20 bill. Each one looked at his bill with disdain, not realizing the value.

With one dollar worth 12.50 Lire in their money, they probably thought the $20 bills were worth very little.

After the boys swam back to shore, I came to realize that I was still in shallow water. I could not move, and my helpers had left the shore. I was desperate. The only way I could move the boat was by the anchor. I paddled the heavy anchor and chain as far out from the boat as I could go. Then I dropped the anchor and went back on board to wench in the chain, getting in and out of the boat each time. When the chain was in as far as I could get it, I then took out the other anchor, paddled out, dropped it and repeated the same process as before. I repeated this procedure over and over for at least three hours. In all, I may not have moved CILIN II more than a hundred yards. It was late in the night when I gave up. I lay on the deck exhausted. When I awoke I looked up to see a cloud cover that gave the appearance of the inside of a huge tent. There were no stars to be seen and though it was dawn, the sun had not yet broken over the horizon.

I rose to find CILIN II still aground. I waited for a long time until a small fishing boat came out from shore. He recognized my situation very quickly. He took a line and was able to pull me a long distance until the depth finder showed 30 feet of water. I thanked him and handed him my last $20 bill. He seemed no happier with it than the boys had been earlier.

By that time I felt the strong urge for more rest. I thought my safety was assured and I was still very tired from the night's activities. I dropped anchor and slept. When I awoke I observed a fishing net spread out a couple of hundred yards ahead of me. As I prepared breakfast of coffee, toast and a bowl of oatmeal, I noticed that instead of being in front of me as it had been before, the net was now about 20 yards behind the boat. That was of no great concern to me until I started to pull up the anchor. It was then that I realized CILIN II had dragged the anchor and the chain was over the fishing net. I saw that the net looked new and well constructed. It was a very expensive net and if damaged could cost a lot of money to repair. I was in trouble again!

I also noticed that the net was made of heavy web material and about 15 feet deep. There was no way I could get over it.

The current was against me and if I tried to pass over the net, it would snag on the keel. So again I sat and waited.

I did not have to wait long until two young boys appeared in a fishing boat. They saw the problem quickly and tried to pull the net free, but with no success. As they could speak no English and I could speak no Italian, we could not communicate. The only thing I could tell them in sign language was already obvious. The anchor line was over the net. At last they gave up and motored away. It was not long before another boat appeared with two larger boys. Their efforts were the same as before and they soon withdrew. I could only imagine what they thought of me. Surely they had a good laugh about my situation.

It was afternoon when an old man with two helpers finally made the scene. He made no effort to communicate and I had the feeling that he was completely disgusted with me. Though he did not try to communicate, he knew exactly what to do. He directed his helpers to take one of my lines under the fishing net, attach it to my anchor chain and then release the other end of my anchor chain. It worked perfectly. CILIN II drifted away from the net, I pulled in my anchor and was on my way after the very worst night of my sailing experience up to that time. Had I known how many more such nights I would experience as I sailed the seas, my sailing might well have ended that very day.

MALTA

It was nightfall by the time I sailed along Cape Passero to head across the 58-mile channel to Malta. Though I was in a busy shipping lane, I laid down in the bunk for some sleep. At some time during the night I was awakened by the sound of a large ship. I jumped out into the cockpit and saw the lights of a ship that appeared to be coming directly toward CILIN II until I could see the green running light on the starboard side. It was going away from me but I could only guess how close it had been when it passed me. The only thing I knew for sure was that it was close enough to awaken me out of a deep sleep. I remained awake until dawn, watching while other ships passed in the distance.

Since leaving the big harbor at Catania, the trip had been rather hectic. First, there had been confused sea and winds taking up several hours before CILIN II was moving in the right direction. Then there had been the matter of running aground, and lastly the entanglement with a fisherman's net. With the breaking of a bright new day, I expected smooth sailing into Valletta Harbor, Malta. But there was still the problem of how I would get into the harbor without an engine.

The skies were clear blue as I approached the island at about mid-afternoon when I heard a disconcerting rumble in the distance. Could it be a storm? I did not think so, but it did increase with intensity. A couple of years before there had been a serious storm in the western

Mediterranean which had destroyed a number of boats in Italy. I hoped that this was not another one. My fears began to increase as the ominous rumble continued. By this time, there were no other boats or ships to be seen in any direction. Maybe they had been warned of an approaching storm. I turned on the VHF radio and it was not long before I heard, "All ships at sea! All ships at sea." Then static garbled the remainder of the message. Fearing the worst, I needed to do something.

The rumbling and roaring in the distance became even more intense and I became very uncomfortable. What was it? The sky was clear in every direction, but I felt I must learn if a storm was approaching. I called on the VHF. "Valletta Harbor Master, this is CILIN II, a sailboat. Would you please tell me what time the storm is expected to reach Valletta?"

The answer came back quickly, "No storm is expected. The weather is calm."

It was something else then. The rumblings were coming from the shore but I had no idea what was causing them.

About five miles out I called the harbor master again to report that CILIN II was approaching Valletta Harbor without an engine and would need help to get into the harbor. He reported that he understood my message and that I should call again when I was closer to the harbor. Then a call from a yacht that said that it was approaching the harbor from the northwest. It would arrive about the same time as CILIN II and would tow me into a mooring.

Soon I saw a sailboat in the distance approaching in my direction. He joined me, took me in tow and delivered me to a mooring in the marina. The crew was made up of four young men who not only helped me into port but then they treated me to a fine dinner at a nearby restaurant.

By that time, it had become apparent that the explosions and rumbling were coming from the city. "What in the world is all of that noise?" I inquired.

"It is coming from various churches celebrating their anniversaries," came the answer. That was it! I learned from my new friends that each Catholic Church on the Island of Malta saves up money throughout the year for a big weekend of pyrotechnic displays. I was told that the number of fireworks burned up on the three-day weekend would cost as much as $10,000 to $15,000. During the week before the celebration, workers are busy laying out the explosives on the ground, including numerous rockets, pinwheels and every kind of design for the most elaborate display. It all starts on Friday night, then resumes on Saturday with the finale on Sunday. Since nearly all of the people are Catholic, there are a large number of Catholic churches. On any given weekend there would be three to five churches celebrating their anniversary.

I did not like it because it reminded me too much of World War II when I was under devastating bombardment for weeks at a time by the Japanese. Also, I was sometimes concerned that the falling embers from the rockets might land on the sails. In addition to that, I wondered about the economics of the business and wondered if the money spent on fireworks might find a better use for education, sanitation or even for improving the streets and roads. I found I was in the minority with my thoughts. Everyone I questioned about it thought the fireworks were a great idea.

It was the summer of 1988 and I had been retired from my law practice in Indiana for a couple of years. Like many other retirees, I had the feeling that I should be doing something productive in my life, so I decided to return to the U.S. while the boat was in the shipyard of Valletta for a major overhaul of the engine. The 1988 presidential campaign was in full swing, so I went to Washington, D.C. and volunteered to work in the George Bush campaign for the Presidency.

I went to the Bush/Quayle campaign headquarters at the corner of 17th and H Streets. There I was told that I should go to the eighth floor. From the eighth floor I was sent to the sixth floor. But when I was told to go back to the eighth floor, I gave up. I decided to walk to the Treasury Building, a short distance away, to talk to Secretary of the Treasury, James Baker. It was well known that the secretary would have a key role in the Bush Campaign and I felt that he could help me. I knew the office well because I had been there a number of times with my wartime buddy, Dayton Drachenberg. His wife had been secretary for Secretaries of the Treasury for more than 20 years. With her there, I would be able to meet all of the office personnel. To my dismay, she was no longer there. A huge African-American receptionist asked me if I had an appointment. When I said that I did not have an appointment, he said I would have to write Mr. Baker a letter with my request.

That avenue not working, I sought out a friend, Mary Ellen Miller, who quickly got me an assignment as Deputy Director of Senior Citizens for the Bush/Quayle campaign. I had begun my quest as a volunteer.

I worked 7 a.m. to 7 p.m. each day, helping establish Senior Citizens for Bush/Quayle organizations in each state of the union. It was an interesting job with fax machines, computers and WATS telephone service to every state in the nation. These are all innovations that had not been in use during my campaign for Governor of the State of Indiana only 20 years earlier. Among other things, I had the duty of phoning members of the National Senior Citizens Committee for Bush/Quayle, which included National Chairman Bob Hope, Arnold Palmer and Jimmy Stewart and a whole host of celebrities to arrange their security clearances for a reception at Bob Hope's Hollywood home.

On the day of the famous debate between vice presidential candidates, Benson and Quayle, Dan Quayle appeared in person on the eighth floor to speak to the volunteer workers of the Senior Citizens for Bush/Quayle. He was completely muzzled by the Bush managers. Instead of allowing him to walk around and shake hands and visit, he was perched on a platform just outside the elevator door to give a canned speech to the volunteers.

Before Quayle spoke to the crowd, I passed him a hand-written note stating, "Cope and Woerner want to be your body guards when you are elected." He read it and quickly pushed it into his pocket. He knew Donald Cope and Dave Woerner very well, as members of the Pizza and Beer Drinking Society back in Indiana.

At the end of my efforts for the Bush/Quayle Campaign I received a nice letter from the Bush/Quayle Committee, advising me that since I had been a member of the campaign committee for President George Bush, I might be interested in applying for a position in the Bush Administration. After weighing the matter very carefully, I wrote back saying, "I have a sailboat in the Mediterranean Sea where life is a dream. Unless you have something better than that, we have nothing to talk about." With that, I packed up and flew back to CILIN II in the shipyard at Malta.

CHARLOTTE'S LEGACY

AFTER AN EXCITING INTERLUDE BACK INTO THE world of politics in 1988, I was back in Malta to take up the sailing trip where I had left off. CILIN II was still moored at the Malta Shipyard, waiting for repairs to her engine. On the first night back, I was awakened at 3:00 a.m. by someone knocking on the deck. I jumped up to find the security guard with a well-dressed man. It was a surprise having a visitor at that time of the morning.

"Have you seen a yacht by the name of CHARLOTTE'S LEGACY?" the guard inquired.

I thought for a moment and replied, "Yes, I have seen that name, but at the moment I do not remember where."

The guard thanked me and the two men departed. After that I could not get back to sleep as I was trying to remember where I had seen that boat. At last I was up and dressed and on my bicycle searching for CHARLOTTE'S LEGACY. My search was unsuccessful, but I did meet up with the guard and the man he had in tow. Then I learned that the man had flown from London with the intention of spending his fortnight vacation sailing with a friend from Malta to Barcelona. I could tell that he was weary and discouraged at not finding the boat.

"Listen," I said, "I know you are tired. I have an extra bunk where you can sleep until morning. Then you can find your friends."

He agreed, and climbed onto CILIN II for some rest. At dawn he was on his way to locate CHARLOTTE'S LEGACY.

I did not see the stranger until later in the day, and he had found his boat. It was owned by a 67 year old man and his two sons, ages 18 and 20. Things were looking up for him and he was confident he would soon be on the way to Barcelona. Days went by and I kept seeing the fellow from time to time. Then one day he told me there were delays caused by mechanical problems and already half of his vacation had expired. Life aboard the CHARLOTTE'S LEGACY was not very pleasant for him. There was much bickering between the father and his two young sons who were spending most of their time in the English pub across the street from the dockyard. He seemed more desperate from day to day.

At last I suggested, "I am going to sail to Gozo. If you are not going to get to go to Barcelona, you might enjoy a few days of sailing on CILIN II. The idea pleased him because, as it turned out, he had been to Gozo before. With that, he moved his luggage onto CILIN II and we headed for the tiny island of Gozo, only 20 miles from Valletta.

It was evening when we anchored in a little bay on the south end of the island. We spent the night aboard, and then caught a bus to Victoria, the capital of the island. We then transferred to another bus that would take us to the place the Englishman had been before. It turned out that the place was a huge stone structure surrounded by a high stone wall. The three-story building had eight bedrooms, a large kitchen and dining area completely furnished and with a colorful garden within the walls. The view from the deck at the top of the structure was spectacular, with gently sloping terrain down to the sea a mile away.

The place was named Fort Appleby and I learned that it was owned by a lady named Appleby in London and that she made it available to her friends who wanted to spend a fortnight vacation on the ancient island. All that she required was that her guests replace any items that were used and tip the maid for keeping the place in order. That seemed like a fair proposition. We remained there overnight. I sailed back to Valletta alone because my nephew, Jay Dolfuss, from Burbank, California was planning to visit me.

It was a happy day when Jay, his wife Carol and two young sons, Jason, age 10 and Andy, age 8, arrived. Jay and Carol slept in the cabin.

I slept in an awkward berth behind the navigator's table beneath the cockpit and the boys slept on deck under a canopy.

I knew that my best effort to entertain my visitors was to take them on a sailing trip back to Gozo to visit that picturesque island. We cleared customs and set out on what should have been a four hour trip, but it turned out that the winds were adverse. It was necessary to tack. Instead of making small tacks of an hour or two at a time, I took a starboard tack and held it for several hours. In doing so, we were far out at sea and missed seeing the interesting places along the shore, including the bay where the Apostle Paul was shipwrecked on his way to Rome, where he was later executed. It is said that during his stay on Malta, he influenced the conversion of the population to Christianity. It was surely one of the world's most successful evangelistic efforts because Malta now boasts that 98 percent of its population is Roman Catholic.

Darkness overcame CILIN II as she made her way toward the little bay at Gozo. Then appeared a boat headed on a collision course with us with a bright searchlight and bristling with machine guns. It appeared that he intended to ram CILIN II. Then a voice in the night asking us to identify ourselves. It was a Malta patrol boat. I identified myself and the boat, and then I reported that we were traveling from Valletta to Gozo. I had properly cleared the port at Valletta before departing. They were not satisfied and continued asking questions. When I repeated that we had departed Valletta at 8:30 a.m. and were properly cleared for Gozo, they finally seemed satisfied and pulled away, telling us to pull into the bay.

For me it had been a normal encounter, as I had been stopped many times and gone through the same routine before. But for my passengers, it had been a hair-raising experience. The boys later reported that we had been attacked by Russian soldiers during the night.

Though I was uncertain of the route, we found our way to Victoria and back to Fort Appleby. There we found my friend taking advantage of all that the place afforded. He had met and fallen in love with a British woman who was also on a fortnight vacation. She had formerly served in the British diplomatic service in Malta. We all became one big happy family, the English couple, the Dolfusses, and I.

The Englishman and I went to the market and bought groceries, including lots of vegetables and a dressed rabbit. That night we enjoyed a delicious rabbit stew in the big dining room area.

The following day the Dolfuss family and I toured Victoria and the countryside. The island looked as if it had changed very little in the past hundred years. During World War II, when the mainland of Malta and the harbor at Valletta had been under siege and bombed ruthlessly by the Axis powers, little Gozo, which was of negligible military significance, was bypassed. Though the buildings were ancient, the island appeared to be taking on a new life as more and more people were discovering it as a haven of tranquility.

Upon returning from a day of sightseeing in the village and in the ancient castle, the Dolfuss family and I returned to Fort Appleby to find that our friend and his new love had prepared another feast. This time the main course was chicken stew. The following day the Dolfuss family opted to rent a car and take the ferry boat back to Valletta instead of risking another trip at sea on the CILIN II.

Fort Appleby turned out to be a delightful stop along the way. When I asked the maid what would be a reasonable fee for her services, she seemed delighted with $30 for the two nights that the Dolfuss family of four and I had stayed at the fort.

After that, I sailed back to Valletta alone, but this time I stayed closer to the shore and enjoyed a peaceful return to the marina. The night of my arrival I observed a commotion and a crowd along the street near the marina. I walked over to see that it was a very large procession. A statue was being lowered from the second floor of a church. I observed it to be a statue of the patron saint of the community. Unlike other statues I have seen, this statue had a very pretty face.

A band of musicians led the procession after the patron saint was in place on a carriage, but it stopped after a short distance. The streets were crowded on both sides as I moved toward the front of the procession to see what was causing the delay. There I saw a number of teenage boys, stripped of clothes to the waist, falling in the street ahead of the parade and stopping the procession.

I learned that the youngsters were protesting the selection of the band which had been chosen to lead the procession. Police moved in to remove the culprits. No sooner had they dragged one of the bodies out of the way and gone for another, the first was back on the street again. The police were outnumbered. Their efforts to clear the way was frustrated until the protesters finally grew tired and the impatient procession moved on. It traveled a route of several blocks and then returned to the church, where the patron saint was restored to her perch in the church.

MALTA TO BARCELONA

THE DISTANCE FROM VALLETTA, MALTA TO BARCELONA, Spain was 800 nautical miles and should, I thought, take eight days to sail, good weather permitting. Malta, with its dramatic history of being the last home of the Knights of St. John, had been a very interesting stopover. In a sense, it was a continuation of the story of the Knights after they had been driven out of Rhodes by the Turks in 1523. Being without a base of operation for 50 or 75 years after their defeat at Rhodes, King Charles of the Holy Roman Empire had granted them the Island of Malta.

Upon taking up residence on the island in the Mid-Mediterranean Sea, the Knights who had since their inception at Rhodes performed as male nurses to support European Crusaders en route to Palestine, took to piracy upon the high seas. Apparently a great many of them traded their humanitarian ways for a more adventurous life as pirates.

Turkey was a major power in the Mediterranean Sea, so the Knights took it upon themselves to attack Turkish ships near Malta. In retaliation, the Turks decided to eliminate the Knights one more time. The island was under siege in 1565.

The vicious Turks came on in full force, threatening the continued existence of the Knights of St. John as a viable operation. Life on the island was austere and precarious. The Knights pleaded for help from the major countries of Europe, but no help was forthcoming. The powers of Europe may have considered the Knights were fighting a losing battle and efforts to assist them against the powerful Turks would be useless. Nevertheless, the valiant Knights held on during the dreadful siege until at last the Turks gave up on their effort to conquer the island and withdrew.

Upon seeing the success of the Knights in defending their island, the various powers of Europe then sent aid for building up the fortifications of Malta until a substantial defense system was in place. The Turkish army never came to Malta again, but tourists from over the world have come in large numbers to view the magnificent structures at Malta, just as they have come to Rhodes to see the fortifications built there to protect the Knights from the Turks.

The siege by the Turks had not been the end of the troubles for the residents of the little island. It was bombed mercilessly by the Axis forces in World War II. The island held on tenaciously and refused to surrender. British Prime Minister Winston Churchill called Malta "our only unsinkable aircraft carrier."

I had found Malta to be a very interesting stop along the way, but there were more seas to sail. After departing Valletta Harbor heading for Barcelona, I encountered several days of very rough seas that would test my ability as a novice sailor.

HALLUCINATIONS

THROUGH THE EARLY MORNING LIGHT, I NOTICED two young fishermen on shore about 20 yards away. They stopped their work and called to me in a language I could not understand. My first impulse was that they were Indians but that could not be so. I understood that they were asking if I wanted the police and did I have a radio.

I shouted, "No!" to both questions. I did have a radio but I did not want the police. I looked about to see that my sailboat was beached and lying on its side with the mast at a 45° angle above the water. I climbed overboard into waist-deep water and tried desperately to push the boat into deeper water. It would not budge. It was aground near a sandy beach. After the fisherman gave up on me and sailed away, I sat atop the boat for a long time, wondering where I was and how I got into this predicament. I honestly didn't know.

Slowly it came back to me. I had been sailing from the Island of Malta to Barcelona, Spain, a trip I had considered would take about eight days. Because the seas had been very rough, I had made very slow progress and after three days I was weary and very tired from lack of sleep. The sea was so rough, in fact, that after a few days I decided to put in at Port Empedocles, a harbor on the south shore of the island of Sicily, only 80 miles from Malta.

As the afternoon wore on, it became apparent that I would not make the harbor before dark. After the sun set, a light on shore showed me that I was west of my destination. As I proceeded to the east, I was amazed to find the shore aglow with lights. I started looking for the red and green lights that would show me the entrance to the harbor, but they were not to be seen. I felt secure that I was in the right location though the Sat-Nav refused to give me a fix. Eager to drop anchor in the harbor and get some rest, at last I doffed the sails and went on the engine. Then I saw a thrilling sight. Before me on the shore was a huge airdrome with a magnificent spaceship. I was sure that I had come upon a secret Italian spaceship airdrome. I steered CILIN II in closer to shore to get a better look at the gigantic aircraft. I thought that I could see crew members moving about the craft. I got out the binoculars to get a better look.

Then to my surprise and disappointment, instead of space ships and an airdrome, I saw lights, trees and buildings. There were no space ships and no airdrome. Without the binoculars, the pattern of the light had deceived me.

I motored on and on, back and forth, searching for the entrance to the harbor intentionally far from shore to avoid hitting an unseen obstacle. If I had had radar, it would have been easy to find the harbor, but I had no radar. Finally, I gave up and decided to go out to sea for the night and approach the harbor during daylight. After some time I came to realize that instead of skirting the shore, I was motoring up a river. Far off to the port side was a lonely cottage in the middle of a field and then I saw a very strange sight indeed. A man was sitting in the cockpit of my boat right across from me! He wore a hat, coat and tie and looked straight ahead, never looking at me or speaking to me. He looked like a Russian and I made no effort to converse with him as we motored along. It was all very weird. There was no moon yet I could see clearly. Though we were moving along at a good speed, the house in the field was still as when I had first seen it.

Then came a sight that was even more strange, but it did not disturb me at the time. There was an automobile driving up the river ahead of us! After a while it stopped. A man climbed out of the passenger's side of the car, walked to the rear of the automobile, examined something, then got back into the car and proceeded up the river.

After that I noticed a large number of cars coming into the river from a side road and proceeding up the river ahead of us. Far ahead, the top of a hill was aflame with bright lights. For some reason I thought it was a mountain villa and the automobiles were headed there for a big party. I did not want to attend a party. What I wanted more than anything else was to get some rest and sleep.

We had left the little house in the field in our wake, but then there appeared a gigantic vision of a human head in blue mist atop a peak off to the starboard. It was a handsome, stoic figure and I felt certain that it represented the person who was holding the party. My passenger was still looking straight ahead and paying no attention to me. Somehow I felt that I was under his control.

Up ahead I saw a wide place in the river that would give me room to turn the boat around and head back toward the sea. I had no intention of going to the party at the villa, but I wondered if my passenger would react to my action. When I reached the wide place in the river, I swung the boat around 180° to the port and headed back downstream. A glance at my passenger showed me that he was unmoved by my action.

As we proceeded back downstream, we came to a fork in the river, which I had not observed on the way upstream. Which way to go? I was uncertain. I took the fork to the left for no reason other than that I had to go one way or the other. It was not long before I realized my mistake, because soon I again saw the figure in the blue mist high above the mountain. A handsome face it was and I felt certain it represented a member of the Mafia who was holding the party at his villa. Then again I was at the little house in the middle of the field down by the sea. Then a bump. The boat stopped. After a short time it jolted forward a short distance.

During all this time I had a weird feeling that some Mafia person was controlling the boat. Then there came the feeling that there was a giant Indian under the boat pushing it along from time to time. He would keep pushing until I was safely afloat, back on the sea.

Much to my surprise, my passenger had disappeared as mysteriously as he had first appeared in the cockpit. He had never spoken to me or me to him.

On the starboard shore I saw a girl sitting on the porch of a small cottage as CILIN II was moving steadily toward the sea. To the starboard was deeper water and I felt confident that my helper under the boat would take me in that direction. It did not work that way.

The boat moved to the port where the water was shallower and stopped moving.

It was then that the fisherman had offered to call the police but now they were gone and I was alone. With nothing more important to do, I climbed into the cabin to get something to eat. The gimbaled burner on the stove was at a ridiculous angle but it worked. I made a cup of coffee and then had a bowl of cold cereal. Though I was very tired, there was no way I could lie down and be comfortable because of the angle of the boat.

I sat out on top of the boat and little by little came to realize that I had been suffering from wild hallucinations through part of the night. After failing to find the entrance to the harbor the night before, my head had played tricks on me and the boat had run aground near the mouth of a river. The cars I had seen were traveling along a road beside the river. There had been no cars in the river, no figure in blue mist above the mountain and no Russian in the cockpit with me.

The hallucinations had been unlike anything I had ever experienced before. I had no idea that such a thing could happen. The things I imagined I saw were as real to me as if they had really happened. It took a while for me to understand that it had been imaginary.

I came to realize that my condition was a result of fatigue and because I had been pushing myself to go without sleep and proper food. I resolved that I would not let myself get in that condition again, a resolution hard for a solo sailor to keep.

After I had come to understand what had really happened, I turned my thoughts to the condition of the boat. Had it been damaged so much that I would not be able to continue sailing? Had my sailing days come to an end? Would I have to abandon the boat and fly back to my home in Indiana? Prospects for the future were very depressing.

As I was mulling these things over, my thoughts were interrupted by the sound of a helicopter approaching from the west. It circled the boat numerous times and as he came lower, I could read CAPITIANA and assumed it was the Captain from a nearby Italian navy station. As he drew closer I stood up in the cockpit and waved my arms to let him know that I was all right. When he came very low, I stepped into the cockpit and was drenched from head to foot by the wash from the propeller blades. After that he gained altitude and headed back to the west.

As I sat contemplating what the future might hold for CILIN II and for me, I observed a ship approaching from the west. It was still a great distance away when it stopped and launched a large dinghy with five men aboard. Upon their arrival at CILIN II, it was quickly apparent that no one could speak English, but they were able to convey that the Lieutenant would arrive soon.

In due course a fine looking young officer who spoke fluent English did arrive from the west on the same navy ship as before. Again it anchored out a couple of hundred yards and delivered the Lieutenant to CILIN II via the dinghy. He asked me if the boat was strong. I assured him that it was strong. Then he asked for a face mask and went under the boat to access the damage, if any. Apparently he found none. I was still under the illusion that a Mafia figure was in control of the situation. In my mind the Lieutenant was asking questions to try to appraise the value of the boat.

Back in Malta a retired British admiral had advised me to never let another boat tow me with his lines. He had told me that under maritime law, your boat might be considered salvage and the boat that towed you might recover an amount up to the value of the boat. I felt certain that the questions had to do with assessing the value of the boat. Other sailboats cost $50,000, $75,000 and $100,000. Nobody would believe that CILIN II had cost only $13,000.

After examining the situation, the Lieutenant departed for his ship and sailed away, leaving five Italian sailors sitting on the side of the hull of CILIN II. We waited for a long time until at last the ship reappeared upon the horizon. Again he anchored far at sea. This time the Lieutenant mustered three small fishing boats with outboard engines to try to pull CILIN II into deeper water, but they were unable to move her.

Again the Lieutenant sailed away on his ship, to return a couple of hours later with three larger vessels. The same scene was re-enacted as before with the same results. Again the navy Lieutenant sailed away to the west, leaving me alone. It looked very much as if CILIN II could not be recovered and my sailing days were over. The thought of losing her was devastating and I was very much discouraged. What should I do?

While we were waiting for the Lieutenant to return again, I was summoned to the shore where a group of people had been watching the rescue efforts. There, another Italian Navy Lieutenant, who let me know that he liked to be called Captain, announced that his friends with a fishing boat would be willing to help. I let him know that the other Lieutenant was in charge of the operation and went back to CILIN II to wait.

It was growing late in the afternoon when a large Italian Navy vessel came to within 100 yards and hooked his line onto CILIN II. Then the Lieutenant from on shore had his fishermen put their lines on CILIN II. There was no purpose in it whatsoever. It was clear that the big Italian Navy ship needed no help from the tiny fishing boat.

When the signal was given, the big Italian vessel took CILIN II with one mighty swoosh. She was afloat in deep water. I raced into the cabin to make sure that no water was coming in and gave the ship the signal. The fishing boat disengaged his lines and the Navy ship towed me a long, long distance to the Navy headquarters. I was surprised to learn that it was the port at Porto Empedocles, the port I had been seeking the night before.

I tied CILIN II along a wall and fell into my bunk to sleep. It was not for long. Someone knocking on the boat informed me that the Captain wanted to see me, so I followed him to the Captain's office. There I was informed that the American Consul in Palermo wanted to talk to me on the phone. The call was put through quickly. The American Consul greeted me and expressed his pleasure that my boat had been rescued from the beach. Then to my surprise he stated, "You are going to have to pay the fishermen who helped you."

I argued, "But they were not necessary. I did not need them. There was no question but that the Navy ship would do the job."

"Yes, but they say they were necessary and they helped you. You are going to have to pay them." I assured the Consul that I would take care of the matter and headed back to CILIN II. Outside the door of the Captain's office waiting for me was the Lieutenant who wanted to be called Captain.

"The fishermen have to be paid." He announced. We walked along the path toward my boat until we came to a spot where the two fishermen were waiting.

"How much are they charging?" I asked as we drew near. I could not help but notice that one of them was wearing an expensive gold necklace.

"One million Lire," was the answer.

I was stunned and delighted at the same time. Stunned because they had the nerve to ask for anything at all, and delighted because the amount was so small compared to what they could have asked. In American money that was $800. But they could have asked for much more, and with the American Consul on their side, they could have gotten it.

I paid the money, went back to the boat and slept through the night. In the morning I learned that I was indeed in the port I had been seeking when I went to sleep. I had sailed eight miles down the coast before the boat ran aground on the beach.

There was a request for a letter of commendation for the two Lieutenants. I wrote it because I was grateful to the first Lieutenant for working so diligently in spending the full day in three attempts to extract CILIN II from the beach. I could not resist stating that the Italian Navy, *with the assistance of a fishing boat*, pulled CILIN II off the beach. I regretted that later, because it was not fair to the first Lieutenant. He should have received a medal. My real appreciation was for the Italian Navy. It could have charged a whopping fee for getting the boat afloat and towing me eight miles to Porto Empedocles. It charged nothing.

I stayed a couple of days with CILIN II moored along a wall at the Italian Navy station, then decided to go into the city to get some money on my Visa card. Then I ran into an unexpected problem. In other ports I had visited I had always found it easy to find someone who spoke English, but not so in Porto Empedocles. I approached person after person on the street with the question, "Do you speak English?" The answer was always the same until one man surprised me by answering me in perfect English.

"Where did you learn to speak such good English"? I asked.

"Oh, I worked for 20 years in the United Nations in New York City," was the proud reply.

"My goodness!" I responded. "What did you do?"

"I was a night custodian," he answered, almost boastfully.

I knew immediately that this was a man I wanted to talk to. Besides finding a bank, I was also interested in getting a Sicilian's opinion of the great General George Patton, who had spearheaded the American military forces across Sicily in World War II.

When I asked the question, he answered excitedly, "Oh, General Patton made a great mistake."

I knew the general had been accused of slapping a G.I., but that was surely not the mistake he was talking about. "What did he do?" I asked.

"He should have put up an American flag and made Sicily the 49th state in the union," was his matter of fact reply.

I could tell the man was sincere and saw no point in arguing the case, but in my mind I wondered how acceptable his idea would have been to our allies. I got my directions for finding the bank, and after drawing some money on my Visa card, I returned to the boat and made preparations for the trip to Barcelona.

COSTA DE SOL

THE SOUTHEAST COAST OF SPAIN, KNOWN AS the Costa de Sol, with its warm weather and many days of sunshine, is a haven for Europeans during the cold winter months on the continent. It was there that I had some unusual experiences.

In Cartagena, Spain I suffered a major disaster. At the end of a hard day of sailing, I tied up along a wall in the harbor adjacent to a public park area. The wall stood five feet above the deck of the boat. I was awakened late in the night when I heard someone jump down from the wall onto the top of my boat. Thinking that he had jumped back up on the wall, I went back to sleep. The next morning I learned that my wallet with a couple hundred dollars in cash, my Visa credit card, driver's license and all had been stolen. The thief had entered the cabin while I slept and lifted the wallet from the navigator's table. Fortunately, my passport was in a different location at the time and it was not taken. I reported the theft to the city police. When I went to warn the couple on the boat moored ahead of me along the wall, I learned that their boat also had been entered during the night while they were sleeping. The thief had taken a radio from them. From all of that, I learned of the difficulties that stem from being in a foreign country with no money. It caused me no end of trouble for many weeks. I did phone my bank in Indiana and waited several days for enough money to tide me over until I reached Gibraltar.

A few days later, when I moored in the small port of Marbella, on down the Spanish coast, I took a walk in the evening along the city streets to view the sights. As I strolled along, a small fellow who appeared to have been looking in shop windows stepped back and bumped into me. He then started dancing around me and muttering something I could not understand. Thinking that he was trying to apologize for bumping into me, I kept saying "No hablar español." Then suddenly I realized that he had his hand in my left pocket. I grabbed it and shouted, "You had your hand in my pocket!"

It was no surprise to him. Of course he knew it. Then I said, "I ought to call the police."

That did seem like a good idea so I screamed "Police! Police!

My friend quickly faded away down the street and then, for the first time, I observed that he had a companion who had been in close range to assist him in case he needed help. It was a great relief to me when I found that I still had the $55.00 that had been in that pocket, the only money I had until I reached Gibraltar.

GIBRALTAR

APPROACHING GIBRALTAR FROM THE EAST GAVE THE illusion of an island in the sea. For hours, the portion of land connecting it to the mainland of Spain remained below the horizon until I actually had the feeling for a long time that it was not connected. This huge rock of myth and legend seemed actually to float on the surface of the water. Finally, as my boat came closer, a thin fringe of land appeared between the rock and the mainland.

Prospects for visiting this historic bastion of British might brought a certain excitement and curiosity. What would it be like? Who might I meet? What adventure might it have in store? Arrival seemed to take forever but at long last I was looking up at large slabs of cement on the side of the hill which I recognized to be water catchments. The sea chart showed a large area in the southeast part of the port as being occupied by the British Navy. Following the markers, I came to a long channel that led to two marinas. I was almost there. Then a cruiser pulled alongside with the Captain shouting, "Get that Spanish flag down. Don't you know that you are in British waters?" I did not know that I was in British waters, but the Spanish flag had been the least of my worries until that time. I was concerned about finding a place to moor CILIN II in the midst of heavy traffic in the two marinas ahead of me.

First, I must draw alongside the customs and immigration office. There I found the officials friendly and efficient. I also noticed the officer who shouted at me so rudely about the Spanish flag, visiting with some of his fellow officers in the Spanish language.

Then there was the matter of choosing between one of the two marinas. That became easy when someone ahead of me guided me to a mooring place. Once ashore, I promptly went to the marina office to explain that I had been robbed in Cartagena and that I would not be able to pay the moorage fee until I was able to have money transferred from my bank in Indiana. That was easy. The clerk agreed that there would be no problem.

Since it was late in the afternoon, it was necessary to wait until the next day to go to the bank and request that $2,000 be forwarded to me from my home bank in Seymour, Indiana. With the matter taken care of, I strolled about the city, viewing the shops and buildings. Among other things, I was delighted to learn that there were two very large Safeway supermarkets stocked as fine as any I had ever seen in America. They were in stark contrast to the so-called supermercados of the Mediterranean Sea, which many times were tiny rooms sometimes as small as 20 feet square. I soon learned that people from all along the Spanish coast flocked to Gibraltar on weekends and holidays to shop in the free markets because the socialistic government of Spain could not provide the bountiful items at reasonable prices that were available in the Gibraltar markets.

One of the most important items on my list of things to do was to climb to the top of the rock; a rock that long has been a symbol of ability and permanence, a rock claimed by a prominent American insurance firm as its logo. On the third day, I started on what I thought would be a difficult climb. It was not. It was long, taking about an hour, but it was an easy climb. From the top I could see far up the Spanish coast where I had sailed, and across the channel to the south was the country of Morocco, on the northern coast of Africa. More awesome to me was the sight to the west of the channel that I would soon be traveling on the way to the Atlantic Ocean. Storms in the Atlantic had held up a number of yachts waiting for better weather. I knew that there would be storms. The prospects for bad weather loomed up as a major concern about the crossing. How violent might they be? How might my small boat react? Would my life be in danger?

On the way down the hill, I passed the famous pack of monkeys that have occupied Gibraltar for centuries. I talked to them in my best monkey-talk, but they just stared back at me with that "What is the matter with that guy?" look in their eyes. Getting no response, I made my way back down the hill to CILIN II.

Back at Shepherds Marina, little groups of anxious sailors gathered from time to time along the quay discussing the prospects for a break in the weather so they could go sailing. There were interesting speculations about prospects for storms in the Atlantic to subside. I knew a number of the sailors from previous stops along the way in the Mediterranean and stopped to listen in on their conversations.

It was a bit intimidating to me when I learned that most of the captains had been sailing on the ocean for years, many since childhood. Some were graduates of the Coast Guard Academy or other maritime institutions. It became obvious that I had less experience sailing on the sea than any of them. Through all of the conversations, another thing became obvious to me. It was that everyone I talked to was planning to sail around the world. They were not just concerned about crossing the Atlantic Ocean. They were talking about sailing around the world. I had never thought seriously about that. My head started swimming. I thought of nothing else and the more I thought about it, the more excited I became. Around the world! What an exciting thing it would be to do!

I had come to the Mediterranean Sea to view and learn about the wonders of that great Greek civilization of some 2,000 years ago. It had been far more interesting than I ever could have dreamed. Imagine how much more I would encounter sailing around the world!

I know my boat well and I had endured some fierce storms in the Aegean Sea. I felt I could handle the storms in the Atlantic. I finally decided that I would give it a try, but in the back of my mind was one disquieting note. Someone along the quay had mentioned the danger of whales capsizing small sailboats. A young lady in the group expressed her concerns saying, "I would never go the Atlantic Ocean in one of those small boats because whales have been known to capsize them."

That got my attention and I spoke up, "You mean a whale can upset a sailboat?" I asked.

"Yes, it has happened. One couple had their boat capsized by a whale and they spent weeks in their dinghy before they were rescued."

That was a danger I had never heard of before but it seemed like a remote possibility to me. It was a chance I would just have to take. In my travels in the Mediterranean Sea, I had sailed as far east as Tel Aviv, Israel. I would take that as my starting point and sail west from Gibraltar until I reached Tel Aviv again. In leaving the Greek Islands and sailing into the Atlantic, I suddenly became aware that I would be sailing into a world which was totally unknown to the people who inhabited the Greek Islands 2,000 years earlier. Marco Polo, a Venetian traveler, had acquainted the Greek world with the existence of China hundreds of years after the death of Aristotle, Socrates and Plato.

Of more immediate importance at the moment than my dream of sailing around the world was the matter of getting my money transferred from my bank in Indiana to Gibraltar so I could pay my moorage fee at Shepherds Marina.

On the third, fourth, and fifth days, I had applied to the bank to see if my money arrived. It had not. Equally often, the money collector from the marina office came by the boat, demanding that I pay my moorage fee.

"But I have no money. I explained that when I first arrived," I pleaded. It did no good. Then I went to the marina office and requested that they stop harassing me.

"But you must pay the moorage fee," he stated flatly. The only thing that relieved my concern was that at no time did the marina officials demand that I move out of the marina.

I became more concerned about my money when a fellow yachtsman told me that he once had to wait for two months for the transfer of $26,000 from his home bank account. With the pressure from the marina office for payment, I felt helpless. I went to the telex office and asked how long it would take my message to get to the U.S. His answer was, "It is instant. It is received in the U.S. within a second of the time it is sent," he stated.

With that I went back to the bank for my fifth trip. The teller went into a back room as he had done each time before. The answer was the same. "I am sorry Mr. Whitcomb, but your money has not yet arrived." I was disturbed and I was mad to think that the bank might be holding my money. I had talked to other sailors and they believe the banks held money from people like me in order to draw interest on it. I decided that was the case. I was also embarrassed that I could not pay the marina for my moorage fee, so I made up my mind to take action.

On the sixth day, when the teller returned from the back room with the sad news that my money had not arrived, I let him have it. "All right," I said, "that does it. I am going to report this to the banking officials right away. I have had enough," I threatened.

"Let me look again," he requested. After a few minutes he returned again, telling me that the money had not yet arrived.

"All right," I said. "I am going to the banking officials right away." I turned and started toward the door when I heard my name.

"Mr. Whitcomb, Mr. Whitcomb," another man called as he walked from the back room. "Mr. Whitcomb, your money has just come in."

I thought it was some coincidence that the money arrived just as I was on the way to report to the banking officials. In truth, I had no idea who the banking officials were or where they might be, but it mattered no longer.

The marina bill was paid and I had money in my pocket. I walked along the street, feeling much better about Gibraltar. In a park I listened to a British Army military band in full uniform. It seemed to be a remnant of the old powerful British Empire. Along with this were rumors of pressure by Spain for possession of the rock.

GAS FOR COOKING

THE BOTTLE THAT PROVIDED FUEL FOR THE two gas burners on the stove in the galley was getting low. I wanted to get it topped off before setting out on the trip to the Canary Islands. I had previously understood that camping gas was available everywhere. Not so. There was no place to fill the bottle on Gibraltar and I was advised that the customs officer would not allow me to take it across the border into Spain. But a young hippie-type man with long hair told me that he would carry it across the border in his backpack. "I have already been across and back a couple of times and they never checked my backpack," he volunteered.

"OK. I'll take my bicycle and we will make the trip," I said, glad that I had found a solution to the problem. We set out to cross the big international airport that separates Gibraltar from the mainland of Spain. The customs officer was on the Spanish side. The street to Spain crosses the middle of the busy airport. Upon the arrival or departure of planes, bells, whistles and lights are activated and gates are closed to clear the runways.

I peddled slowly and my backpacker friend moved along with the crowd crossing the runway until we reached the customs officers. We showed our passports and then, to our surprise, the officer asked, "What do you have in the backpack?"

My friend unzipped the backpack so the officer could see the gas bottle. "OK," said the officer. "I'll let you take the bottle in, but you will not be able to bring it back." That was a victory of a kind, but next we needed to get it filled before worrying about how we would return it to Gibraltar.

At the office of the gas company in the city, the lady was furious at the idea that we would try to purchase camping gas. That was a French gas container and she would have nothing to do with us. She did not even want to talk about it. We had failed. The cost of gas was very low because it was subsidized in Spain, but that was of no consequence to me. Getting the tank topped off would be worth a lot.

On the return to Gibraltar I placed the gas bottle in a paper sack in the bicycle basket, showed the customs agent my passport and rode across the airport back to the boat without incident.

Upon discussing my problem with friends back at the boat, I learned that there was a gas plant four kilometers west of town and there was no question but that I could get the bottle filled there. Early in the morning of the next day I rode through the customs gate with the bottle still secure inside the bicycle basket. It was an easy ride to the gas plant, but I was alarmed to see a crowd of soldiers in uniform about the place. A labor union strike had brought out the troops to maintain order.

When I finally found the man in charge of dispensing gas, I was advised that he dispensed gas to gas trucks only. I should go to a location a mile north of town. That was the place where small bottles were filled. So I peddled the bike back into town and a mile north to the small tank distribution center. The operator was very friendly and explained that there was no problem in filling my bottle, but first I would have to go into the city to get a paper authorizing him to fill the bottle. He obligingly wrote the address and I was on my way again. Upon reaching the address he had written on the paper, I was dismayed to see that it was the office where I had been so rudely treated the day before. I decided to let bygones be bygones, walked in and explained to the lady that I needed a paper in order to get my bottle filled. This time she did not say a thing but turned her back and looked away. I got the message and left the office and peddled the gas bottle back to CILIN II. Whatever gas remained in the bottle would have to suffice until I reached the Canary Islands, 800 miles away.

Preparation for the crossing consisted of examining every fixture of the rigging to make certain that there was not a hairline crack or break that might cause an accident at sea. Ropes (called sheets and halyards) that were worn and frayed needed to be replaced. Sails needed to be examined and replaced or mended wherever there might be a small rip or tear. Then, last but not least, there were the supplies, including food, which would be necessary for the trip. My problems were relatively simple since I would be traveling alone. Yachts with passengers and crews numbering six, eight or ten had to load in many times the food and water that I would need. Grocery shopping was convenient for the surprising fact that there were two Safeway Supermarkets in Gibraltar, finer than any stores I had seen along the Mediterranean shores.

After days of waiting for favorable weather, the time finally arrived when many of us would be heading for the Canary Islands on the first leg of the journey that would take us across the ocean. For the most favorable passage through the Strait of Gibraltar we were told that we should be heading out two hours before high tide. That happened to be at 11:30 a.m. With a three knot current against us and a headwind, it would be slow traveling at best. Fortunately, I was able to sail for the first three or four hours without the use of the engine. Then it became necessary to take down the sails and go on the engine. Other boats with much more powerful engines passed me as if I were standing still until there was not another sailboat in sight. There was, however, heavy traffic through the Strait by large commercial vessels.

By the time darkness came, I had traveled only about thirty miles. Then an unexpected thing happened. A fishing boat nosed up beside me, then shifted around and followed me for a long time. I became worried. Was he trying to see how many crewmembers were aboard? Why was he following me? Finally I turned on my VHF radio and called for anyone who might answer. There was no response. I called again and again. Finally, a voice broke the silence. It was the Spanish traffic controller for the Strait of Gibraltar. He asked for my location and confirmed that he was able to identify me on his radar. Then he asked me what I wanted him to do. I did not know what to tell him. I was petrified with fear but somewhat comforted just knowing that I had someone to report to. I was of the impression that he would send a boat to help me if I was really in distress but I was not sure. I asked him to stand by and I would report any developments. After some time, much to my relief, the fishing boat faded away into the night.

I did not sleep all night long, but instead kept an eye out to see if the intruder would approach me again. By mid-morning the next day the winds subsided. I took down the sails and slept until the middle of the afternoon. It was then that I noticed two fishing boats sitting rather close together about half a mile ahead of me. When I put up the sails, a third boat appeared from somewhere. He moved close to the other boats and then headed in my direction. He was following me. I became more and more worried as he drew closer. Again I did the only thing I knew to do. Even though I felt that I was out of radio range from the traffic controller, I gave it a try. Much to my surprise he answered. Again, I explained that another fishing boat was following me. Again he asked me what I wanted him to do and I told him that I would like for him to stand by. I stood in the hatchway with the radio-telephone speaker in my hand to be plainly visible to the fishing boat. I felt that they were probably listening to my conversation and that they would be less likely to attack me knowing that I was in radio contact with someone. For whatever reason, the boat finally left me. I was deeply grateful to the Spanish traffic controller for his patience and willingness to assist me.

THAT EVENING THE WIND DIED JUST AS the sun set. The sails were hanging limp from the mast while I was lying on my stomach examining the rudder in an effort to determine what was causing it to make a knocking sound. Then I heard an unusual "swish" sound.

Thinking that it was probably the mainsail raking across the lifeline, I stood up and shouted, "Do it again!"

(I talk to myself when I am alone at sea. My friend Zig Zigler down in Texas says that it is all right to talk to yourself. He even says that it is all right to answer but if you hear yourself saying "Huh? What did you say?" you are in trouble).

Just as I said "Do it again" a spray of water went up with another "swish" and I saw two giant whales side by side about 50 feet from the boat.

Without taking a second look I jumped through the hatch into the cabin below, grabbed a bag and started preparing an emergency survival kit. I was fearful that the whales would attack the boat and dump me into the sea. I grabbed everything I could get my hands on while my heart was pounding and I was breathing heavily. It was nonsense. I realized that I had little that would be of lasting value to me in case I had to leave the boat.

I dropped the bag and rushed back to the deck to find that the whales had completely disappeared. That was a relief beyond description.

After a while a breeze came up. I raised the sails and I sailed on into the night. I had hoped that I would be far enough out to sea that there would be no more fishing boats, but though I was 50 miles at sea off the coast of Morocco there were numerous fishing boats plying the waters. They appeared like farm tractors plowing big fields in the night, but none of them came close to me.

About noon the next day, all the fishing boats were gone except one I spotted in the distance to the north. He seemed to be heading in my direction, as he drew nearer he appeared to be on a collision course with me. I watched and waited. Then, when he was really close, he stepped out of the hatch into the cockpit. He waved for me to move out of his way. It made no sense whatsoever with the big ocean and all the space available that I should be in his way. I did not argue. I made an abrupt turn to let him pass and was much relieved until, after a while, he turned and headed toward me again.

By that time I knew that I was completely out of range of the Spanish traffic controller's radio. What could I do? I was deeply concerned because the only individual I ever knew personally who attempted to sail the Atlantic alone was Dean Carl Jackson from Indiana University, the one who had recommended to me that I should have a 30-foot boat to sail the seas. On his effort to sail from England back to America, his boat had disappeared somewhere along the Spanish coast. Later a part of his boat had drifted ashore but he was never found. I considered the possibility that he might have been attacked by pirates at sea, like the ones who had been harassing me.

I started up the engine and put the throttle to the wall faster than I had ever run it before. I might burn up my engine but if I were to be attacked, the engine would be of no use to me. I watched to see if I were pulling away from him. From time to time it seemed that we were maintaining about the same speed. Then at last I could see that I was pulling away from him. From time to time he would alter his course. Sometimes he would be coming directly toward me. Then at other times he ran parallel to my course.

This continued for more than two hours while I prayed that my little Volvo engine would not overheat and blow up. At long last, when I was far ahead of him, he turned on a different course and left me. From that time on, I never saw any more fishing boats along the coast of Morocco. I was, however, in a busy shipping lane with the danger of being run over by the big freighters.

The Atlantic crossing could have come to an end on November 6th, 1989. That was my 72nd birthday. Sitting on the deck I noticed that the main halyard was over the side and dragging in the water. When I attempted to pull it in, I found that it was fouled in the propeller under the boat. It needed to be freed or it could cause serious trouble. The only thing to do was to stop the boat and get it loose. Stopping the boat when the sails are up is accomplished by "heaving to". That is a maneuver where the sails are set so that the boat loses its forward motion. It then tends to sit and rock gently in the water. I never did learn to do it properly. When I thought it was in shape, with my safety harness on and the tether snapped on to the lifeline, I dropped over the side of the boat to free the rope. To my surprise I saw the boat go rushing by me and the tether jerked rather violently on my harness. I had not heaved too properly and the boat was still sailing and dragging me along through the water. Had the snap on the tether given way, I would have been watching CILIN II sail away, leaving me a hundred miles out in the ocean alone. I quickly went under the boat to release the rope from the propeller and pulled my body back up on the boat, somewhat shocked as I realized what had happened.

In Don Street's *Cruising Guide for Crossing the Atlantic*, he had written of the sheer effect of the winds by the mountains of the Canary Islands. I reasoned that I could avoid this problem by passing the islands to the east and approaching the south side of the Island of Grand Canaria from the east. I could not have been more wrong as it turned out later. The greatest effect of the sheer winds is to the south of the islands. Passing between the Canary Islands and Africa in the evening time after a good day of sailing, I felt certain that I would reach my destination the following day. I sat at the table with a paper plate full of spaghetti and meatballs with the feeling that it would be my last dinner at sea before docking the boat the next day. It was almost dark when a bright light suddenly illuminated the cabin. As I rose up to see where the light originated, the leg of the table collapsed. I grabbed the plate of hot spaghetti and meatballs and looked out to see a Spanish patrol boat approaching. After disengaging from the table and dumping my meal in the sink, I jumped out onto the deck, I was embarrassed that I had not turned on the boat's running lights earlier, but that was not the problem. It was a routine stop by the Coast Guard.

Then the usual questions about who I was, where I was going, etc. I had been stopped a number of times by patrol boats in various countries who wanted to make sure I was not in narcotic traffic or smuggling. At no time had any crew members come aboard for an inspection, and only once did a patrol boat require me to show my boat papers. By now these stops had become routine. The officers were always friendly but businesslike. These officers were no exception and they departed, leaving me to prepare dinner all over again.

After clearing Fuertaventura Island I headed west and was hit by more than one heavy gust of wind sheering off the mountains. I was south of Grand Canaria the next night but did not want to approach the port in the dark. I cut the engine and hove to, but in the morning I could tell that the strong wind during the night carried me a long distance to the south.

In the morning I started the engine and headed toward shore. After about an hour, the engine stopped dead. I tried everything I could think of to restart it but my efforts were in vain. With a wind out of the north it would be necessary to tack my way in to the marina at Port Mogan. Progress was slow and it was pitch dark before I reached the shore.

The lights on shore presented a spectacular sight. Bright lights from sea level to the top of the mountains glistened in a "V" shaped pattern. With so much light I decided to enter the harbor at night. As I approached, masts of a large number of yachts were visible. But as I drew nearer I could see a wall between the boats and me, but there was no entrance. There was an inlet but it was not connected to the boat basin. Even though I had no engine, I decided to enter into the inlet in hopes that I would see the entrance to the boat basin.

The wind was very light as I proceeded. There was only a beach but no sign of an opening to the marina. Miraculously I was able to turn the boat and sail back into the sea. Then I decided to follow the wall to the east in hopes of finding the entrance, but that was in vain. (I later learned that if I had traveled a little farther, I would have found the entrance).

The only safe thing to do was to go back out to sea for the night. Then I thought of the VHF radio. I would call the harbormaster and ask for instructions. At first I got no response. Then a gruff voice asking me to identify myself. "What is your call number?" he asked.

I gave the only honest answer I could give. "I do not have one", I replied. With that he refused to communicate with me any further. The truth was that I had purchased a new VHF radio at Rhodes, Greece when I had first taken possession of CILIN II. The radio was installed and I had sailed for four years in the Mediterranean Sea without anyone ever asking me for my call numbers.

ARRIVAL IN CANARY ISLANDS

IT WAS A LITTLE AFTER NOON THE next day when I finally reached a harbor on the south shore of Grand Canary. On the port side was a large dock that was clearly marked, "Ferry Boats Only". With my engine dead and no place else to go, I pulled alongside and secured my mooring lines. Then came voices from different directions telling me what I already knew – that I could not stay there because it was a place where ferryboats moored. Then the dock master with the same good news. I explained that I had a dead engine and did not know where to go.

"The ferry boat will arrive here at four o'clock and you will have to move", he announced sternly as he turned and went back to his office.

That was good news because it was only about two o'clock. That would give me time to scout around the marina and find one of my friends who had sailed from Gibraltar. He would help find a place to moor CILIN II. I hurried down the line of sailboats along the quay without seeing a familiar face or even a boat that I recognized. What I did not know at the time was there were many marinas on the islands and my friends could be at any one of them. After about an hour I reluctantly gave up my search and headed back to CILIN II much discouraged.

Then I did an unbelievable thing. I cannot believe I did it. Being very tired and weary, I climbed aboard and into the bunk and went to sleep. I had not been there very long when a rap on the hull woke me out of a deep sleep. It was the dock master and I expected him to be furious, but instead he said, "Release your mooring lines and I will tow you with my dinghy to a slip on the other side of the channel." I wondered why he had not thought of that sooner but I was, nevertheless, grateful for the fine assistance he gave me. Very shortly after that I heard the horn of the ferryboat and saw it pull into the spot where I had been moored.

At last, I was securely moored in a place away from the wind and the waves and expected to relax. But then another rap on the hull. What will it be this time, I wondered. I looked out to see a young man about 25 years of age. After apologizing for disturbing me, he introduced himself as Dieter Klinkhart and asked if I were headed for the Caribbean Sea. He then offered to serve as a deck hand in exchange for his passage if I were making the trip. I told him that I intended to sail to the Caribbean Sea but that I planned to sail solo. Then I invited him to come in for a visit. It had been 21 days since I had talked to anyone except the Coast Guard Patrol and I was glad to have someone to talk to.

He told me that he was a steel worker from Germany and that he and his younger brother, Stefan, planned to go to the Caribbean for a few weeks' vacation. In our conversation, I told him that I had been at sea for a couple of days with a dead engine, trying to get to shore. That interested him and he wanted to look at the engine. I had tried everything I could think of to find the problem, but after examining it for a short time, he found the problem. I could not have found it in a week.

My new friend found that the flexible fuel line from the tank to the engine had ruptured so that instead of sucking fuel in, it was sucking in air. With an extra flexible fuel line installed, he soon had the Volvo diesel engine running smoothly. It reminded me of an old adage that a German boy is born with a monkey wrench in his hand. It was no doubt coined because German boys have a mechanical aptitude. For me, the whole episode was like making a cloudy day sunny again because, until that moment, I had no idea how I could get the engine running again.

While I was reveling in my joy about the engine, there came yet another knock on the hull. This time it was the German boy's brother, Stefan, but he was not alone. With him was an attractive young lady. I took her to be one of the many backpackers who travel so easily about Europe.

I invited them to come into the cabin and then suggested that if they had not eaten dinner, I would be glad to prepare spaghetti and meatballs. Everyone seemed agreeable to the idea. It was one of my favorite dishes on the boat and I had become very proficient at preparing it. It was a big help that sauce came in small jars and meatballs came in cans.

Soon I was enjoying a good meal with my new friends. I offered seconds and then explained that I thought that I already had more than my share. I was surprised when the girl spoke up and told me that I had eaten only five meatballs while the others had each had six. It occurred to me that the matter of division of food is important to hungry backpackers.

Having a nice dinner with young people was a pleasant interlude for me after being on the sea alone since leaving Gibraltar. They departed after a couple of hours with Dieter volunteering to return in the morning to sail with me to Mogan Marina about five miles to the west. He did return the next day and sailed with me. Then he and his brother Stefan returned to the boat daily, helping with many chores, and putting the boat in shape to sail the Atlantic. With all of the help they gave me, I thought they might insist that I let them sail with me, but they accepted my statement that I intended to sail alone.

Mogan Marina was an ideal place to wait for the trade winds to set in. As we sailors waited, we were getting closer and closer to the Christmas season. It was an easy decision when many of us decided that we would rather be enjoying Christmas and New Years in that luxurious marina with our friends than at sea during the holiday season.

CILIN II was moored in a slip about 150 feet in front of the Irishman's Restaurant and Café which became the central gathering place for our group of sailors who had met in the Caribbean Sea and at Gibraltar.

A Canadian musician by the name of Tony entertained the crowd nightly at the Irishman's Restaurant. Accompanied by his guitar he sang old favorite songs, much to the delight of his audience. At the front of the restaurant a wide deck provided a dining area and a view

of the entire marina full of luxurious yachts and, beyond that, the wide
Atlantic Ocean.

I particularly enjoyed the company of Bob and Carole Hamilton,
Harvey Atkinson, his mother and ten year old daughter, Leah.
Everyone was helpful in getting CILIN II in shape for the next leg of
my journey.

Dieter and Stefan came by regularly to assist in getting CILIN II
ready for the trip. They seemed to understand my desire to sail solo and
never asked again to accompany me, but they did solicit other boats for
a ride. At last, they gave up and on December 10, 1989, they returned
to Germany. Their greatest pleasure in coming to the Canary Islands
had been in working on the boat and helping me get ready for the trip,
for which I was very grateful.

My stay in the Canary Islands was much longer than I had planned
and it became necessary to restock the supplies. For provisions for the
30 to 40 day trip to Antigua in the West Indies, I had the following:

30 gallons of diesel fuel
2 gallons of engine oil
2 tanks of propane gas for the cook stove
30 gallons of fresh drinking water
4 dozen green bananas
Potatoes, onions and two heads of lettuce
2 dozen apples
4 pints of honey
24 cans of Coke
12 one-liter paper cartons of fruit juice
8 cartons of long life milk
8 canisters of Quaker Oats
3 pounds of rice
8 packages of spaghetti
2 dozen eggs
40 paper packages of soup

After four seasons of sailing the Mediterranean, I had a good idea
of my requirements, with a little extra for insurance.

When I realized I did not have adequate foul weather gear for the trip, Harvey Atkinson offered me a suit that looked brand new. It was too small for him but just right for me. When I asked Bob Hamilton how much I should offer for it, his response was "Don't offer him money. He would be insulted. Just take him to dinner."

That evening I saw Harvey's mother and told her I would like to take her, Harvey and his daughter, Leah, to dinner on Friday evening. The next day, being Wednesday, I went fishing in a canal near the marina with Leah when she proudly announced, "Daddy and I are having steak for dinner tonight."

"What about grandma?" I asked.

"Oh, she is having dinner with you", was the answer.

Until that moment I had no idea that grandma was a little hard of hearing. She had misunderstood my invitation to her, Harvey and Leah for dinner on Friday evening and thought I was inviting her to dinner that evening.

So grandma and I had dinner at the Irishman's that night and the four of us had dinner at the Irishman's on Friday night. The foul weather gear was well paid for.

In preparing for the trip, I encountered a problem that I could not solve. The red and green running lights on the bow did not illuminate when I flipped the switch to the on position even though the voltmeter showed there was current to the lights. In an attempt to solve the problem, I installed new light bulbs. That did not solve the problem. There were still no lights.

I needed help so, knowing that Bob Hamilton was an engineer, I turned to him. For him it was simple. "You have a load on your electric line, possibly due to corrosion at some connection", he explained. "There is enough power to register on the voltmeter but not enough to illuminate the lights."

It did not make sense to me but I installed new wiring from the switch box to the bulbs. Presto! The running lights came on brightly. Then it occurred to me how fortunate it is that there is usually someone around a sailboat marina to give advice on any problem having to do with sailboats.

During the long stay in the Canary Islands I received a FAX message from my brother, Charles, in Miami, Florida, in which he included a copy of an article from the Indianapolis Star newspaper telling of this 72-year old man who was going to sail the Atlantic Ocean alone. I began to think about that. I had never thought of myself as being old but I could remember a time when I considered anyone in his 70's to be old, old, old. Anyway, I had been sailing the boat through difficult conditions and had confidence that everything would be all right. My age was not something to think about.

In preparing for the trip, it occurred to me that I might make some changes in my Last Will and Testament but there was a problem of finding a witness who might be available when needed. Then a thing that I never could have imagined. Quite by chance I came upon a couple of sailors by the names of Judy and Lee Bochen from Brownsburg, Indiana, about 70 miles from my home in Indiana.

I learned that they had sold their home in Brownsburg eight years earlier, bought a sailboat and spent the time since then cruising the ports of Europe. When I visited with them, they willingly signed as witnesses to the Codicil to my Will. They did not wait for the trade winds to set in but set sail for the Island of Barbados in the West Indies on November 29, 1989.

I learned years later that they had encountered such rough seas that they turned back and resided in France for a couple of years before returning to their home in Indiana. I got a taste of those rough seas later.

It was long after my years of sailing that I happened to be in Brownsburg, Indiana when I thought of the couple from that city who had so generously signed the Codicil to my Will just before I left the Canary Islands on my solo trip across the Atlantic Ocean. I decided to check the phone book to see if I could locate Lee and Judy Bochen and see what had happened to them. I found the last name but none by the name of Lee or Judy.

In answer to my call to one of the Bochen listings, a cheerful young man answered. I told him that I was Ed Whitcomb and that I had been sailing in the Atlantic some years before. His response surprised me. "Yes, I know about you. I read about you in the paper."

He then told me that Lee Bochen was his uncle. "But my grandmother knows a lot more about them. She is in a nursing home but you had better not call her yourself. When she finds out you a Republican, she will hang up on you."

I did learn that both of my sailor friends, the Bochens, were then deceased and that was the end of that story.

A MEMORABLE EVENT WAS WHEN HARVEY ATKINSON invited me to participate with him on his boat in the Boxing Day on the day after Christmas. It has nothing to do with boxing or sailing for that matter. It is more like Christmas all over again, with people giving gifts and celebrating. But for us, it was a big sailboat regatta on the largest sailboat I ever sailed on. It was exciting and though we came in last, we got an award for being the best in our class.

GiGi

SHE APPEARED ALONE IN THE IRISHMAN'S RESTAURANT two days before my scheduled departure from the Canary Islands. I had spent six weeks at Port Mogan preparing for the trans-Atlantic crossing and waiting for the trade winds to set in, but I had not, during that time, met anyone so attractive and charming. GiGi was a 34-year-old Lufthansa airline stewardess, five foot two, well packaged and with a cute German Accent. She had vacationed in the Canary Islands over the years and was well acquainted with the place. I did the only polite thing to do. I invited her to have dinner with me. So at seven o'clock we were seated in a Spanish restaurant across the street from the marina with another couple who were friends of hers.

As we had entered the restaurant and while walking through the bar, I noticed a burly fellow who would remind you of Vincent Price, if you were old enough to remember the $64,000 Question on TV. Our meal ordered and visiting with my new friends, the lady excused herself to go to the powder room. In a short time she returned disturbed and in an agitated state, blurted, "Do you know what happened to me?"

GiGi spoke up quickly. "Yes, I know. He grabbed you and tried to rub your boobies and kiss you." Our friend was as much surprised as I was. Apparently the bartender was able to get by with such unseemly conduct, unhampered by the local officials, while he provided unsolicited entertainment to his unsuspecting guests.

Nothing more was said of the incident while we enjoyed a delicious Spanish cuisine and departed. For further evening entertainment, GiGi suggested that we attend a parlor to play "Foosball." I had seen the game before but never played it until then. It is played on a rectangular table about four feet long where two or four participants twist a wooden dowel which allows an attached mallet to strike a ball toward the goal line on the opposite end of the field from the player. We teamed up with some local players for the game. It soon became apparent that the local players were experts in the field. One in particular was so good that if he were your partner, you would win against all comers. If he opposed you, you had no chance. I thought to myself that if he practiced the violin until he developed such finesse, he would qualify for any symphony orchestra, but Foosball was his thing. The game went on into the night but at 1:30 a.m. we decided to depart.

We were out the door, walking along the dark road toward the marina when GiGi announced that we had reached the path which led up the hill to her apartment. With a quick goodnight, she disappeared and I was on my way back to the lonely boat.

I was having lunch on the patio of the Irishman's Restaurant the next day when GiGi appeared at my table. Would I have dinner with her that night at her apartment? It would be my last night ashore before undertaking one of the greatest adventures of my life. Why not? I had checked and double-checked everything on the boat, the fuel, the water and provisions. Everything was in shape. Dinner at her apartment and an evening with GiGi would be an ideal sendoff for the trip.

"The apartment is small. We may have to sit on the bed to eat," she volunteered. I could tolerate that. I had been eating and sleeping in the cramped quarters of CILIN II for the past four years. No problem.

Before she departed, she said, "Wolfgang will come by your boat at 7:00 to show you the way to my apartment." That was fair enough. I knew Wolfgang, a German lad whom I had seen from time to time at the Irishman's. I never did know if he was a sailor or just someone in the area on vacation.

At the appointed hour of 7:00 p.m., there was a rap on the boat. It was Wolfgang, there to guide me to GiGi's apartment. By this time it was dark and I followed him along the path GiGi had taken the night before. We wound our way through the darkness along the narrow path to the top of the hill overlooking the bright lights of the marina and the dark Atlantic Ocean. I was glad to have Wolfgang for a guide, but when we arrived at GiGi's apartment, he too came in. It was not a tiny apartment and I could see three place settings at a table on the patio. We were not going to be sitting on the bed. We were going to be sitting on the patio for dinner, all three of us.

It was an enjoyable evening. The food was good and the conversation interesting, but come 11:00 p.m., which was well past my usual bedtime on the boat, Wolfgang dutifully escorted me back to CILIN II.

In the night I thought a lot about the trip. Surely everything was in order; I had stopped by the Irishman's early that morning and enlisted a couple of early morning coffee drinkers to come by the following morning to cast off my mooring lines for departure.

Dawn on February 8, 1990 saw me approaching the Irishman's Restaurant to alert my line handlers that I was ready to cast off. Back at the boat, I made a last minute check. The mooring linemen were in place and I was prepared to turn the key to start the engine when I heard footsteps on deck above me. Protocol on yachts is like protocol in a home. People do not come aboard until they make themselves known and are invited. I looked out the hatch to see the smiling face of GiGi. She had a box of cookies and offered me one. I took two, thanked her and told her that I was ready to shove off. She wanted to hug me and kiss me goodbye. I had no time for that. All I could say was, "Thanks for last night. I have to go."

It was not easy getting GiGi off the boat. The line handlers waited patiently. At last I was back in the cabin. The engine started perfectly. The four mooring lines were cast off and I was backing out of the slip and into the channel when backward motion ceased. Something was wrong. I accelerated the engine. Then there was a thump and the engine died. The boat was drifting out of control. Finally, I managed to get a line ashore and have CILIN II pulled back into the slip. It was then that I learned that in my agitation I had failed to release the starboard mooring line at the stern. By this time a number of people had gathered to watch the proceedings.

GiGi was back on board with her box of cookies. "Leave it. You can get a new start tomorrow," she suggested. I was not about to leave it. Putting all modesty aside, I stripped my clothes to my jockey shorts and dropped over the side to find a very heavy rope twisted firmly about the propeller. I pulled and twisted, coming up for air about five times. Each time GiGi was telling me to let it go. "You can go tomorrow," she insisted.

Persistence won out. At last I was able to wrestle the rope from the propeller. The engine started but I had no way of knowing what damage might have been done to the propeller.

CANARY ISLANDS TO ANTIGUA

On February 8TH, 1990, I was on the way along the channel from my dock and headed out toward the sea when an unexpected noise filled the air. I was surprised because I did not think anyone knew of my departure except the marina officials and my early morning, coffee drinking line handlers. It seemed that everyone in the marina had gathered with tin pans, whistles, bells and horns, waving and screaming good-bye messages. I had made many new friends on the island but felt certain that many of the people did not know me except that I was a lone sailor in a little sailboat headed out on a trip of some 2550 miles of open sea. It gave me a good feeling and for a while, I did not seem so alone.

The boat jibbed shortly after I got away from the island; I was embarrassed and hoped that my well wishers had returned to their boats without seeing me as the boat jibbed time and time again. The combination of the troubled waters at the southern end of the island together with the sheer effect of winds off the mountains made for difficult sailing for about half an hour. Then CILIN II settled down to normal sailing. I remembered that I had faced the same problem upon departing Canary Islands and for the same reasons, sheer winds off Mt. Etna and troubled waters.

Before I arrived in the Canary Islands, I had no idea of what to expect. I had never been there before but had seen the seven islands many times at night while flying the Atlantic from New York to Casablanca on Air Force transport planes during World War II. At that time, the coastal areas were rimmed with faint lights at night but I felt certain that by 1990 those lights were much brighter due to the many resorts and marinas along the coast.

After about half an hour, sailing got back to normal with a good wind. I set the self-steering device on a course of 270 degrees and relaxed after a very busy morning of getting under way. At twilight time, the hills of the Canary Islands faded into the evening haze as a big red sun slowly sunk into the western sea. It seemed that the whole world was at peace as little CILIN II made her way toward the island of Antigua, far across the sea to the west. The wind was strong and the waves picked up but the sky was clear and full of stars. With things going so well, I decided to use the working jib and the full main sail. That all worked well until about 2:00 in the morning when the wind became much stronger and the sea became much rougher. That found me on a pitching deck in the black of night replacing the working jib with the storm jib and putting a couple of reefs in the main sail.

That was not the worst of it. The exact same thing happened on the next two successive nights. The night had been so clear without even a hint of a storm blowing up that I left up the full sails again, tuned on the self-steering device and climbed into the bunk for a good night's sleep. Again I was up in the middle of the two following nights, changing the sails. But I learned my lesson and from that time on I sailed at night with a storm jib and three reefs in the main sail until I reached Antigua.

Sailing with the trade winds was a new and wonderful experience for me. They were strong and sometimes steady for long periods of time. But then at times the sea became very rough. Fortunately, the two gas burners for cooking were in a cradle so that liquids did not spill when the boat rolled. At times the sea was so rough that I had to brace myself in a corner while eating and it turned out that a pan with a handle was better for eating oatmeal, rice, spaghetti and other cooked foods, rather than a plate or bowl.

After a time, my body grew tired from holding on and bruised from being knocked about the cabin. I was really surprised at how rough the sea was and how long it remained that way. All of my clothes became wet and the bedclothes damp because whenever it was necessary to go on deck to change the sails, I would be drenched.

It was little comfort to me when I determined on the 16th day out that I still had 1440 miles to go to reach my destination. But on the 20th day the wind abated and the sea became calmer. At last I was able to sit out on the deck again and the clothes I wore and the bedclothes dried. Sailing was pleasant again. Never in my years of sailing thereafter did I encounter such rough seas.

ANTIGUA

THE LIFE OF A SOLO SAILOR CAN be lonesome at times but that was not what the island of Antigua had in store for me. After spending the night outside English Harbor so I could find my way in during daylight, I found it a very easy approach. Once inside the harbor I was greeted with a sight I had never experienced before in four years of sailing in the Mediterranean. There were yachts everywhere flying the American flag. I was back home in America.

I sailed near one boat and asked "Where can I anchor?" The friendly voice responded; "just drop your anchor anywhere. There is 20 to 30 feet of water." With that, I dropped the anchor and sat back to enjoy the scenery about me but that was not for long. Cheery voices from a nearby yacht called, "Get your papers together and we will take you to customs."

It was Neil McLean whom I had last seen when he had sailed away from the Canary Islands more than a month ago. We exchanged greetings and rode in his dinghy to shore to check in with the authorities. When we found that my papers were in order, I looked out to the shore to see a familiar couple coming to greet me. I could not believe my eyes. It was Bob and Carole Hamilton from London. When I had left them in the Canary Islands I thought they were sailing back to London.

It turned out that they had become concerned about me sailing the 1900 miles alone with my lack of experience on the sea and decided to come to Antigua to see if I made it. The day before, they had talked of sailing away but then decided to wait one more day just in case I made it.

Needless to say, it was deeply appreciated – the thoughtfulness of my British friends. This was not the first time Bob had helped me because it was he who had taught me back at the Canary Islands why my running lights would not illuminate even though the volt meter indicated electricity in the line. After a good visit, the Hamiltons +were on their way back to London. It had been a warm welcome to Antigua, first by Neil McLean and then by the Hamilton's.

After they had departed, I straightened up CILIN II and took a nap. It was near noon when I pumped up the six-foot inflatable dinghy and paddled around English Harbor, feasting my eyes on the many luxurious yachts moored in the area. One took my eye when I read the name ARCHTURAS on its bow. Could this be the yacht of General George Patton, the son of the famous World War II general? I could not believe it.

Months before, at a board meeting of Veterans Life Insurance Company in Florida, he had told me that he had a boat in the West Indies. He boasted that its name was ARCHTURAS, named for the brightest star in the heavens. In navigation school I had been taught that Sirius was the brightest star, but who was I to dispute a three-star general?

Without hesitation, I paddled over to his yacht and rapped on the hull. There appeared on the deck the tall, handsome figure of General George Patton. Immediately, I could tell that he did not recognize me with a month-long growth of whiskers on my face and sunglasses.

"Could you use a deckhand, sir?" I asked.

"No, we don't need anybody," was his curt reply.

"But I'd really like to work for you," I insisted.

With that he turned and started back to his cabin, repeating, "We don't need anybody."

Then I shouted, "Is Joanne aboard?" His jaw dropped as he turned and stared at me. Then he let out a yell that could be heard all across English Harbor. "Governor Whitcomb!" I could not have had a greater introduction to English Harbor. He called his wife, Joanne, and we had a short visit just before they sailed away. He had a party aboard and I had interrupted his departure.

That was my introduction to English Harbor, where I spent many wonderful days after that rough Atlantic crossing. English Harbor's history went back 200 years, when a brash, 26 year old British Naval Officer named Horatio Nelson had been assigned to enforce regulations against trade with the United States. The local people wanted U.S. business and Nelson became very unpopular with the people of Antigua.

English Harbor was a well-sheltered harbor with a dry dock where damaged warships could be repaired without the necessity of returning to England. Years later, when Nelson became the most celebrated officer ever to serve in the British Navy, the government of Antigua honored his name by establishing a national park by the name of Nelson's Dry Dock.

I continued my sightseeing tour until I came upon a coffee shop near the water's edge. There were only three diners. So I joined them. One was a Doctor Bartolet, a retired veterinarian from the military service, his wife Grace, and their attractive daughter Joanne. There being no other customers, we visited and I learned that a vacation in Antigua was an annual affair for them. Knowing that I was also retired military, he said, "You know, there are a couple of space "A" Air Force flights a week from here to Patrick Air Base." "That is good news," I answered. "I'll be taking a flight one of these days, but first, I need to see about storing my boat in the boat yard on the north end of the island."

It would be hard to find a more delightful place in the world for cruising than English Harbor and Nelson's Dry Dock, because of the many interesting sailing destinations near at hand. But as fine as the place was, I became interested in another facility on the north end of the island. I learned that there was a fellow who had a sailboat and would be glad to help me. His name was Charlie Wright, a civilian Security Guard at the US Navy station. I found him and he gladly agreed to guide me on the trip. Knowing that the waters to the north were littered with coral reefs, I enlisted Charlie Wright to accompany me to a place called Crabbs Marina. It would be an easy trip, so we invited Joanne, the daughter of vacationing Dr. Bartolet to accompany us on the trip.

The doctor and his wife, Grace, would meet us at Crabbs Marina at the end of the day.

We sailed out of English Harbor at mid-morning, headed west with a 20 knot wind, then turned north following the west side of the island to the north. It was not long after we turned north that I noticed a line of dark clouds approaching from the east. It fit all of the descriptions of what a sailor had called a line squall. The water became very rough and the wind strong, making for unpleasant sailing.

When the squall passed us by, I noticed another formation approaching from the same direction. In a short time it hit us just as the other had done.

With the rough seas and storm conditions, our progress was much slower than we had planned. My log book showed that in the course of the trip we were hit by eleven line squalls.

By the time we reached the north end of the island to head eastwardly to the marina, we found ourselves facing a headwind and lowered the sails to go on the engine. We arrived at Crabbs Marina in a pitch dark night to be greeted by Joanne's worried but happy parents. We had endured more line squalls than I experienced in the 31 days crossing the Atlantic Ocean.

CRABBS MARINA

CRABBS MARINA ON THE NORTH END OF Antigua appeared to be a suitable place to put CILIN II on the hard while I returned to Indiana for a rest from the sea.

Back home in Indiana, I was greeted with much acclaim and was treated as if I were the first person to sail the Atlantic since Christopher Columbus had done so 500 years earlier.

At home I was invited to speak a number of times to various organizations including the Rotary Club, the Lake Monroe Sailing Club and at a "Safety at Sea" seminar at Indiana University. There I recognized only one couple in the audience of 80 people. It was Dr. Ian Templeton, an outstanding surgeon from Seymour, Indiana, and his wife, Jane. I knew of their many trips to Florida sailing in the Gulf of Mexico and was glad to see them.

In my talks, I endeavored to cover matters concerning possible hazards at sea, but it was irony of the worst kind that Dr. Templeton later suffered a tragedy worse than anything I could ever have imagined. He suffered an infection from a coral cut and lost his life.

After nine months of being back home in Indiana, it was time I returned to my sailing odyssey. After my extended vacation at home, I returned to Crabbs Marina to find CILIN II where I had left her and apparently in good shape. When I climbed aboard and into the cabin, I found two feet of water and mud inside the boat, requiring many hours to bail it out. It was consoling, as I bailed water, to realize that I was on dry land instead of at sea.

The water was not the worst part. It turned out that a small collision with another yacht months earlier, when I had first arrived in English Harbor, had resulted in a small crack on the deck. I did not notice it at the time but dust from a road nearby had washed into the boat and left five inches of mud and water.

And even that was not the worst part. A number of cans of vegetables had rusted and ruptured from the tropical heat, leaving a putrid odor that seeped down between the plastic lining and the hull so I could not scrub the area. For a time I wondered if I could ever get rid of the odor but little by little it disappeared, leaving me with only an unpleasant memory.

THE WEST INDIES

Sailing in the West Indies was an all new experience compared to sailing in the Mediterranean Sea. During the four years in the Mediterranean, I had been intrigued by Greek history and mythology as I traveled from island to island. In the West Indies I found a cruising paradise of more than 7,000 islands and reefs. There were long stretches of sea sprinkled with spectacularly beautiful tropical islands. I also enjoyed the company of a number of friends who came to sail short trips with me. There was John Lindley, a retired politician district chairman from southern Indiana. We had much to talk about of the good old days in politics. At first he said he could spend a week with me and I told him that he should spend a month, which he did. He later said it was one of the most wonderful months of his life.

My nephew, Sidney H. Showalter, a veteran of two years aboard the aircraft carrier SARASOTA in the Mediterranean Sea in WW II, came to sail for a couple of weeks. He enjoyed deep sea scuba diving at Cousteau National Park. In addition, he was my most entertaining guest though he did not intend to be entertaining. He became sea sick each time he came aboard CILIN II and could do nothing about it. I did not want to laugh at him but I soon learned that my laughing was uncontrollable for me as his vomiting was for him as he hung over the rail feeding the fish.

The strange part of it was that he loved to sail with me on CILIN II and he had joined me for short hops more than any other person during my time at sea.

Also joining me in my sailing trip in the West Indies was Wayne Stearns, an experienced sailor and boat owner from near my home in Indiana. They both provided good company as I hopped from one island to another in the magnificent West Indies.

It was good having wonderful friends spending time with me but after their departure I received word that my daughter, Ann and her husband John Guggenheim, would be arriving with his parents on May 29 aboard the giant luxury liner "Song of Norway". I waited 10 days for their arrival spending a lot of time getting CILIN ll in shipshape. Ann would be the first family member to be aboard the boat since her sister, Shelley, had jumped ship on July 14, 1968 at Rhodes, Greece.

Time went fast as I awaited Ann's arrival. Soon I saw the "Song of Norway" on the distant horizon looking as big as the moon. She glided into her mooring and I was soon pulling along side with 30ft.CILIN II.

We wasted no time in getting Ann and John aboard for a cruise across the bay and back. Then we had lunch on shore before Ann and John were boarding the big ship to complete their cruise. Though it was a very short visit, I remember it as one of my most pleasant days on my cruise.

After Ann's departure, I sailed along the North Coast of South America to find a mooring at Caracas, where I hoped to find a long-time friend, Neil Malloy, and his wife Patricia. After mooring the boat in a marina, I was delighted to hear his voice after the first ring of the phone. I had known Neil when he was employed by the Shanghai Power Company in China and I was in the U S Military. We had remained in touch over the past 45 years. He moved to Venezuela when the Communist took over China.

Neil picked me up at the marina in his chauffer driven car. On the way back to his home it was necessary to stop by his granddaughter, Elizabeth's school and watch her while she completed her equestrian lessons.

When we arrived at his home I could see the years had been kind to his wife, Patricia. She was beautiful as I had remembered her 45 years ago. To my surprise it turned out I was in for more than a visit with my old friends. Neil and Patricia had invited a number of friends for a party with Indiana connections.

I wondered where in the world I could stop on my sailing trip and find such warm hospitality.

It was almost a week before I convinced my friend my sail boat was anxiously awaiting me in the harbor. After I bid Patricia farewell with much gratitude, we packed my bag into his chauffer driven car and Neil escorted me to the marina.

I boarded the boat to put my bag into the cabin. When I came out I saw a sight that chilled my soul. In the marina the boat sometimes surges with the surf. I saw the boat gently pulling away from the mooring with Neil's arms outstretched attempting to hold the boat back. As a result Neil fell on his face into the water about 6 ft below. He did not realize that he could not hold the boat back or that it would soon stop moving when the mooring lines reached their limit of a few inches.

To his credit Neil maintained his composure until a young man and I assisted Neil back on to the boat. This was an ironic twist of fate after Neil had been a generous and cordial host to his old friend.

From Caracas, I sailed past the beautiful islands of Bonaire, and Aruba to reach Deutch, Curacoa.

CURACAO TO PANAMA

WHEN I DECIDED TO LEAVE SARAFUNDY MARINA in Spanish Waters on the Island of Curacao to return to Indiana, I learned that it was necessary to have someone designated as being responsible for CILIN II. A Dutch gentleman by the name of Lars Noorlander and his son had agreed to repair the engine during my absence, so I asked him if he would be in charge of my boat during my absence. He agreed, and we prepared a document showing his authority. CILIN II was left swinging at anchor while I flew back to Indiana.

It was a happy day for me when my unmarried 30 year-old son, John, agreed to come back to the boat and sail with me. We would fly back to Curacao and sail to Panama and then on the Hawaiian Islands. That was something I had dreamed about since General George Patton told me that he had sailed from the U.S. to Hawaii with his father.

John had sailed with me from time to time in our 19-foot Lightening sailboat and I felt that he would be comfortable at sea. In addition to that, he liked to cook and I was sure we would get along well.

We encountered our first obstacle when I attempted to buy a one-way airline ticket for him from Miami to Curacao. The female clerk at the ticket counter in Miami also informed me that it would be necessary to purchase a round-trip ticket for myself. It was an airline regulation brought on by the fact that highly desirable tourist resorts in the island do not want tourists stranded without means of leaving when their visa expires.

I explained to the clerk that we would be departing the island on my sailboat, which was on the island. Then she asked me if I had any evidence that I had a sailboat there. I did not have any. Then I thought of the letter I had given Lars Noorlander back at Curacao, authorizing him to look after CILIN II during my absence.

I was not sure that I had a copy, but all of my possessions were packed in my sea bag. It was drawing near flight time when I moved out of the check-in line, dumped all of the contents of the sea bag onto the floor and searched frantically for that paper. At last I found it and displayed it to the clerk.

"That is good for you but nowhere does it mention him as a passenger or a crew member." I would have to buy him a round trip ticket.

"But he is with me and we will be sailing together," I insisted.

It was just seconds before the call for boarding that her heart softened and she quickly wrote out a one-way ticket for each of us.

It was great getting back to CILIN II and finding her in excellent condition. The only problem was that long strands of grass had grown from every link on the anchor rode.

After five years of sailing alone, it was good having my son for company. We visited Willemstadt, the capitol of the Dutch Island of Curacao, taking in the sights. Back at the boat in Spanish Waters, John swam 150 yards to a shallow spot and returned with the report that he had spotted a number of lobsters. Later, he and a German lad off a nearby boat captured nine lobsters, which provided a fine dinner for us, John and me, the German lad and his father.

Of more interest to John than the lobsters was Darlene, the beautiful daughter of John and Johanna Lindholm, a Swedish couple sailing the Caribbean Sea. Darlene was a New York and Paris model on vacation visiting her parents. She and John spent some evenings together.

On Wednesday, May 4, 1991, I took a bus from the marina to Willemstadt to clear out the following Saturday. It was a long walk from the bus along the dock area, but the officer told me I would have to come back at a time closer to my sailing date.

On Saturday I took the bus again to Willemstadt with my clearance papers. This time the indignant immigration officer hit me with two questions. "Why did you not get permission from the Port Director to moor in Spanish Waters?" and "Why did John Whitcomb not report his arrival in Curacao to the Port Director?"

The answers were obvious to me, but the Captain of an ocean-going sailboat should never have to say, "I did not know that we were supposed to do that."

With that bit of education in international travel, we were authorized to depart the island where we had spent an enjoyable two weeks, and we departed the Sarafundy Marina on Sunday, May 12, 1991. We motored the long, long channel of Spanish Waters to the open sea and then enjoyed the quietness when we cut the engine and felt the wind tugging at our sails. During the first night out we passed the lights of the Dutch resort island of Aruba off the coast of Columbia.

The Cruising Guide for the Western Caribbean told us we should stay 60 miles out from the coast of Columbia because of the danger of pirates. It was said that sailboats would be useful to Columbians smuggling illegal drugs to the U.S.

We made certain that we were more than 60 miles from the Columbian shore, but in the darkness of the night we suddenly observed a boat that appeared to be following us. We had no way of knowing what kind of vessel it might be. All we could do was watch and wait to see what might happen. We had no guns to defend ourselves. The only thing aboard the boat that would give us any protection was a rusty old fishing spear gun. I dug it out of the locker, even though I realized it would be of little use if armed pirates attempted to attack us.

Our intruders appeared to be standing off as if they were watching us to see what we would do. Then after a long time the boat disappeared in the night, as quietly and mysteriously as it had appeared. We kept a watchful eye throughout the night and were glad when the light of a new day showed us there was no boat in sight.

We later learned that the cruising guide we were using was obsolete and there was little danger in sailing along the Columbian Coast. We also learned that some of our friends from Spanish Waters had sailed to Cartagena and been greeted with warm hospitality by the Columbian people.

John prepared all of our meals and seemed to be enjoying our cruise. I thought he was enjoying one of the wonderful experiences of his life until one day he appeared to be unusually quiet. I did not say anything about it until the second day, when I said, "John, I think something is bothering you. What is it?"

Then he confessed. "Dad, I don't like it. I didn't like it when we used to sail on Lake Monroe back home in Indiana."

A dagger in my heart would have been less painful as I remember the times our family of five young children, Tricia, Ann, Shelley, Alice, and John with their mother had sailed in our nineteen-foot Lightning sailboat on Lake Monroe. We had enjoyed picnic lunches aboard, swimming and sailing in what I had thought were good times. Now I was learning that maybe I had been the only one who had enjoyed it.

It was a painful decision for me when we agreed that John would leave the boat as soon as we reached Balboa, Panama.

There was a certain excitement at the idea of arriving in Panama. It had been ten days since we departed Curacao, but little did I realize it would be two full years before I would sail from Panama into the Western Pacific to continue my dream of sailing around the world.

As we sailed along in a calm sea about one day out of the Panama Canal, we could see land off to our port. Then John said excitedly, "Somebody is flashing a mirror from shore. Maybe it is a distress signal." We decided to sail toward the shore to investigate.

But then John suggested, "Maybe it is a trap. Somebody may be trying to lure us into a trap."

With that, I turned on channel 16 on the VHF radio and called, "This is CILIN II, a sailboat. We see a light flashing from shore. Do you read me?"

An answer came back immediately. "CILIN II, we read you. We are waiting for friends, and we thought you might be them. Thank you."

After I hung up the speaker, John exclaimed, "That was John from back at Spanish Waters! I recognized his voice."

With that, I re-established contact. We exchanged greetings, and he invited us to come in to shore for a visit. We accepted the invitation, and on shore we found a veritable Shangri-La, the kind of place dreamers dream of. An American by the name of Michael Starbuck had notched out his little bit of heaven there on the coast off Panama. He, his beautiful Filipino wife, and tiny baby lived on the shore in a Filipino-type home, surrounded by tropical vegetation. He had a generator to provide lights as well as an extravagant sound system to flood the area with beautiful music. In addition, he maintained a VHF radio with which he kept in touch with yachts plying the area.

A couple of other yachts arrived, including the friends from Spanish Waters, to enjoy an evening ashore in a tropical paradise.

The following morning John and I sailed past historic Portabella without stopping until we reached the very long Cristobal breakwater, where we saw many commercial ships waiting to enter the Panama Canal.

It was evening when we finally moored in a marina at Colon alongside other boats. We welcomed the idea of a fresh water shower and dinner in the Marina restaurant.

When we asked a waitress where we could purchase some provisions, her answer was, "There is a good supermarket about six blocks down the street. You can walk there, but you had better take a taxi on the way back."

"We don't mind walking," I replied.

Her quick answer was, "If you want to get back with your groceries, you had better take a cab." The presence of a couple of guards patrolling the isles of the supermarket with sawed off shotguns when we arrived there lent credence to her warning. It was said the unemployment rate in Colon was about 75 percent and crime was rampant.

We traveled to the immigration office without incident, but there I encountered an unexpected problem. A very large Panamanian lady behind the desk advised me that my ship's papers were not in order. It was a fact. In six years of sailing I had never had CILIN II registered in my name. During the first year of sailing from Greece to Turkey, Cyprus and Israel, I had only a bill of sale from the ship's previous owner. The contract under which I had purchased the boat provided that it would be "free and clear of all encumbrances", and it had taken the Italian government a full year to report that the title was clear. By that time, I had arrived in Israel. There the American Counsel by the name of Julian L. Bartley had provided me with a duly authenticated document stating that Edgar D. Whitcomb was an American citizen and the owner of CILIN II. This document was provided under U.S. State Department regulations for a fee of $40.00. That, with my bill of sale, was good enough to get me by immigration officials in Italy,

Spain, Gibraltar, Antigua and Venezuela. But they did not get me past the efficient Panama Canal immigration lady.

It would be necessary for me to take a bus 50 miles to Balboa at the other end of the canal to get a certificate to be notarized by the American Counsel, that I was the owner of CILIN II and that I would, at my first opportunity, obtain a proper registration for the boat.

At the reception desk in the American Counsel's office was a picture of Dan Quayle, Vice President of the United States. I wondered and thought that he might be amused at the predicament of his former employer. He had worked for me in the Indiana State House as an administrative assistant.

With the affidavit in hand, I made my way to the Panama Minister of Foreign Affairs. After obtaining two stamps at the bank across the street from his office, one for one dollar and the other for twenty cents, the minister authenticated the signature of the U.S. Counsel.

My new friend, the immigration lady, was well satisfied with the affidavit and I was ready to transit the Panama Canal. But first there were a few little details that had to be attended.

At that point we found ourselves in the clutches of a giant bureaucracy, the Panama Canal Commission. Though we were only a 30-foot yacht, we would be required to follow the requirements of the giant commercial transports transiting the canal. There was a form for me to fill out listing possible cargo of my boat, including the number of tons of coal, steel, cotton, and many other items.

Then there was the admeasure, a measurement of the boat to determine the tonnage of the vessel. To accomplish this, an attractive young lady of Chinese extraction came aboard and very efficiently measured CILIN II from bow to stern at the waterline and also overall length and breadth. It measured 30 feet long and 10 feet wide and the net weight was seven tons, as had been reported at each stop along the way from Tel Aviv. Here it had to be confirmed for the Panama Canal Commission to determine the cost of my transiting the canal.

There was also a matter of acquiring four, 100-foot lines and four line handlers to manipulate the boat while in the locks. As a practical matter, only two lines and two line handlers were ever used because in the 110-foot wide locks, several yachts were rafted together so that only the handlers on the starboard and the port side of the raft had any responsibilities.

It was also necessary to employ a canal pilot for the trip through the canal. The name of our pilot was Carlos. He was very friendly and accommodating, but from time to time he would say, "Can't you make it go any faster?" I would speed it up with the accelerator, but invariably the speed would drop off, making me very uncomfortable. I was well aware of the Panama Canal Commission rule that if it became apparent that the vessel was making less than four knots, it would be turned around and returned to the starting point and an aborted transit charge would be billed to the craft.

It was a relief to me when we made a stop at a place called Gamboa for the night. I was certain that we would not be turned around and returned to our starting point from there.

The following morning, we had an easy trip through the Pedro Miguel Locks and on to the Balboa Yacht Club on the Pacific end of the canal. It was different than any marina I had ever seen. We moored at a buoy on the open sea adjacent to the canal. There we waited patiently for a water taxi from the marina to take us to the pier. High on the shore above the marina stood a large structure, which turned out to be the marina office, and a restaurant where we were warmly received and given a membership card to the Balboa Yacht Club.

It had been several days since John had expressed his dislike for sailing. In the meantime, we had experienced the excitement of seeing a light flashing from shore, which led us to an enjoyable party at Playa Blanca. Then there had been the interesting experience of transiting the Panama Canal.

Nothing had been said about his leaving the boat and abandoning our plans for sailing to Hawaii. I hoped that he was now enjoying the trip and would change his mind about leaving.

But it did not happen that way. As soon as we were settled in at the Balboa Marina, John was busy making arrangements to fly home the following morning. He was in a taxicab at 5:00 the next morning. It was devastating for me because then I knew for sure that instead of my dream of a sailing trip to Hawaii with John, I would be facing the rigors of the sea alone when I sailed into the Pacific Ocean.

DANCING WITH DEBBIE
—YOUNG GIRLS AND COLD COFFEE IS
THE EARLY DEATH OF THE SAILOR

PANAMA OFFERED MANY SURPRISES FOR A LONE sailor who had struggled with language difficulties through a dozen countries. It was a paradise with almost everyone speaking English. In addition, there was no problem with currency or the rate of exchange because U.S. money was acceptable everywhere. The best part of all was the large U.S. community made up of all branches of military services, Army, Navy, Marines, Air Force, Coast Guard as well as civilian personnel and business people.

The Balboa Yacht Club offered a view of the wide Pacific Ocean from the club room and appeared to be an ideal place to stay while preparing to sail on, but then I learned that because I was retired military, I was eligible to moor the boat at the Rodman Naval Station, about a mile back up the canal.

The day after John departed I motored along the canal to find the Navy station on the opposite side from the Balboa Club. The Navy Marina, like Balboa, was open to the canal with a constant flow of canal traffic, night and day.

I moored CILIN II and set out on foot to explore my new home and was delighted with what I found. In easy walking distance was a fully equipped basketball gymnasium with fresh water showers and all kinds of exercise equipment. There was a sailors club with a fine restaurant and a Marine Exchange about a block away. It all seemed too good to be true after all of the inconveniences I had suffered in foreign ports.

A couple of days after my arrival, a sailor stopped by the boat for a visit. His name was James Papineau and he was a Lieutenant with the Navy Seals and on the way to a very large boat that was moored between my boat and the canal. Before he departed he said, "I live in an apartment and will invite you for a meal sometime."

That sounded good to me and I looked forward to it, but he paddled his dinghy past me day after day without ever mentioning it again. I was sure he had forgotten he had ever mentioned it until one day, about three weeks later, he announced, "We are planning for you to come for dinner tomorrow night."

That was the invitation I had been waiting for and I was able to follow his directions the next evening to his apartment. The walk along the beautifully manicured base was a pleasure as I walked past Building 40 where I had been attending religious services, and up the hill from the Officers Club with its Olympic-sized swimming pool.

In the ground floor parking area I noticed a motorcycle that I assumed belonged to my new friend. Then I found him and his wife Cheryl, and their two infant children, Russell and Lauren, living in a spacious third floor walk-up apartment. That was the beginning of a long and lasting friendship. From that time until the time I left Panama, their apartment became my home away from home. I had many more meals with them, baby-sat for them while they attended parties, and spent evenings writing a manuscript for a book on their dining room table.

During the ensuing months we had a number of trips on his big sailboat, out the long shipping channel to the south to the resorts of Taboga and Peerless Island.

At a sunset party at the Balboa Yacht Club one evening I met another Navy Lieutenant by the name of Lt. Deborah G. Dunston, a Port Service Officer of the Rodman Navy Station. She was tall with light brown hair and looked immaculate in her white navy uniform. I was more than a little surprised to learn that she shared an apartment with her mother, Claire, one floor below the Papineaus.

Like the Papineaus, she invited me to dinner with her mother at their apartment. It was then that I learned that the motorcycle on the ground floor parking area was hers and that she had recently made a solo round trip to the other end of the canal on her cycle. In addition, I saw on the wall a certificate qualifying her as a parachutist which she had acquired during a tour with the Italian Army while on duty in Naples, Italy.

Debbie and I and her mother enjoyed other meals together at the Sailors Club, the Officers Club and a variety of other restaurants. Life in Panama was a delight that account for my spending two years in the area before continuing the trip around the world.

Though Debbie was neat and proper in every other respect, profanity flowed from her lips as easily as if she were saying pie and cake. In other words, she swore like a shipwrecked sailor. It made no difference where we were dining. Debbie, before taking a bite of food, would bow her head reverently for a moment of silent prayer. Upon raising her head, she resumed conversation with her foul, "sailor talk". That caused me to wonder what kind of language she might be using in addressing her Holy Father. Her mother never admonished her in my presence, but a gradual decline in her foul language made me wonder if her mother might be encouraging her to tone it down a bit.

The highlight of the social season in Navy circles was the annual Navy Ball, when ladies appear in their finest gowns and officers in their dress uniforms, displaying their medals and awards from various military campaigns. I was surprised and honored when Debbie invited me to be her partner at the ball. I had no uniform but my dark suit appeared acceptable under the circumstances. I was painfully aware that I had not attended a dance for many years and that younger people danced differently than we had danced, when I was younger, 30 or 40 years earlier. Then it occurred to me that most of the people who would be at the dance were not yet born at the time I had last danced.

It happened that there were some unusual conditions coupled with Debbie's invitation. Since she was chairperson of the dance committee, I would be transported across the big All American Bridge to the ballroom in Balboa by a couple of Debbie's friends. I was uneasy upon arrival at the crowded hall and wondered what the evening would be like. I was a stranger in a crowd where everyone seemed to know everyone else. After they visited over a few cocktails, dinner was served, and it was then that I got to see my dance partner for the first time that evening. She had been busy taking care of arrangements. We ate and visited until at last the band struck up with a flurry. My big moment had come. We walked to the floor, hand in hand, but when I reached out to embrace her she was gone. I looked around and attempted to dance the way other people were dancing in an effort to attract as little attention as possible. It seemed to work, because everyone else was busy wiggling and shuffling about the floor as if they were off in another world, but Debbie was gone. Maybe she had gone back to check tickets at the door, but then I saw her shuffling and wiggling in my direction on the crowded floor. Then I lost her again.

What had happened to dancing, as I knew it, when you held your partner in your arms and got a squeeze from time to time, and maybe a little kiss on the cheek during slow music? This kind of dancing was all new to me. Whatever anyone may have thought of this 74-year old trying to keep pace with a younger generation, not one person made any sign of noticing my discomfort. They were all too busy. If they had thought anything about it, they would never have thought that I had once danced with the great Ginger Rogers.

The last dance was a great relief to me but was not "Good Night Sweetheart" or "I'll See You in My Dreams." The music stopped and the dance was over. Debbie was back again, taking care of arrangements and my escorts, who were to drive me back to Rodman, appeared and delivered me back to my boat in the marina. It had been a memorable Navy Ball, but I did not see Debbie again until the day I sailed away from Panama.

Many months later, in the far Pacific, I met a new friend on the Isle of Tahiti by the name of Bill Roberts. While paddling my dinghy across the bay to get fresh drinking water in my jerry can, I spotted a flag that I recognized as the flag of Antigua on a big, beautiful yacht. Since I had spent several months in Antigua, I thought it might be someone I would have met there. I had not met Bill Roberts before, but we became friends immediately when I learned that he too had spent a long time in Panama. Like me, he had spent many evenings at the Balboa Yacht Club. He knew many of the same people I had known there, but when I mentioned Lt. Debbie Dunston, a cloud fell across his face.

"That is very sad," he said.

"What's sad?" I asked.

Dancing with Ginger Rogers

Then he related that Debbie had been visiting friends in Virginia Beach, Virginia. One person had a motorcycle and Debbie had asked to take it for a spin. She sped away and disappeared down the road but she never came back. Then after a long wait, a search party set out to find her. When they found her, she lay on the ground unconscious, 15 feet from the cycle. An ambulance was called, but tragically, she was pronounced dead upon arrival at the hospital.

As the words left Bill's lips, I felt a shock of sadness as my mind took me back to those wonderful days in Panama and to the high-spirited young Lt. Debbie Dunston, who had lived life to its fullest and was now in a different world.

THE DOLDRUMS

ON SUNDAY MORNING, DECEMBER 1, 1991, CILIN II unceremoniously departed the mooring buoy at Rodman Naval Station, Panama and headed for the romantic Hawaiian Islands. There were no well-wishers to see me off, though I had made many acquaintances in the military community of Army, Navy and Marines during my 24 month stay in Panama. U.S. Navy personnel and other yachters had been very helpful in preparing CILIN II for the voyage.

The boat was well-stocked for the long trip with diesel fuel, fresh drinking water and the usual foods for long crossings except for one interesting addition, which I had never enjoyed before – 24 cartons of Meals Ready to Eat (MRE'S) procured for me by Lt. Papaneau. They were substantial meals used by the military and required no refrigeration and a minimum of preparation. It was comforting to add them to the stock of foodstuff.

CILIN II motored under the magnificent All American Bridge as I had done so many times during the stay in Panama, past Fort Amador, the Balboa Yacht Club and for five miles to the end of the buoy-marked channel. It would be another five miles at 210° to the tiny island of Taboga, which we had visited many times. I passed many large transport ships lying at anchor, waiting to travel the canal from the Pacific Ocean to the Gulf of Mexico.

At first I headed for the northeast side of the island where we had previously anchored on a trip to Taboga from Panama, but noticed five sailboats at the south side where there was better protection from the wind. It was 3:30 p.m. local time when I arrived. I did not go ashore or visit any other boats, but settled in with a bowl of chicken noodle soup and spent the evening and night on the boat.

The next day, while doing some last minute checking, I noticed that two of the 3/8 inch lines to the self-steering device were frayed and worn. I could not imagine how I had overlooked that detail while inspecting the boat. They were vital and had to be replaced. There was no question about that. I quickly pumped up the inflatable dinghy and paddled to shore in search of some replacement lines. I roamed from place to place in my search, but it was all in vain. There were approximately 100 well-kept dwellings, a couple of grocery stores and restaurants and an ancient Catholic Church, but not a sign of a place to buy the lines. Soon it became very clear that it would be necessary to sail back to the Rodman Naval Station to get the lines.

The trip to Hawaii was getting off to a very slow start. First, my hope for crew, my son John, had deserted me and returned to our home in Indiana. After that I had found Panama to be such an enjoyable place that I had stayed there much longer than I had first intended. There had been sailing trips to Taboga, a flight to the San Blas Islands to the north of Panama in the Gulf of Mexico where the Kuna Indians occupied many of the 365 islands and lived much as they had lived hundreds of years ago. I attended church regularly, sometimes at Rodman and other times at various other churches. There were several clubs at Rodman that served fine meals, held dances, and provided entertainment. With all of this, there had been little incentive to sail on. Then when I did start to sail on, I had to return ten miles to Rodman to find ten feet of 3/8 inch line to run the self-steering device. It turned out that Jim Papineau had just what I needed on his boat, and soon I was making my way back to Taboga on the way to Hawaii.

The new lines were installed on the self-steering device and they worked perfectly. I had mushroom soup and canned turkey for dinner and slept on the boat anchored off the shore of Taboga.

The following morning I weighed anchor at 0:900 and headed out to sea toward a buoy two and one half miles to the south, into the Pacific where Magellan had sailed years before with no sea charts, Sat-Nav, radio, or G.P.S. A following wind came up at about 20 miles per hour and took us on our way with CILIN II clocking five and one-half knots with full sails out until 11:00 p.m. At that time the wind abated and the sails hung limp. I gave up on sailing and slept a couple of hours.

I planned to sail at 180º for about 100 miles in order to get out of the busy shipping lane and past Point Malo. I saw very few ships during the night, but there were some highflying planes passing over the following morning. Also, there were very few sea gulls to be seen, but a number of frigates souring about the sky.

Saturday, December 7, 1991 turned out to be a beautiful day with low clouds and a 20 to 25 mph wind. I listened to President George Bush on the radio commemorating the 50th anniversary of the Japanese attack on Pearl Harbor.

The Sat-Nav and the self-steering device worked perfectly and I was able to sleep during the day to make up for lost sleep during the night before.

Toward evening the wind and waves picked up with five-foot waves splashing over the deck from time to time. Then at 6:00 p.m. the sea calmed. I put two reefs in the mainsail and installed the storm jib in preparation for whatever the night might bring.

What it would bring was far beyond anything I could have imagined. I was to learn about sailing in the Equatorial Convergence Zone.

After a good night's sleep, I was awakened by the flapping of the mainsail as the boom swung with the rise and fall of the swells. The wind had died for the first time since leaving Panama. It was Sunday, December 8, when I turned the radio on to listen to a sermon by a Lutheran Minister, Meyers, from Fort Wayne, Indiana, and for a while I was far away from the unpredictable winds and waves of the Pacific Ocean.

A delicious breakfast consisted of pancakes cooked with three ripe bananas as the boat moved along very slowly in the water.

After a mid-day siesta, a bird flying out of the cabin startled me. He had been perched on the navigator's table while I slept. It flew out and around the boat for a while and then finally perched on the rail at the stern, as if to see what was going on. The bird, about the size of a sparrow, had a cream-colored body with a little red on his neck.

It was surprising that the bird was not afraid because when I went back into the cabin, it flew in and perched on the radio headset where it had been before. It no doubt felt the need for a rest, since we were 65 miles from the nearest land. When I returned to the cabin from readjusting the sails, the bird was gone. I had enjoyed his Sunday visit on the boat.

Any thoughts that I would have a fair weather trip into the Pacific were shattered at one o'clock in the morning of the fourth day out from Taboga. A squall with heavy rain and strong wind interrupted the night's sleep. With two reefs in the mainsail and the storm jib up, the wind became so violent that I felt it necessary to lower the mainsail. In the black of night, with the wind howling and the little boat bobbing up and down, I managed to lower the mainsail. When the wind finally abated, I decided to leave it down until daylight when I would be able to see the condition of the sky. At dawn I raised it again.

The Air Force meteorologist at Howard Air Force near the Rodman Naval Station told me that I would miss a lot of bad weather by sailing to the south on a direct course to Hawaii. By 9:45 a.m. on December 9, CILIN II was 110 miles south of Panama at 5° 45' North and 81° 38' minutes West. I had a cup of coffee, oatmeal and the last piece of fresh pineapple.

The sun did not shine all day, and with low winds, progress was painfully slow. Just before dark, heavy black clouds appeared to the west. Then the rains came, heavier and heavier. Again, I was taking down the mainsail in the dark in a driving rain. With no sails up, the boat was hardly habitable in an unstable sea. Everything that can fall on the deck falls; things that do not fall, rattle and clatter. The boat lurches and rolls. A person cannot relax and roll with it because the roll is not rhythmic and sleeping is difficult but it helps escape the noise.

At dawn on December 10, while raising the sails, a sea gull flew in and perched on the dinghy engine, which was mounted on the stern. It showed no fear or interest in me though I tried to talk to it. After a while it flew away, circled the boat a couple of times and landed back on the engine for a short time. Maybe it had decided to be sociable and talk to me. But after a while it took off again and left me.

After that, six fat porpoise swam alongside the boat for about ten minutes. They were not particularly entertaining and gave the impression that they just happened to be going in the same direction as the boat until they left me.

A fix on the Sat-Nav told me that in five days since leaving Taboga I had traveled 250 miles. At that rate I figured that it would take 86 days to reach Hawaii, a very dismal prospect.

In the late afternoon of the seventh day out of Taboga, some fat porpoise came to perform for me. They came in pairs until there was a crowd congregating ahead of the boat. Some were diving and slapping their tails on the water, but the big attraction came when some jumped above the water and came back down for a belly flopper. I wondered if they thought I was a talent scout for the Sea World Marine entertainment park and they were auditioning for a job. The show was spectacular and unlike the antics of other porpoise I had ever seen anywhere. After about half an hour, they disappeared as quickly and quietly as they had first come on the scene.

On Friday, December 13, the weather was almost a replay of the day before. Off to the west a gigantic cloud formation appeared. I felt certain it would dissipate and go away. Wrong! It did not go away. It moved over, dead ahead of the boat. There were no heavy winds or waves, but rain poured down all morning. The boat made very slow progress because of the light wind. I filled all of the containers with water and enjoyed a fresh-water bath.

I saw a large transport ship in the distance through the rain, the first I had seen for a week. I feared I might be getting near the shipping lane but saw no other ships. The visibility was so poor I feared a ship might come upon me before I saw it. The wind died down completely in the afternoon, giving me the opportunity to replace a broken batten in the sail.

There was a slight breeze during the night and the self-steering device did not work properly. At various times during the night I checked to find CILIN II far off my intended heading. It made little difference because the boat was moving so slowly.

On Saturday, December 14, the Sat-Nav told me that CILIN II had moved six miles during the night. Progress was so slow that I did not even turn on the Sat-Nav again all day. The truth was really demoralizing. CILIN II was in the doldrums and might be there for a while.

In the morning there were big buildups of clouds all about the sky. I watched for one to move in my direction, but as time went by the clouds dissipated. By noon the day was like yesterday and the day before, a glassy sea with swells, which caused the sails to flap and jerk incessantly. It was maddening. The only remedy was to lower the sails, but then the boat would pitch and roll with the swells. To me it was the worst part of sailing the seas. The one bright hope was that a good wind would come up and carry us out of the doldrums.

My hopes that Sunday, December 15 would be a better day were wasted. We were seven degrees north of the equator but it was not a better day. The sea was glassy again. I sighted a sailboat at 60° from me and for a moment had hopes of making contact, but was disappointed when it headed off to the southeast.

Nathaniel Bowditch (1773-1838), in his fine book on navigation, defines doldrums as "the belt of low pressure at the surface near the equator...Wind speeds are light and directions are variable. Hot, sultry days are common. The sky is often overcast, and showers and thundershowers relatively frequent; in these disturbed areas, brief periods of strong wind occur."

He could not have described conditions better. I had hot cakes with Del Monte peaches for breakfast.

On Monday, December 16, the sea was dead calm. Gray haze hung over the horizon in every direction and it appeared that CILIN II was in the center of a huge bowl with sails hanging limp. I had coffee and Quaker Oats for breakfast.

The air was warm, with a faint breeze. CILIN II was doing more drifting than sailing. Up ahead of the boat I saw what looked like the head of a whale in the water. I had the feeling that it was waiting for me, and with the direction we were drifting, we would come very close to it. It was very real to me. I panicked and jumped into the cabin to check my emergency survival gear, added a bag of the army field rations and grabbed a life jacket. I also strapped a hunting knife to my belt and moved back up on deck, waiting, as we slowly approached the whale. Unless the current changed our course, we would come very near to the whale.

Sometimes we appeared to be getting closer to it, then at other times we seemed farther away. At last I grabbed the binoculars to get a better look, but they only made it look larger. Then I was relieved when I felt we were drifting away from it, but up ahead there appeared three or four objects like the one we had passed.

It was a great relief to me when one of the objects I took to be a whale turned out to be a very large white bird sitting on the water. From time to time it dove under the water for long periods. The other objects looked like rock protruding above the water, but the sea chart showed no such things. Again CILIN II was drifting toward what I had taken to be a whale. The big surprise came when, with the binoculars, I was able to make out the form of a giant sea turtle. It was no whale!

I had been at sea alone too long under the most frustrating of conditions and my mind was playing tricks on me. The reality of my situation was shown by a morning fix with the Sat-Nav. CILIN II had progressed 15 miles in the past 24 hours. She had traveled only 42 miles the day before that. At 3:00 p.m., a delightful breeze picked up and we had superb sailing most of the night.

Tuesday, December 17, was another slow day with wind so light that again the self-steering device did not work.

With slow progress in sailing, I had thought that I might possibly reach Acapulco, Mexico by Christmas. That thought faded when I looked at progress over the past five days when CILIN II had averaged only 38 miles per day. At that rate, it would be mid-January before I could reach Acapulco. I saw a ship in the shipping lane during the morning, but was unable to contact him by radio. Even though sailing progress was slow, the weather was very pleasant so that I was able to wear shorts and a T-shirt every day. It was very pleasant living with no pesky insects.

I was so discouraged with progress on Wednesday, December 18 that I decided to put in at Punta Quspos, Costa Rica, 90 miles to the north. Sailing was very good on the new bearing but I was unable to see land even after four hours of sailing.

I was able to contact a large transport ship during the night. I had worried that the radio was not putting out a signal. The operator on the ship came in loud and clear, giving me a good weather report.

Upon hanging up the microphone in the cabin, I heard an unusual noise up on deck. I jumped up and was shocked to see the mainsail all across the deck. I could not image what had happened. Then upon examination I could see that the clip of the main halyard had broken. It was dangling high at the top of the 37-foot mast and I could think of no way to get it down. It was the clip that Navy Chief Mike Pine had installed for me at the Rodman Naval Station in Panama. I had confidence in him because he previously had been a boat rigger at the U.S. Naval Academy at Annapolis. Then I considered that the boats he dealt with in the training fleet there had been smaller and that clip had been adequate for them.

My situation was desperate. I needed the mainsail. My first reaction after getting over the shock of losing the use of the main halyard was that I was glad that the accident had happened when I was only about 90 miles from shore instead of many miles at sea. At first I secured the mainsail and lowered the jib so I could motor in to land. With the engine, we could make 5 M.P.H. and that would take about 18 hours to reach land. But after the first hour, the engine became very hot so I cut it off and raised the mainsails again by using the line that holds the boom. It worked well except for a couple of small problems. The new line rested over a shroud cable and was certain to be cut. The other problem was that the sail could be raised only part way up. The weather remained good and a bright moon made for a pleasant but slow night of sailing.

At daylight the next day, I looked out to see hundreds, maybe thousands of small-sized ducks spread out across the water as far as I could see. They were not disturbed by the sailboat as CILIN II drifted among them.

After four days, I finally limped into the port at Puntarenas (point of sand) Costa Rica, and anchored near a large, rusty, steel pier. There I pumped up the inflatable dinghy and prepared to go ashore to clear in to the port. When I called the port captain, he warned me to be prepared for a three to four knot current. That did not seem like a problem to me until I boarded the dinghy over the side and started to paddle.

Suddenly I realized that the current was carrying me backward. A couple of strong strokes with the paddles showed I was making no progress. I grabbed the gunwale just in time to avoid being swept away by the current. Knowing that the tide changes every six hours, I decided to wait for a while before attempting to go ashore again. So I put my boat papers aside and laid on the bunk for a nap. When I awoke, it was late in the afternoon. Then, when I tried to call the port captain again, the radio was dead.

Slowly I came to realize that it was December 24, Christmas Eve. The port captain had retired for the night and there was no way I could clear into the port until he was back on duty. It was almost a month since I had departed Panama. I wanted desperately to contact my family and exchange Christmas greetings, but that was out of the question. I could not legally leave the boat and go ashore without clearing in with the port authorities.

I prepared a Christmas Eve dinner of Teriyaki Chicken with long grain rice, and looked across the water to the activities along the shore. I had no way of knowing that Puntarenas was a resort city with a long beach, but I could sense a festive atmosphere on shore.

Then I saw a beautiful luxury yacht anchored about 100 yards down the coast and decided to give it a call on the radio. The captain quickly replied and told me the name of his yacht was THE OTHER WOMAN, and that his passengers were preparing to go ashore for a Christmas Eve party. He also told me that he had sailed around the world alone in his youth.

Soon I saw the party, dressed for an evening of celebration, boarding a large dinghy and heading for shore. This made me feel even more alone and wanting to go ashore. At last I reasoned that any port official would be very hard hearted who would penalize me for going ashore to call my loved ones on Christmas Eve. In the late evening I dressed and lowered the dinghy over the side into the water. By that time the current had slowed up and it was easy rowing in to the big steel pier where I secured the dinghy before climbing to the top deck.

I walked the long deck of the pier without seeing a soul. On shore there was a long row of tents with refreshment stands and the usual activities of a carnival with vacationers milling in all directions. I walked for a couple of blocks down the shore before I came upon a telephone booth. It was all so simple. With my telephone credit card, I was able to make a call to my daughter Ann, in Indianapolis.

By this time family members were used to receiving telephone calls from me at unusual times from unusual places. Ann was fine, everyone was fine and the weather was fine with five inches of snow on the ground in Indianapolis. It was the usual greeting but to me it was very precious, making that contact with the family before I walked back along the pier, paddled the dinghy back to the boat to spend Christmas Eve alone, and listening to Christmas music on the radio.

BREAKFAST IN PANAMA

IT HAD BEEN MORE THAN THREE WONDERFUL weeks since I had departed from the Jungle Club at Golfito, Costa Rica. I had waited until too late in the sailing season to make the trip to Hawaii, so I was making my way back to the Rodman Navy Station in Panama to prepare for crossing the Pacific Ocean on a more southern route.

The supply of fresh drinking water was growing low and I needed to find a village where the supply could be replenished. The sea chart showed a small village up the coast, so I decided to make a stop from the sea. I could see a large number of small fishing boats outfitted with outboard engines swinging at anchor along the shore at a place I took to be Pedasi, Panama.

Had I foreseen the hectic problem I was to encounter I would surely have sailed away as fast as I could go. But instead I circled among the small boats until I found a place I considered suitable to anchor. After throwing out the anchor, I saw that CILIN II was snared in a long fishing net. With the aid of the gaff hook, I endeavored to release the net. At that time three men in a small fishing boat came to my rescue. They advised me to start the engine and move the boat backwards. That I did, only to find that the net was dragging along with the boat. Then they advised me to go under the boat, so with my facemask on, I went below and was able to disengage the net.

With that matter out of the way, my helpers offered to escort me to a proper place to anchor down the coast. I could tell that they were preparing to go fishing, so I requested that they bring me a fish upon their return. It was agreed that they would bring me a fish at 6:00 in the morning. I thanked them and they sailed away. From my new location, I was too far from the village to paddle the dinghy because of the wind. I decided to settle in for the night and wait until the next morning.

While I was relaxing, I heard a thumping sound on the side of the boat. I jumped up to find a man in a dugout canoe. He was taking orders for tropical fruit. I talked with him by sign language but also requested that he stop his canoe from bumping into the CILIN II. He pretended to understand but made no effort to stop it. I ordered a papaya, some coconut and some bananas to get him on his way, but when he returned he had only five husked coconuts. He had nothing else, so I paid him two dollars and he departed.

With all of the excitement out of the way and safely at anchor, I settled in for a night of rest. It was about 10:00 p.m. when I heard another thumping on the boat. I was sure it was the man in the dugout canoe. What did he want at this time of the night? I jumped out of the bunk and onto the deck, but there was no one to be seen. The night was pitch black. I walked from one end of the boat to the other. Surely he had disappeared into the night.

Back in my bunk, a few moments later, there was more thumping. This time I recognized it. The tide was going out and CILIN II was bouncing on the rocks. I quickly hoisted the sails in hopes of sailing into deeper water. When that did not work, I fired up the Volvo engine. It was all in vain. She would not move.

After a long time, fishermen passing by saw my plight and offered to help. They anchored about 50 feet from me in deeper water and attached a line to CILIN II but after a long time their efforts were in vain. Then they hailed a second fishing boat and had him anchor out farther and attached a line to his boat.

All the while I saw that a crowd had gathered in the dark on shore to watch the proceedings. I had a great feeling when CILIN II finally started moving, ever so slowly, out into deeper water.

The captain of the first boat directed me to a place to anchor safely in deeper water. I handed him a fifty dollar bill with the thought that he would share it with everyone who had helped. I later had reason to believe that it did not happen.

What next, I wondered, as I finally put my head on the pillow to sleep. I slept well and early the next morning I looked out at the peaceful village where I had stopped to get some water. All was at rest. I was out farther from the shore but even closer to the village than before. The tide was out and I saw many large boulders in the water that had not been visible at high tide.

CILIN II was in good shape and I was in good shape. For breakfast I had a bowl of oatmeal, some fruit juice and a cup of coffee. After breakfast, when I was preparing to paddle the dinghy ashore to get some water, a fishing boat appeared alongside CILIN II. It was the fisherman from the night before with the fish that he had promised. So having no ice or refrigeration and no way to preserve the fish, I decided that the best thing to do would be to cook it. I knew from past experiences that if I waited until I was underway again; the fish would not be cared for. I pan-fried it and it looked so good that I decided the best way to preserve it was to eat it then and there. It was delicious and a very good second breakfast.

With the five-gallon plastic jerry can in the dinghy, I paddled ashore where a few fishermen were congregated. One young fellow walked up to me as I was dragging the dinghy ashore and offered to assist me. He then took charge of the water can and let me know that he would help. I tried to explain that in addition to water, I wanted to buy some food.

My helper led me up the hill to a street lined with neatly kept cottages. He stopped at a house across the street from a store and introduced me to a lady who promptly brought a straight chair to the porch for me. Though I could not understand any of the conversation, I assumed that I was to wait there until the store across the street was open for business.

I did not wait long before the lady reappeared at the door with a smile and a plate of fish, beans and rice. Though I had no appetite whatsoever, I could not turn down their generous hospitality, so I ate my third breakfast of the morning while people passed by on the street, politely paying little attention.

When I finished the meal, my helper led me across the street to what I had thought was a store. It turned out to be a tavern. I let it be known that I was interested in buying food, so my friend led me down the street to a small store which was across the street from the church where people were assembling for religious services. Young and old people in their Sunday attire crowded the area. I assumed that it was a special day.

Inside the store I was reminded of what people in the islands throughout the Mediterranean Sea had referred to as a supermarket. Many times they would be very small with a limited supply of merchandise. That fit the description of this store, which offered for sale about the same number of items which were on CILIN II and many of the same things. I purchased a dozen eggs and some onions. When I asked for mangos, there were none, but my guide let me know that he could get some for me. As we headed down toward the shore he took me into the yard of a big house where we found many mangos on the ground. In addition, there was a good supply of limes on another tree.

Next we went to a well where the jerry can was filled. My helper hoisted it onto his shoulder and led me back to the dinghy. Not a word of English was spoken and I had gotten everything I needed, including a third breakfast, which I did not need. My guide helped me get the dinghy back in the water but graciously declined my offer to compensate him for his generous assistance.

Back on CILIN II I was preparing to weigh anchor and sail away when another fishing boat approached. He tied his boat onto mine and let me know that his was the second boat of the two that had pulled me off the rocks the night before. He had not received any compensation. The operator of the first boat had apparently kept the money I gave him without sharing with the second boat crew. In my wallet I had only $13.00 and a $100.00 bill. I gave him the $13.00 and then he started pointing to objects on the boat that he would like to have. He entered the cabin, though uninvited, and again started pointing to things including some canned vegetables. I gave him half a dozen cans, which he gladly accepted.

As he started to leave the boat he spotted two large plastic garbage bags on top of the cabin and let me know that he would like to have them. They both contained dozens of smaller plastic bags of trash, which had accumulated in the three weeks since I had departed Golfito. In my mind I visualized him taking them ashore for me. In his mind, he would search every one of the tiny bags to see if there was anything useful to him. Almost before I realized what he was about, he had strewn dozens of the little bags over the sea. My first impulse was to jump in the dinghy and gather up the bags, but there were too many of them. They would be a soggy mess. I decided that the best thing to do was pull the anchor and be on my way.

As I started sailing to the north I saw a shocking sight. The men from the shore were boarding their fishing boats and heading in my direction. I observed more and more of them with the thought that they were coming after me for littering the sea with my trash from the boat. CILIN II was moving but I knew that the little fishing boats with the outboard engines could quickly overtake me.

They were lined up in a column of two, headed straight toward CILIN II. I was in a quandary. What would they do to me? What could I expect? In my frustration I was a little amused as I pictured myself as the villain in an old movie picture, with the natives in hot pursuit for the wrong I had committed.

Then much to my relief and surprise, the column veered off to the left, forming a big circle in the sea. I breathed easier as I realized they were oblivious to my presence. I then had reason to believe that the column of boats had been participating in a ceremony connected with religious activities at the church.

They could not have been concerned that the occupant of a boat was throwing trash into the sea. To them that is the way to dispose of trash.

PONTRENAS TO PANAMA

WHILE LISTENING TO THE RADIO ONE DAY I heard a report that got my attention. It said that an American had won a half million dollar award for finding a means of eradicating screwworms from cattle in feed lots. The worms were causing the loss to cattle owners as they nested in the hide of cattle and caused infections. That may seem to be a strange item to interest a sailor at sea, but it did interest me. I owned a 150 acre farm on the Ohio River in southern Indiana where I planned to retire when my sailing days were over, but the place was infested with little insects called ticks. I reasoned that if this man could eliminate screwworms from feed lots he could eliminate ticks from my farm and possibly mosquitoes, which cause malaria fever around the world.

For a time I was more excited about this new discovery than I was about sailing my boat. I listened to the radio for more reports about it but there were none. Then I determined as soon as I reached Panama I would learn more about the discovery.

Upon mooring the boat in the Rodman Naval Marina, I was off to Howard Air Force Base Exchange in search for the article concerning the eradication of screwworms. At the Exchange, I scanned U.S. News and World Report, Time, and Newsweek magazines, but my search was all in vain. Then I recalled that Navy Chaplain William Wildhack kept back copies of the Miami Herald, all neatly arranged in chronological order in his library. With a full month of papers, I was certain to find an article of such importance.

Fortunately he was in his office and I told him the purpose of my visit. I was surprised when he told me that when he was young, the grandfather of one of his pals was working on something like that. Then he invited me to help myself to his newspapers.

I searched through every paper carefully and could not believe that such an important item would go unpublished. A half million dollar award should attract some attention. In addition, the possibility of eradicating harmful insects was truly significant. I could find no item relating to the matter, so I went back to the boat, much discouraged.

After a short nap, I paddled my dinghy back to the marina office where the secretary told me that the Chaplain had been looking for me. Without hesitation, I hastened back to his office, where he gave me exciting news. He had called his mother in Arlington, Virginia, and learned that it was his childhood friend whose grandfather had made the discovery that had collected the half million dollar prize. It was E. E. "Knip" Knipling who had worked for two decades as director of Entomology for the U.S. Agricultural Research Service. He had written, "If they continue to rely on insecticides, I think they are going to have hazardous problems continue indefinitely. Nature has created good parasites for nearly every pest we have and these parasites don't harm people or animals or anything else."

I wondered that a young entomologist with the zeal and tenacity of Mr. Knipling might find a means of reducing the millions of deaths from the deadly mosquito.

To me, here was a possible means of eradicating wood ticks on my farm in Indiana but also those pesky mosquitoes that bear germs causing malaria fever.

I wondered where in the world I would find a naval station where I would find so complete an answer to my problem. The Chaplain gave me the phone number for Mr. Knipling in Arlington, Virginia.

In my excitement to explore this possibility, I placed a phone call to Mr. Knipling. Then I received the disappointing news. His answer was that his system would work well in a confined area such as a cattle feed lot. It would not work in open areas such as fields or forests. Maybe, just maybe, in the future some scientist will build upon Mr. Knipling's program and actually eliminate pesky insects.

SAILING WITH MISS FINNEGAN

SINCE THE FIRST DAY I STARTED SAILING the seas in 1986, friends and relatives insisted that I should not sail alone, but should have a crew or a sailing companion. "What if something should happen to you? What if you get sick? Don't you get lonesome?" Those all seemed good reasons to have somebody along.

On the other hand, there is much compensation in solo sailing that in my mind outweighs the benefits of having someone along. In sailing alone you have the free run of the boat. It is like the difference between living in a single room and having to share it with a roommate. You can sleep, read, eat, listen to the radio or even sing at the top of your voice at anytime of the night or day without disturbing anyone. I particularly enjoy the moments of solitude out on deck, watching the sea and sky, the sunrise and sunsets and the dolphins when they come up alongside the boat to play. Among the other compensations of solo sailing for a person who is hard of hearing is that you do not have to keep asking, "What did you say?" or "Please repeat that."

I had spent months in the Panama Canal Zone in preparation for my trip into the Pacific Ocean, including the false start when the clip on the main halyard failed. While I was moored at the Pedro Miguel Boat Club, a young lady by the name of Juanita Finnegan from Perth, Australia showed up to serve as cook on a boat moored next to CILIN II. She and a man from Denver had responded to an ad in "Cruising World". In a short time they had made sailing trips to the Peerless Islands south of Panama and the San Blas Islands to the north. These trips had turned out to be exceedingly unpleasant for Juanita, the cook, because the men argued incessantly. When the man from Denver decided to leave the boat, Juanita decided that she would do likewise. We visited and I decided to ask her if she would like to sail with me to Galapagos Islands. From there she could get her flight back to Australia.

And so I thought, "Worry no more, my dear friends and relatives. I have a crewmember who happens to be a cook. I will be lonesome no longer and nothing is going to happen to me out on the sea alone."

Juanita Lucille Finnegan was a 48-year-old schoolteacher of Irish-Catholic ancestry, deeply religious and of unblemished virtue. She spoke with a crisp Australian accent that would have been difficult for me to understand even if my hearing was not impaired. It became necessary for me to ask her to repeat almost everything she said, but it was to her credit that she never once raised her voice or shouted at me.

Juanita Finnegan

Though Juanita had limited sailing experience, it soon became apparent that she intended to be the Captain of CILIN II. It was not long before she was telling me when to trim the sails, when to go on the engine, and which way to steer the boat.

On Saturday, April 3, 1993, CILIN II cleared the Rodman Naval Station at Panama, sailed under the towering All American Bridge and headed for the paradise island of Tobago, ten miles out in the bay off Panama. There we anchored for little more than a week in final preparation for the 600 miles to Ecuador and then on to the Galapagos Islands.

Included in preparation for the trip was a final scraping and painting of the hull below the water line. This was accomplished at the island of Tobago by lashing CILIN II alongside a sunken ship near the shore. We then waited until the tide came in and out again before applying a coat of anti-foul paint to the hull. Everything went like clock work; I had scraped and painted the hull many times before but never in the sea. Soon my sailing companion and I were sailing south of the Bay of Panama.

On this trip I had something I had never owned before. At the Rodman Naval Station in Panama my good friend, Lt. James Papineau, had presented me with a fine fishing pole with a Penn Senator reel and a good supply of lures. In all of my days of sailing I had no luck at fishing, but I was soon to learn that was because I had never owned proper fishing gear.

I had let out about 75 feet of line behind the boat as we were sailing along at a good clip. After some time I grew weary of waiting for a fish to strike, parked the pole in a holder and, leaving Juanita at the tiller, retired to my bunk in the cabin. Sometime later I was jarred out of my semi-conscious state by a sound much like the whine of the siren of the patrol boat off the coast of Greece which had admonished me for flying a Turkish flag in Greek waters. But it was not a siren. It was the reel of the new fishing pole I had left unattended while I dozed.

I dashed from the cabin to the cockpit, grabbed the fishing pole and started to reel it in, but something really big was tugging on the line. If I reeled it in too fast it would surely snap the line, so I reeled in only when there was slack enough to avoid too much pressure on the line.

From time to time the fish broke out above the water, just as I had seen in TV shows, but I had never experienced such a thing before. It did it time and time again until my arms grew tired. How long it tugged and ran with the line I could not imagine and in my mind I thought that I would never get so big a fish in the boat. The line would snap and he would be gone. But at last it was beside the boat. I screamed to Juanita to hand me the gaff hook. With it I was able to lop the fish into the cockpit.

Juanita was as excited as I and we at first worried that it might somehow flip out of the boat. It was a funny looking fish, unlike any I had ever seen before, and certainly unlike any that swam in the creeks and rivers back in Indiana. It was a Dorado, one of the finest fish in the seas.

Knowing that none of our friends would believe that we caught such a fish, we hung it up and snapped a picture. Then there was the job of cleaning it. Juanita meticulously skinned and butchered the fish. Then we came to realize that it was a waste of time. We had no refrigeration and no way to preserve it, so we cut off a generous portion and threw the remainder back into the sea. The catching and landing of our first fish was an ordeal. We estimated its length to be about five feet and weighed between 30 and 40 pounds.

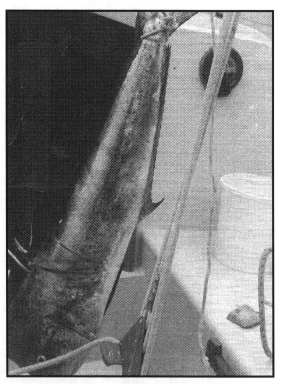

Our first catch - a Dorado fish

Juanita was sleeping the next morning when, at dawn, I saw a sight that made my hair stand on end. Dozens of sharks four to six feet long were darting to and fro about the boat. I quickly called Juanita and admonished her to be quiet. When she asked me why she should be quiet, I was at a loss for an answer. Maybe I thought that a noise would make the sharks mad, but that did not make sense. There was no way they could harm us as long as they were in the water and we were on the boat, yet it was a weird and somewhat frightening experience. It was as if we were in a big aquarium and the fish were watching us. Then after about half an hour they departed as quickly and silently as they had first appeared. Why had they been attracted to our boat? Afterwards we could only speculate that they had been attracted by the blood that had run over the gunwales and dried when we cleaned our fish the day before. From that time on, we made sure there was no dried blood left on the hull whenever we cleaned a fish.

On April 19, I observed that we had made no forward progress in the course of the day though we had been sailing and motoring all day. We had, in fact, been swept backwards. It was then that we first became acquainted with the equatorial current which flows along the west coast of South America. Our concern about that melted when Juanita called from the cockpit, "We are not moving!"

"What do you mean, not moving?" I shouted as I bolted from the cabin to see that the boat was sitting still in the water though the engine was running at normal cruising speed.

Something was definitely wrong. I pushed the inflatable dinghy overboard and moved to a position where I could see that the propeller shaft had pulled away from the engine. It was a disastrous situation. The same thing had happened off the Coast of Greece, but that had been more than 5,000 miles ago. At that time CILIN II was only a few miles from the Greek mainland. Now she was a hundred miles off the coast of Columbia, South America, and far out of commercial shipping lanes. I had learned a lot about the boat and engine since that first time the propeller had separated from the engine.

From the dinghy I was able to pound the propeller shaft back into position with a rubber mallet. It was tedious work since it was all done in the water under the boat. With the shaft secure, I started to climb back into the boat, but with too much weight on the end of the dinghy, it flipped and spilled me into the water. With the memory of those dozens of sharks in the water, I made quick work of pulling myself into the dinghy and onto the boat. Back in the engine compartment I found that the bolt, which had held the propeller shaft to the engine, had sheared off. With good fortune, I was able to find another one to take its place. I worked late into the night and part of the next morning until I was satisfied with my work securing the propeller shaft.

At that point, Juanita and I discussed the matter of whether we should attempt to proceed on our course toward Ecuador or return to Panama where we knew that we could obtain the expert mechanical assistance we needed. It was an easy choice to make, so after sailing south for more than a week, we turned and headed back toward Panama.

Sailing back to the north was slow. We were far from land and far from commercial shipping lanes and we had not seen another ship for more than a week.

On Sunday evening, April 25, black clouds gathered and a storm from the south hit us just about dark. In Panama I had fashioned what is known as a lazy jack which is something of a cradle to hold the mainsail in place while it is being lowered. I was proud of my work because it had worked so well, but with this sudden storm blowing up, part of the sail hung up in the lazy jack so that the top portion of the sail flapped violently in the wind. It continued to flap for a couple of hours while heavy rains poured down and the storm raged about us. I felt certain that the sail would be damaged and the battens lost. Though the storm lasted most of the night, I was delighted in the morning to see that no damage had been done to the sail. I was also relieved that the storm had passed us by. But my relief was short lived as I saw more dark clouds closing in upon us from the south. It looked like the makings of another tropical storm. At 9:00 a.m. the next storm lashed its fury upon us with heavy winds and rain lasting about three hours. It was comforting at last to see the storm subside with the prospects for clear weather ahead.

Then from the cabin Juanita called, "The Sat-Nav has stopped working". That was no problem. I would find what was wrong and have it working in a minute or two. First, I pushed the on/off button, but nothing happened. Then I turned on the voltmeter switch. I was stunned to see that it registered zero voltage. The battery was dead and we had no electricity to run the engine, the Sat-Nav or the lights. To make matters worse, when I turned on the key to attempt to start the engine, a puff of smoke came from the underside of the engine. That suggested that the electrical system had been flooded with rainwater and had shorted out. That left us in a precarious position for trying to sail back to Panama, about a hundred miles away. We would be entering heavily traveled shipping lanes with no lights, no radio and no engine.

The atmosphere was still hazy from the storm which had passed us by, limiting visibility appreciably. Since we had intentionally been sailing out of the shipping lanes, it had been more than ten days since we had seen a ship.

There was nothing to do but sail back to Panama. Then the most miraculous thing occurred. Up ahead, through the haze, there appeared an image of a big blue ship sitting still in the water. It was like a dream or another one of my hallucinations. I could not believe it, but Juanita saw it too. As we drew closer, it became more real.

We passed the ship by and sailed along its leeward side to avoid a collision. As we passed, we saw 10 or 15 sets of eyes staring back at us, apparently as surprised to see us as we were to see them. After passing the ship I made a 180° turn to bring CILIN II back alongside the blue ship. Maneuvering CILIN II was tedious because we were under sail without the benefit of an engine. On the second pass of the ship I called out, "No electricity. No electricity." On the third trip past the boat, a man I assumed to be the captain came out to us in a dinghy. He handed me a card upon which was printed the geographic coordinates of our location and "Eighty Miles to Tobago."

I explained our problem and he quickly returned to his ship. In a moment he was back with a long line to secure CILIN II to keep her from drifting. He also had an electrician in tow. The electrician acted very efficiently. He cut the insulation off both ends of a wire about 18 inches long and poked around under the engine. He then installed a 12 volt battery which he had brought along, turned the key and had my engine running in no time. I thanked them profusely, but before I could get out my wallet to offer some money for their fine assistance, they were off CILIN II and on the way back to the big blue ship.

Our "dream ship" was a mother ship for a tuna fleet named ISABEL TUNA out of Manta, Ecuador. She had been sitting in the water waiting for the tuna boats of their fleet to off-load their catch to be hauled back to Ecuador. To us, she was truly a dream ship. We did not want to think about what might have happened if she had not been at that place at that time.

We sailed toward Panama, our next destination. We had no other mishaps. With the engine running smoothly and the sails in good shape, we decided to bypass Panama and sail to the north to Golfita, Costa Rica. It was much further, but I knew of a machine shop there that could repair the problem with the propeller shaft. I knew that the Jungle Club would be a good place to stay while the work was being performed. Sailing went well, and it was an uneventful trip.

When we arrived in Golfita, Juanita said her good-byes to me and made preparations to visit her sister in Montreal, Canada. I left Ms Finnegan waiting for a bus that would take her to San Jose, where she would catch a flight to Montreal, Canada, and then on to her home in Perth, Australia.

As we parted, I realized that her dreams of cruising the tropical islands had surely not lived up to her expectations. She could not have imagined the ferocity of the storms we endured or of being caught at sea with a dead engine, no lights, and no radio.

Nor could she have visualized the miracle of a beautiful rescue ship appearing from nowhere to assist us. Junaita Finnegan had been a brave soul throughout it all. Now she would be returning to Perth, Australia, and back to the classroom as a teacher with enough exciting memories to last her a lifetime. She had been a courageous shipmate, and now I knew I would be sailing 4,400 miles alone to Tahiti.

COSTA RICA TO TAHITI

THERE WAS AMPLE REASON FOR APPREHENSION ABOUT the trip even before CILIN II weighed anchor at Golfito, Costa Rica. Two attempts at the Pacific had ended in near disaster. The first had been the effort to sail from Panama to Hawaii when the clip on the main halyard had given away, dropping the mainsail onto the deck. It had happened on the 13th day out. The second happened nine days out from Panama, on the way to the Galapagos when the propeller came off.

In preparation for the trip to Tahiti, it became necessary to repair the propeller shaft. It had to go to a machine shop and be fitted so the propeller would remain attached to the engine. At the Jungle Club in Golfito, Costa Rica, there was a stall where at low tide the shaft could be removed. The hole was then sealed to keep water out until the shaft was replaced. It all worked out as planned except that a storm blew up during the night. As the tide raised, the waves would lift the boat and then drop it, so that it crashed against the bottom over and over again. It became so violent that I was certain there would be structural damage to the boat. Up and down it crashed, again and again.

At last, through the driving rain in the darkness of the night, I called the proprietor of the Jungle Club on the VHF radio to report what was happening. His residence was less than 100 yards away. His wife answered and told me there was nothing they could do. My propeller was off and they did not have a boat large enough to pull me out of the stall in the face of the storm.

The storm continued with unabated fury and for me, each jolt was a nerve-shattering experience. I felt that my third trip into the Pacific was ending before it got started. I was sure the boat was being destroyed. I was alone in the darkness of the night until the storm finally subsided and it was a relief to know that the boat was not taking water.

In the morning, when the tide went out, I observed nothing unusual about the hull, and I felt there was a chance that no damage had been done. If that had been the end of it, there might be a chance that there was no structural damage, but the second night another storm came in, causing the keel to hammer against the bottom even heavier than the night before. Again in the morning I observed no damage to the hull from the exterior.

The following day, June 19th, the propeller shaft was restored and CILIN II moved out into the bay. Retired Navy Captain George Wales volunteered to conduct a survey of the boat. This was a real bonanza because a boat survey on a boat the size of CILIN II can cost up to $500.00. This was free and I was delighted with the offer. It nevertheless was cause for some concern. I could not make more than three or four of the 20 changes he recommended before setting sail. I had already spent five weeks in preparation for the trip, and I was eager to get started.

Aboard were 30 gallons of drinking water, 30 gallons of diesel fuel, together with a bountiful supply of rice, spaghetti, ten loaves of bread that had been toasted on the deck, and a good supply of canned goods. I also had four dozen packages of army field rations which were packed in hermetically sealed plastic bags, known as Meals Ready to Eat (MRE).

As I headed out of Golfito Bay, a pretty Polynesian girl I had never met before from a Hawaiian Catamaran drove her dinghy alongside and handed me a loaf of delicious, home-baked banana nut bread as a going-away present. What a treat! Other than that, there were no whistles, bells, horns or people waving and shouting as there had been upon leaving the Canary Islands on the way across the Atlantic Ocean. That seemed a little strange because this trip would take me 4500 miles, while the Atlantic crossing had been a mere 2980 miles.

There were no meteorological records of having been a hurricane in the route I took across the Atlantic at the time of my crossing. In the Pacific it was different. Weather patterns in the past few years had not been so reliable for reasons that have not been satisfactorily resolved. There are theories that major climatic events in various parts of the world may be caused by "El Niño". The theory is that dust from the gigantic eruptions of El Chichonal in Mexico, Mt. St. Helens in the U.S. and Mt. Pinatubo in the Philippines have weakened the heat from the sun on the tropical Pacific, thus triggering "El Niño". What this all means is that past records are unreliable in predicting weather. Hurricanes and tropical storms may appear at times and places they have never appeared before.

With all of these happy thoughts to reflect upon, I headed out of Golfito Bay. The tide was receding and the current was with me.

Golfito had been a very interesting and enjoyable stop for me. There at the Jungle Club, nestled at the far corner of the bay, Whitey and Barbara Helton took care of the needs of sailors headed for Panama or the Pacific. They are known far and wide among sailors for the hospitality of the club where one night a week there is a pitch-in dinner.

On other nights, the club serves chicken, fish, or steaks with Barbara's home-baked bread. Whitey would provide diesel fuel to your boat, potatoes, onions, bananas, canned goods, and a wide variety of other items. During the time I spent at the Jungle Club there were from 15 to 20 boats anchored in front of the club daily.

Across the bay about one mile was the city of Golfito, with a variety of shops, restaurants and bars. According to one observer, the town is full of American promoters with little to promote but themselves. There are also a lot of solid citizens. Pat O'Connell, a Hoosier from Lake County, Indiana, promotes the American Legion. He also has dealt in gold for years with prospectors scattered about the mountains. His hobby is hunting crocodiles and I was the beneficiary of a crocodile dinner with him at Mike's Restaurant.

Paul and Judy owned the Sanbar Restaurant where we watched Michael Jordan in the NBA Championship series on a giant TV screen. Then there was a quiet, mild-mannered young Englishman, Shane Ackton, who had sailed around the world in an 18-foot boat that held the record at the time of being the smallest vessel to circumnavigate. On his second trip around, he found Golfito and it is easy to understand why he had made his home there for the past eight years.

A movie producer from the U.S. took over a city block in the downtown area. There he constructed a chapel and invested a lot of money in preparation for making a movie. Rumor was that the local officials made such demands for payoffs that the whole project was abandoned. He auctioned off his equipment to reduce his losses.

With these memories of just a few days spent in a beautiful part of the world, I watched the mountains of Costa Rica fade into the evening haze as I headed into the wide Pacific. On my two earlier ventures into the Pacific, I had spent days in what I thought were the doldrums. Near the equator, the wind had stopped blowing and CILIN II was doing more drifting with the current than sailing. It was not so on this trip. The winds were good and they moved CILIN II at a good pace through the evening and during the night. With the excitement of setting out on such a journey, it was a sleepless night. The boat needed attention because we were crossing a major shipping lane of ships from the West Coast heading to and from the Panama Canal.

At mid-morning of the second day, when the morning haze had melted away, the mountains again became visible in the distance. I was feeling good about our progress when I suddenly observed a fishnet directly in front of the boat. I tried to turn the boat to avoid hitting it, but my efforts were in vain. CILIN II was in the net. Quickly, I lowered the sails and attempted to release the net from the keel and rudder. With great care, I tugged and poked with the gaffing hook; but instead of extricating the boat, it became more tangled in the net. To avoid further complication, it became apparent that the best course of action was to cut the net. I snipped it with a sharp knife, but that did not solve the problem. It became necessary to cut the net three more times before I was completely free from it.

Then the question of what to do. There was no fishing boat in sight, but I visualized a mean and angry fisherman coming down on CILIN II demanding justice. Would they want money? Would I have to buy a new net or just pay damages? I watched and waited, wondering just what to do. There was not a boat in sight in any direction. Realizing that it might be hours before they showed up, I took the coward's way out. I put up the sails and sailed away, but I had not sailed far when I saw a fishing boat in the distance, coming in my direction.

I lowered the sails and watched and waited. The fishing boat headed for the net and started reeling it in. What now, I wondered. When they see that their net has been cut in four places, they will be furious. I waited a while and then finally sailed over toward the net, expecting a raging crew to come after me.

Finally, when I was close enough to their boat to get their attention, by hand signals, I made a confession that I was the one who had cut their net. I repeated my act several times to make sure they understood. The only response from the crew was friendly waves and smiles. I was sure they knew the net had been cut and that I was the culprit. With that, I hauled up the sails again and sailed away, still waving at the fishermen.

It was a happy ending to an awkward and embarrassing situation. It was good for me that it was so because they were the last human beings I would see for almost two

months. The third day out was a glorious day. The doldrums that I had anticipated did not materialize. The southeast trade winds that I had expected to find south of the equator appeared to have moved northward. Sailing was excellent. I sat out on the deck for a long time, looking at the sea and the sky, and then went into the cabin and slept.

That night the sea became very rough, making sleep impossible. Everything that was loose fell to the deck. This is a part of sailing we all live with. Sometimes rough seas last but a few hours. At other times, they last for days.

I did not try my luck at fishing until the fourth day out. I let out an artificial bait about 50 feet behind the boat. It was a couple of hours before the Penn Senator Reel whined like a far off police siren. The fishing pole whipped in the holder until I was able to grab it and start reeling it in. I could tell it was a good one because of the pressure on the reel. When I finally lopped him into the cockpit, it turned out to be a beautiful 21-inch long Dorado. Cleaning a fish that size was something I was not used to. There seemed to be a surprising amount of blood and I soon learned to wash it off the deck before it dried. Once dry, it was very hard to wash off.

For my first fish, I merely cut off small steaks and fried them in a skillet. Later I tried a variety of things with the pressure cooker. There would be fish and rice, fish and navy beans, and fish stew with onions, potatoes, cabbage and carrots. For the first couple of weeks, I caught a fish at least every other day. By utilizing the pressure cooker, I could get four meals from one fish. After taking out a serving for a meal, I would bring the pressure up and turn off the heat, thus creating a vacuum to preserve the fish. It was always amusing to me to think about how family members worried about me getting caught in a storm. I was always more worried that the pressure cooker would blow up than that I would be caught in a storm. Many times, when the relief valve did not go off when I thought it should, I would turn off the heat and start up the heating process again.

From the log on June 22, 1993 – Wind moderate from the south. Going farther west than intended. Mid-afternoon – massive dark cloud up ahead.

I prepared for the worst, three reefs in the main and the storm jib up. Nothing happened. I sailed through it as a path opened up at 5:00 p.m. I decided to retain the sail configuration. At dark, the wind picked up carrying CILIN II at 300°. That was getting us too far north. I hove to and later noticed there was a good wind for a compass heading of 180°, just what I wanted. I sailed south on a miserable, rough sea. A bad night! Everything loose fell to the deck.

June 23 – Wind from the west, good for going south to get out of hurricane belt. Caught a 21" dolphin fish mid-afternoon. Wasted no time in getting it in the skillet. Joy at catching the fish was dampened by a three-foot rip in the mainsail. Took it down and installed back-up mainsail. It worked perfectly. Weather threatening at dark. Hove to and slept. Saw a ship in the distance in the early morning.

June 24 – started mending mainsail. About five minutes of sun. Remainder of day, low hanging clouds in every direction. Light mist all day. No storms. Good progress sailing in spite of the dismal weather. Spent 95% of the time in the cabin. Weather is either bright hot sun or rain. Sailed over 100 miles. One of the best days!

Friday, June 25 – Caught a fish. Had visions of fish stew in the pressure cooker with potatoes, cabbage, onions and fish. When I reeled him in, there was only the head. Other fish had beaten me to him. In a matter of a few minutes, there was another on the line. He was larger than the 19 inch one from Wednesday. When I got him next to the boat, I could see other fish after him. In my excitement to get him in, I lost him. Beautiful sailing day, winds moderate.

Sunday, June 27 – Music for today's devotions provided by Sandi Patti (from back home in Indiana).

The music came from the boats entertainment center, a $29.00 Sony Audio Cassette Player, which provided many hours of pleasure at sea while I sat on deck, enjoying the beauty of the sea and sky. Sometimes the spirits would be aroused by marching music of John Philip Sousa. The occasion of landing a big fish was frequently celebrated by Richard Hammerstein's "Victory at Sea". Then for a touch of class the London Philharmonic Orchestra would cast its spell.

In addition to music, the Sony Radio kept me in touch with world news, much of it making me very happy that I was at sea and far away from the cares of this troubled world.

Monday, June 28 – a note at top of log sheet – "Inter-Tropical Convergence Zone", where northeast and southeast trade winds converge near equator – extensive clouds and rain squalls. Routine – up at daybreak. Coffee, cornflakes and orange juice. Replaced storm jib with working jib. Removed reef from mainsail, then tuned vane for exact course. Heavy overcast, brightening at noon. Spent morning mending the mainsail. Should have it repaired by tomorrow. Though CILIN II is 1º, 30" north of the equator, we are getting effects of southeast trade winds from about 170º. Threw little yellow spoon out with coffee water. Stars bright for first time on this trip.

Wednesday, June 30 – Have not seen another vessel for a week. Am 60 miles north of Galapagos Islands.

Friday, July 2 – This is my sister Laura's 77th birthday. She is a year older than I. I wrote her a long letter to be mailed upon arrival at Tahiti. Had mailed her one just before leaving Golfito on June 19.

Saturday, July 3 – The back-up mainsail ripped across the top. Replaced it with the repaired old sail which worked very well. More bad news. Sat-Nav refused to lock on to a satellite. Will put sextant to test.

Sunday, July 4 – 20 to 25 M.P.H. winds from south. Big waves. Some hit boat with a heavy jolt. Many splashed over the boat. Replaced storm jib with working jib. Everything wet. Wind is howling.

The trip continued on with more and more maintenance problems day after day. There were numerous rips in the sails, which required the tedious chore of mending them with a needle and thread. Many times a pair of pliers was necessary to pull the needle through the fabric.

The boat's Volvo engine was used only for charging the two 12-volt batteries for the running lights at night, but the alternator worked so poorly that it was necessary to use a crank when turning the key to start the engine.

I continued catching a bountiful supply of Dorado fish, but had the 80-pound test line snapped by large fish a number of times.

The trade winds are a sailor's delight, strong and steady much of the time at 15 to 20 miles per hour. The configuration of the sails does not have to be changed for long periods of time with the self-steering device, and the boat maintains a steady course.

I awoke in the morning from a sound sleep. I can tell that it is daylight. I am lying on my back with my head toward the bow. I hear the water rushing by the hull of the boat. More than one time I lay there in my bunk with the weirdest of thoughts. Is this my casket rushing me toward purgatory? Is it a 30-foot long missile racing through the open sea? Out on deck, I see water in every direction as it has been for days on end. Somehow I have the feeling that the water is all mine. There is no one to dispute my claim. It is all mine to do with it as I please, miles and miles of it. But what can I do with it but sail on it and keep on sailing? I am so small that I would not be a speck on the expanse of the map of the Pacific Ocean.

Nobody in the world knows exactly where I am located within thousands of miles. If I were to disappear out here, no one would ever have any way of knowing what happened. This is what happened to Josh Slowny, the first person to sail solo around the world. It happened years after his celebrated circumnavigation. It could happen to me. Only a few would be affected – Charles, Laura, Sally, etc.

My daughter, Ann, in Indianapolis, had once written about how she enjoyed telling her girlfriends about her father's sailing adventures. I could not tell her not to do it but I feared that sometime, when someone asked about me, she might have to answer that I was missing and had not been heard of for a long time.

Atoms Self-steering device

Calamity hit CILIN II on the 31st day out from Costa Rica. It was so devastating that my morale hit an all-time low for all of the time I had been sailing. The Atoms self-steering device broke in a way that it appeared hopeless to repair. Made in France by a company out of business, parts were not available. That meant that I had to be at the tiller at all times when the boat was underway. Then it was necessary to heave to when I needed to do anything other than guide the boat. I had read where other sailors had lashed the tiller so that the boat would stay on a steady course, but that was not for me. I tried it many times but could not make it work.

It was 980 miles to the island of Hiva Oa in the Marquises Islands and I was able to make only about 50 miles on the first day of sailing without the self-steering device. When I hove to, the boat pitched and rolled so that I got very little rest. At that rate of travel, it would take almost three weeks to reach the nearest land. I became very demoralized and very tired. Sometimes, after a rest period, I could sail less than an hour before needing to stop to sleep and rest.

Then I remember that Shane Ackton, the English lad I had met at Golfito, had sailed around the world in an 18-foot boat. He had made his own self-steering device. I thought about it and concentrated my thoughts on it for a day and a half, thinking of nothing else. I was desperate.

The problem was that a stainless steel rod had been welded in place and the weld had broken. There was surely no way to find a welder out in the middle of the Pacific Ocean, but I was able to determine that the thing would work if the rod could be held in place. One problem was that it was on a rack at the stern and not easy to access. It was the rod that the three foot long wind vane rotated on and was critical to the operation of the steering device.

It seemed only fair here to confess that I never did know exactly how the self-steering device worked. All I knew for sure was that it worked and it had worked magnificently over thousands of miles of calm and rough seas. The three foot long wind vane is set so that its alliance is in the direction of the prevailing wind. Any turning of the direction of travel of the boat causes the wind vane to swing on the aforementioned stainless steel rod. This activates a pulley system that turns a small rudder to keep the boat on course.

After that day and a half of concentrated study, I found that the stainless steel rod could be held in place with a small block of wood secured by two standard stainless steel hose clamps.

It was in the evening of the second day when I put my theory to a test. If it worked, I could get back to sailing as usual. If it did not work, I knew that I was in for a long, hard trip.

No experience in my days of sailing gave me the thrill as did that little self-steering device when I learned that it held the boat on a steady course. It worked! I set it and had a long sleep as the trade winds carried CILIN II on her way through the dark of night.

From the sea charts I learned that the archipelago of Tuamotu was laden with coral reefs, so I gave it a wide berth in sailing toward Tahiti. The decision to do so had seemed justified when I learned that a fellow sailor had run aground on a reef three months later. I had first met him in Panama and learned that he entertained with his clarinet in various marinas as he sailed around the world in exchange for his moorage fees and meals. Upon running upon the reef, he had paddled his dinghy out away from his stranded boat to take a photograph to mail to the New York Times newspaper. He kept the world advised of his travels with reports to the newspaper from time to time.

By staying far north of Tuamotu, I found that in sailing south from there toward Tahiti, I was being carried farther west than I wanted to go. I was far from any shipping lanes and wondered why I saw no ships of any kind though I was less than 170 miles from Tahiti. I wondered what could be so great about Tahiti that people would travel so many miles across the sea to get there.

On the 54th day out from Costa Rica I saw an island up ahead in the distance. There was something strange about it. It was unlike anything I had ever seen before. Jagged mountains protruded into the sky. The terrain gave the appearance of the surface of the moon except for the green vegetation. I could see some yachts in the distance and was tempted to go in, but first I must clear in at Papeete, ten miles to the east. I was much too far west and it became necessary for me to turn back to the northeast to reach Papeete.

When I finally reached Tahiti, a new problem arose. There were coral reefs along the shore but my sea chart did not show a passage that I could feel safe with. I sailed back and forth, up and down the coast at a distance from the coral, until I observed some yachts approaching the shore. I followed them and finally found a place to drop the anchor. There was another boat nearby and I worried that I might be too close to him. To put an end to my worries, I paddled my dinghy over and asked the Captain if he thought I was at a safe distance. He assured me that everything was fine, but later in the evening I observed that he pulled his anchor and moved a little farther from me.

Writing a letter is the next best thing to a personal visit when you are far, far away. I sometimes get so involved in thinking about the person I am writing to and the things that I am writing about that I become completely oblivious to my surroundings. I had written to my dear sister Laura, just before departing Costa Rica and then again on July 2, 1993, her 77th birthday.

Upon reaching Tahiti, one of my first missions after clearing in to the harbor at Papeete was to make a trip to the post office to mail letters that I had written. There was a long line of people in the post office waiting for service. After affixing stamps to my letters I dropped them, including the one to my sister, in the post box and entered a nearby glass enclosed phone booth in the same room as the post office. I would call home to tell them that I had made the 55-day trip safely and inquire about family members. When I asked about my sister, Laura, there was the cold, abrupt answer, "She died". I was shocked! I could not believe it. "Tell me the truth". I shouted. Then I sobbed loudly for a long time, without a thought of the people waiting in line in the post office. I asked over and over if it was true.

I stepped out of the booth still in a state of shock, with no thought of what the people waiting there in line might be thinking. They could well have taken me for a crazy man or an inebriate. I did not care. I was alone with no one to talk to. I remembered how Laura had worried for my safety at sea. She had been so nervous when I called her from Antigua after the Atlantic crossing that she could not carry on a conversation.

Having checked in with the port officials at Papeete Harbor and mailed my letters, I tidied up the boat and paddled the dinghy to shore for some fresh drinking water. Before leaving CILIN II, I had observed a young couple visiting on the deck of a luxurious yacht anchored nearby. He was a handsome Caucasian lad about 25 years of age and she was obviously Polynesian, with dark skin and bright eyes. There appeared to be no other people aboard the yacht at the time. As I passed by, the girl rushed to the rail, waived and shouted," You got woman?"

I thought this is Bloody Mary from James Michener's "South Pacific". "No, I got no woman", I replied.

"You need woman!" she declared and withdrew back to her friend.

A fine introduction to the paradise islands of Tahiti, I thought. My preoccupation with the problems of the boat and the sea had fully occupied my thoughts over the past two months and now I felt very much alone.

After filling my jerry cans with water at the dock, I headed back past the yacht with Bloody Mary and her friend. By this time the Captain and his crew had returned to the boat. I visited with them briefly and was invited to join them for dinner on their boat late in the evening.

I rested for a short time back at the boat and prepared for my first meal away from CILIN II for many weeks. I looked forward to a visit but could never have imagined the story that was about to unfold before me.

Aboard their yacht I was introduced to the Captain's wife and the sailing party. The young man I had seen on deck in the afternoon was Shean Kelly from San Francisco, and obviously a guest on the boat. The Polynesian girl was serving a delicious tropical salad before the meal. It was an enjoyable and relaxing evening as we visited and talked of sailing the seas.

The following day I cleared the harbor and I was on the way to Cooks Bay, 10 miles to the west on the Isle of Moorea. It was the picturesque island I had seen on the way to Tahiti. It would turn out to be more wonderful than I could ever have dreamed. It was said that parts of the filming for both "Mutiny on the Bounty" and "South Pacific" had been filmed there, but the real delight was in learning that one of the leading resorts, "The Bali Hai", welcomed transit sailors with free moorage and restaurant, beach and bar privileges. It was a real delight meeting old friends from other stops along the way and making new friends on snorkeling trips and tours about the island and at happy hour at the bar.

It was something of a surprise to see Shean Kelley, the young man I had met on the luxury yacht back at Papeete, at happy hour at the Bali Hai Club. We visited at length, but he made no mention of the other members of his sailing party. I did notice that a couple of times during the evening he sat staring into space, as if he were in a dazed condition. Not knowing him very well I thought nothing of it. Toward midnight, he went his way and I went mine.

The next morning being Sunday, I set out to find a church. At the office of the gendarme I learned that the congregation of the local church en masse was attending another church 25 kilometers away. I gave up the idea of trying to attend church when I came upon the captain of the luxury yacht from Papeete. I learned that he had been in pursuit of Shean Kelley, whose picture had been displayed on TV three times during the night as a missing person.

Shean had been in custody of the captain under an arrangement with Shean's father, a wealthy man from San Francisco, whereby the captain was being paid $1000.00 per day to keep Shean at sea in an effort to cure his addiction to narcotic drugs. The program fell apart when Shean was able to jump ship with the aid of Bloody Mary and convince the gendarmes that the captain had restrained him illegally. His father was contacted and Shean was soon on the way back to San Francisco.

ARRIVAL IN AUSTRALIA

ON THE AFTERNOON OF JULY 27TH, 1994, a dark mound on the distant horizon of the sea meant that CILIN II was approaching the continent of Australia. It was the first land to be seen since sailing from picturesque Port Vila, Vanuatu. Only the Great Barrier Reef lay between us and the port of Cairns, Australia. The reef was not visible above the water but sea charts displayed the Grafton Pass, which we must traverse for safe passage through the reef. After that came the four-mile long channel leading to the Trinity Inlet at Cairns. It was dark by the time CILIN II reached the quarantine area where we were to anchor and wait until the Australian customs officers arrived the next day.

I dropped anchor into the muddy bottom and the 30-foot boat came to rest for the first time in 11 days. Through the darkness I could make out the shapes of other boats anchored about me, and across the water were the bright lights of Cairns. It looked like an interesting and exciting city. It was well known as a center for deep-sea divers from around the world to visit and view the wonders of the Great Barrier Reef.

It was not long before I realized that the anchor was not holding in the soft mud. It was dragging and we were dangerously close to another yacht. It was necessary to pull the anchor, move to a new location and drop it again. The second effort seemed successful. CILIN II was ready to rest for the night until the customs officers arrived the next day.

It was my first time in Australia since our B-17 Flying Fortress Bombers had stopped in Port Darwin on the way to the Philippine Islands in October, 1941. That was two months before World War II had erupted. My arrival in Australia for the second visit could have been much different had I accepted an offer made to me in 1972 when I was Governor of Indiana. There would have been a delegation of distinguished dignitaries, TV cameramen, photographers and newspaper reporters waiting for an interview. A limousine would have been waiting to carry me to a palatial residence where I would have lived in luxury for the next four years. But that was all in the past. It did not happen that way.

It was in the spring of 1972 when I was attending a national governors' conference at Williamsburg, Virginia. A well-dressed man I did not recognize approached me with a very unusual request. Could I go to Washington, D.C. for a meeting with the Vice President of the United States? He explained that a helicopter would be available to take me there. Of course I could not decline such an invitation, but I wondered what the Vice President of the United States would want to talk about with me. I assured the gentleman that I would be glad to make the trip as soon as the conference ended the next day.

On the following Monday morning my wife Pat, Dr. James Kessler, an administrative assistant, and I boarded the helicopter and flew across the picturesque Virginia countryside and up the Potomac Valley to land on a pad at the Pentagon building. A waiting limousine quickly delivered us to the Executive Office Building adjacent to the White House. There I was ushered alone into the office of Spiro Agnew, Vice President of the United States. I had met him many times on the political campaign trail and at various social functions, so it was easy to talk to him.

We visited for a time about the Governor's Conference at Williamsburg. He had been Governor of Maryland before being selected by President Nixon to be his running mate, so he was interested in hearing about the conference at Williamsburg. All the while I was wondering why he wanted to talk to me. Then he came to the point. "How would you like to be Ambassador to Australia?" he asked.

"How would I like to what?" I thought. I was Governor of Indiana with almost a year remaining in my term. I was shocked. Why was I being made such an offer? I had no background or training that would qualify me for the diplomatic service.

While I was pondering over the situation, he opened a photograph album from the desk and displayed pictures of some of the colorful flowers at Canberra, the capital of Australia. Then when he realized I was not reacting affirmatively to his offer, almost apologetically he said, "John Mitchell has asked me to make this offer to you."

"Well, this comes as a surprise to me," I confessed. "I will think it over and you will hear from me soon. I will write you a letter." I knew exactly what my answer would be and I did write him a letter explaining what he already knew, that I still had a year to serve in my term and felt that I should remain in Indiana.

Nothing more was heard about the matter until months later when an old friend, Nyle M. Jackson, explained it to me. Nyle had been executive secretary for Indiana U.S. Senator William E. Jenner, as well as secretary for Arthur Sommerfield, the Postmaster General of the U.S., and I had confidence in him. The answer went deep into Indiana political history.

Paul Vories McNutt, as Governor of Indiana almost 40 years earlier, had instituted what was to become known as the 2% Club. It required each patronage worker on the state payroll to contribute 2% of his salary to the political party in power at the time. The practice had been continued through Democrat and Republican administrations over the years since McNutt was in office. It accounted for large sums of money for the state Republican Party, with a generous portion going to the national headquarters in Washington each year to finance political campaigns.

It seemed patently unfair to me that the patronage workers would be forced to give a part of their salary to the party. They had done more than anyone else to get their party elected. So when I had the opportunity as governor, I put a stop to the practice. Word of my deed brought repercussions from the banks of the Potomac. The Republican National Committee was not getting its usual fat envelope from Indiana. This had all come to the attention of John Mitchell, Attorney General of the United States and confidant of President Nixon. The President was campaigning for his second term with a war chest that was bursting at the seams. But Mitchell wanted more. One way to get it was to get the

Governor of Indiana removed from office so Indiana's 2% Club could be re-instituted.

But it did not work that way, so 22 years later, instead of enjoying the pomp and ceremony of a newly arrived Ambassador to Australia, upon my arrival there, I dropped the anchor of my sailboat into the muddy bottom of the quarantine area and waited for the arrival of the Australian Custom's Officer the next day.

Dr. Cameron Purdie

Blessed is the man that walketh
Not in the counsel of the ungodly,
Nor standeth in the way of sinners
Nor sitteth in the seat of the scornful
But his delight is in the love of the Lord;
And in his law doth he meditate day and night
And he shall be like a tree planted by the rivers of water,
That bringeth forth his fruit in his season;
His leaf also shall not wither,
And whatsoever he doeth shall prosper.

Psalm 1: 1, 2

I HAD MET SUCH A MAN IN the person of Dr. Cameron Purdie when I visited New Zealand a couple of years earlier. He owned a sailboat and was experienced in sailing in the coastal waters of New Zealand, so I invited him to come to Cairns, Australia to sail with me up along the Great Barrier Reef. I sent him a fax message and got an enthusiastic response. One of his married daughters lived on an island north of Australia, so he saw the opportunity to sail with me from Cairns and then have a visit with her.

Dry Dock

At the time Dr. Purdie arrived, CILIN II was on the hard in the boatyard at the Cairns Cruising Yacht Squadron where she had been perched on jacks from August, 1994 until May, 1995. I was a bit uneasy when he arrived because I had not told him that I had also invited Juanita Finnegan to sail with us. At the time I invited her, I had little hope that she would ever sail with me again, after our near disasters in sailing out of Panama two years before, but her answer was also an enthusiastic "yes".

From the moment Dr. Purdie arrived, we were busy scraping and painting the hull with anti-foul paint in preparation for our trip. Then the time came that I had to break the news about the impending arrival of Miss Finnegan.

I finally said, "You may have trouble understanding this, but I have invited a young lady to come along with us." His response was what I would have expected if I had known him better. "Fine," he said.

I had considered that he might be looking forward to a lot of intimate discussions with me on various subjects on a man-to-man basis, but he had said, "fine". He would be glad to have her along.

Then to buttress my position, I said, "She is a lady."

He said, "Is she a lady?"

I answered, "Yes, she is a lady."

Then I repeated a conversation I had with her when I had asked her, "What would you like to be remembered by when you leave this earth?"

She had thought for a moment and said, "I would like to be remembered as a lady."

I thought that was a really wonderful answer and it seemed even more wonderful when I related it to Dr. Purdie.

When Juanita arrived the next day, she and Dr. Purdie got along very well. All of my worries about inviting her were in the past.

Dr. Purdie was very generous when we were purchasing provisions for our two-week trip. He purchased far more than enough food, but in addition, he purchased two new fire extinguishers for the boat. Then, to my surprise, he bought an EPIRB, an electronic device for sending a distress signal to a satellite in the event of an emergency. I considered it an unnecessary expenditure since I had already sailed more than half way around the world with no need for such a device or even for the new fire extinguishers, for that matter.

On June 2, 1995, a monstrous four-wheeled lift put two belts under the hull of CILIN II and lowered her into Smith Creek at the Yacht Squadron. With a bountiful supply of provisions and safety equipment the likes of which CILIN II had never possessed, we faced a problem that we had not anticipated when we were in the water. The engine would not start! There was nothing to do but find the problem. It looked as if our journey had ended before it had begun. I examined every detail but nothing worked. The engine simply would not start. At last I put a new fuel filter in the place of the old one, but that did not solve the problem. Then I put the old filter back in the place of the new one and, to my surprise, the engine ran perfectly.

It was Sunday morning, June 4, 1995 at 10:30 a.m. when CILIN II proudly sailed out of the Cairns Estuary, giving us our last view of the city of Cairns off our port beam. Off our starboard were rows of pilings near the shore serving as moorings for hundreds of yachts and boats used as residences for people who crossed the river each day to their places of employment in Cairns.

It was a clear day with good winds, which would take us the 40 miles to Lower Island. It was a beautiful trip until about 6:00 p.m. when we approached our mooring site. An old bugaboo caught up with us. One of the main sheets had gotten over the side and wrapped around the propeller so that we could not start the engine if we needed it. Unless we could get the boat under control, we would crash into the shore directly ahead; but with the expert assistance of Dr. Purdie, the mainsail was lowered and the anchor dropped just in time.

We sailed for an exciting two weeks along the Great Barrier Reef, with strong winds and currents. Each night we anchored on the leeward side of a reef or an island for protection against the wind and waves.

On our second day we moored in a creek at historic Cooktown, named after the great Captain Cook who had the misfortune of running his boat, "THE ENDEAVOR", upon a reef as he approached the mainland. That was more than 200 years before CILIN II safely passed the reef.

After Cooktown, CILIN II made stops at Flattery's Anchorage, Norwich Island, Morris, Portland Roads, Cape Greenville and Escape River before reaching Horn Island.

Each morning Dr. Purdie was the first person on deck with three teacups, preparing his morning tea. Juanita provided better meals than CILIN II had seen in her years of sailing.

It had been necessary that we find our anchorage each evening well before dark, because we could not chance sailing among the coral reefs after dark. That made for long evenings for the three of us so that we could talk and visit. Dr. Purdie had brought along a collection of books including "Thirty-one Days of Praise", by Ruth Myers, "Dangerous Grace", by Charles Colson, and "The Finishing Touch" by Charles R. Swindle. From these we read passages and discussed them during the course of the evening.

The interesting thing about Dr. Purdie was that he was probably the most religious person I have ever met other than members of the clergy. He lived the life of a true Christian, and from time to time over the course of the trip, he would speculate on what the Apostle Paul might have said about a particular situation.

One of our last big hurdles before reaching Thursday Island would be Albany Passage. I had no idea what it would be like, but I visualized rushing water in a narrow passage. From our cruising guide we learned that we should approach the Pass at high tide.

We moored in Escape River the night before among a large number of racks belonging to a Japanese pearl farm operation. It was necessary that we depart at 3:00 a.m. to make our way out of Escape River and reach Albany Passage at high tide.

Navigating out of Escape River in the dark was delicate but by use of the G.P.S., I was able to keep a very accurate course along the reefs and islands on the way. We reached Albany Passage well after daybreak and found it to be a wide and beautiful scene.

After the passage we saw Horn Island off of our port beam. I gazed at it in awe, knowing that members of my bombardment group had crash-landed planes there during World War II. The world was at peace now and we were happy to have made an uneventful passage. Because of the winds and current, we decided to moor CILIN II just off Horn Island, across the channel from Thursday Island.

I paddled Dr. Purdie ashore from Horn Island so he could take a ferry across to Thursday Island for his flight to visit his daughter. We hated to see him go. Besides being a good sailor, he had been a true inspiration to us with our evening devotions. I was also inspired by the life he had led as a young veterinarian in New Zealand, where he decided to donate 20% of his net income to Christian charities. He set up a trust and made it a partner in his business for 20% of his net income. The New Zealand Revenue Service challenged the arrangement, claiming that it was a tax dodge. The matter went to Court and Dr. Purdie's charitable trust prevailed in what became a landmark case in New Zealand.

The trust started out small in the early days of his practice and Dr. Purdie admitted that he had never dreamed of the proportions it would reach.

Dr. Purdie's delight was in the love of the Lord, and he prospered.

Dr. Cameron Purdie

Sailing with Miss Finnegan, Again?

From the day I first started ocean cruising, I had adhered to an old superstition that said to never start a sailing trip on Friday. But came Friday, June 23, 1993, we were provisioned up, everything was in shape and we were heading out from Thursday Island to Darwin. It would be a long trip across the Gulf of Carpentari and the Arafura Sea to the north side of Australia.

The usual route would take us through a channel between Melville Island and the mainland. From the map it appeared to be studded with coral reefs and relatively narrow in some places. At the time we reached the passage the wind was directly in our face. Not wanting to proceed on the engine, I decided to go around Melville Island. That may have been a gigantic mistake, considering what happened to us during the next couple of days.

As darkness came on, the sea became very rough and the wind howled through the rigging. The G.P.S. indicated that CILIN II was doing a little more than nine knots. I had not experienced that speed before and was concerned that it might increase too near our safe hull speed. With the fury of the storm I did not want to risk going on deck to adjust the sails, so we sailed on into the black night until the storm finally subsided.

With the dawn we found everything intact, with no noticeable damage except that the cover on the anchor well was missing. That presented a problem, because with rough seas more water came into the bilge than I was able to pump with the bilge pump.

I was in the cockpit at about 5:00 a.m. when Juanita shouted from the cabin, "We're on fire! The boat is burning!" Very quickly smoke billowed out from the hatch and Juanita lunged out into the cockpit.

I was able to reach one of the fire extinguishers Dr. Purdie had purchased, but I was unable to activate it. Without my glasses I could not see to read the instructions. I quickly handed it to Juanita so that she could show me which lever to press. With that I jumped into the cabin, opened the hatch to the battery compartment where the smoke appeared to be coming from and emptied the entire contents of the extinguisher. I slammed the hatch closed and retreated to the cockpit to breathe some fresh air.

It took but seconds to realize that the fire had not been extinguished. Then it became necessary for me to dash to the other end of the cabin where we had secured Dr. Purdie's second fire extinguisher. With it in hand I opened the hatch to the engine and sprayed grey powder over the engine until there was no more smoke, all the while holding my breath for protection from the noxious fumes.

It became obvious that the wires from the battery to the engine had shorted out and burned into a molten mess. This left us without an engine, navigational lights or a radio.

At the time CILIN II was 70 miles northwest of our destination of Darwin, Australia. A good brisk wind blew from 135°, the direction we needed to sail. I set the sails to tack and made some headway toward Darwin, but after several hours back and forth we were no closer to our port.

One of the big problems confronting us was that we were approaching the juncture of three ocean shipping lanes leading into the busy port of Darwin. With night coming on, we could find ourselves in a precarious situation with no navigational lights and no radio.

As the day wore on, it became obvious that we needed to do something to improve our situation. I considered that if the waves subsided we might put in to the island of Bathurst. But Juanita was acquainted with the territory and she insisted that if we found any people, they would be aborigines and there was certain to be no telephone or communication facilities. I was not completely convinced but gave in to her warning.

EPIRB

At last there came the issue of whether or not we should activate the EPIRB. It would send a distress signal that would be picked up by satellite and help would be on the way. I pointed out that it was a thing to be used only in a case where life is in danger. I did not consider that we were in that much danger.

Finally she read the instructions on the EPIRB, which indicated that if you lost your radio and your navigational lights, it would be reason enough to use the EPIRB. I held off while considering every possibility while Juanita kept insisting.

At last she said, "Let's have a discussion."

I said, "All right, what do you want to discuss?"

"I don't want to die," was her answer.

It was about 2:00 in the afternoon when we read the instructions on the EPIRB, attached it to a stanchion, extended the antenna and pushed a button to activate the signal.

It was a bright, sunny afternoon and we had no clue as to whether that little box known as the EPIRB was going to be of any help to us. We had no way of knowing that our distress signal had been picked up at

Canberra 2000 miles away and a Danish transport ship, M/B Cambira, sailing from Indonesia to Darwin, had picked up the following signal:

"Confirmed 121.5 MHZ emergency beacon detected vicinity 11 degrees 49 minutes south 129 degrees 52 minutes east at 02-7327. Vessel within 30 miles please report position and check equipment. Report any active beacon. Search operations under way. Report via CRS or direct Telex 7162025."

Nor did we know the air/sea rescue organization at Darwin had been alerted and provided with our coordinates of latitude and longitude and help was on the way.

About an hour and a half later, we saw a twin-engine aircraft that appeared to be heading in our direction. As he passed overhead at about 500 feet we waved to let him know that we were in good shape. Then to our surprise, he continued to pass back and forth over us at his original altitude with no effort to communicate with us. We fashioned a bed sheet with the words "FIRE IS OUT". The usual procedure would have been to communicate by VHF radio, but that was not available to us. His winging back and forth became monotonous to us and we wondered why he continued it until we observed a helicopter coming from the direction of Darwin. The twin-engine plane departed immediately and we watched and wondered what would happen next.

The big hatch on the starboard side of the helicopter was open and a crewmember attempted to communicate by hand signals. As he went through his various gyrations we were unable to make out his signals. Then suddenly a projectile thrown from the copter hit in the middle of the cockpit and bounced off into the sea. It had been a perfect pitch, but if the object had hit either of us, it could have caused great bodily harm. We later learned that it was an effort by one of the crewmembers to deliver a hand held VHF radio to us.

That effort having failed, Juanita said, "He wants to know if we want him to come down."

I told her that there would be no purpose in that. Later she said, "He wants me to come up into the chopper."

"Can you swim?" I asked her. She nodded her head in the affirmative and stepped up to the rail in preparation for jumping overboard.

Then she said, "They want me to put on a life jacket," which she did. Then she kicked off her slippers and slacks. I grabbed up the slacks from the deck and stuck them inside her life jacket.

"You might need these later," I said. With that, she held her nose with one hand and with the other raised in a "Hail Mary" pose, jumped overboard.

All the while the helicopter hovered at about 100 feet above the sea some 50 yards from CILIN II. She swam to a point under the helicopter while a long cable with a sling was lowered for her. The pilot was unable to see her location and for a long time Juanita floundered through the choppy water caused by the churning of the helicopter blades. There was a question as to whether Juanita had the endurance to continue while the helicopter pilot endeavored to get the sling to her.

At last she reached the sling, hooked her arms over the bar and was raised into the cabin of the helicopter. Aboard the helicopter, Juanita was grilled at length about the condition of CILIN II. A second radio message received by the Danish transport reported:

"Marsar 951 267 Beacon Alert.

A020930Z July 1995 a helicopter winched one crewmember off from the Yacht in position 11 degrees 56 minutes south 129 degrees 54 minutes east. Yacht has extinguished a fire on board and has no navigational equipment, no electronics and no radio. The lone crewmember is currently steering 150 degrees, speed unknown and requests an escort to Darwin. Darwin water police are responding with a rescue launch SALLOO. If possible request you attempt to rendezvous with the Yacht and assist as required and/or provide backup to police vessel."

At the end of her interrogation, when the helicopter crew appeared satisfied with Juanita's description of the situation, she indicated that she was ready to return to CILIN II, but the crew member in charge put his finger to his lips as if to silence her and informed her that they were headed for Darwin.

The helicopter took off to the southeast, leaving me alone. By this time it was late afternoon of a very busy day. With nothing more important to do, I set the sails to carry me out of the shipping lane and slept. It had been a long, hard night and day and I slept soundly until I was awakened sometime in the night by a bright light that illuminated the cabin as if it were daylight. Rushing to the cockpit, I saw what appeared to be a great wall beside my boat. I called out but got no response. All was still.

Back in the cabin, my chronometer told me that it was 1:30 in the morning. I had slept about five and one-half hours. After about ten minutes, I heard voices, but they were not speaking English. I took it to be German.

Then a voice in English informed me that the ship next to me was M/B Cambria, a Danish ship. Its executive officer would board CILIN II with a VHF radio and the ship would tow me to Darwin, now 80 miles away.

M/B Cambria

I learned that the M/B Cambria was a cattle transport ship with the capacity to haul 1000 head of cattle from Australia to Thailand and the Philippine Islands. She was due in Darwin at 7:00 a.m. to take on a load of cattle, but had diverted her course upon receiving my distress signal. CILIN II was nowhere to be seen, but her captain, Anders Christian Pedersen, dutifully searched until he located us 20 miles away. Two huge lines from M/B Cambira were attached to the bow of CILIN II and we were under way toward Darwin. The way was difficult for the big transport trying to hold its speed to something near six knots.

At a point about five miles from Darwin, we were intercepted by SALLOO, a motor launch of the Darwin water police. M/B Cambira detached her lines and went on her way, many hours late for the appointment to take on a cargo of 1000 head of cattle.

The Darwin water police towed CILIN II another 15 miles and left her at anchor in Fanny Bay, where more than 100 other yachts lay at anchor in preparation for the annual Darwin/Ambon Race. There were no docks or slips at the club.

CILIN II came to rest a quarter mile from shore for the first time in ten hectic days. I faced a dismal prospect for the future and with nothing more important to do I fixed myself some breakfast. It was past noontime and I could not remember when I had last eaten. After my breakfast of oatmeal, orange juice and coffee, I sat gazing at the sea, wondering what would happen next. What happened next was a water taxi approached CILIN II and there appeared the smiling face of Juanita Finnegan. In the peace and silence of being alone, I had forgotten all about her.

Her story was exciting. The first helicopter ride of her life took her to an airport in Darwin, where for a time she was the center attraction, being a lone lady, barefoot, and disheveled from ten days at sea. For the press, she judiciously had no comment.

Juanita remembered a long, lost cousin who she knew had settled in Darwin as a veterinarian, and she was able to reach him on the telephone. The conversation went something like this:

"Hello, Dr. Black. I am your cousin, Juanita, Juanita Finnegan."

"Are you the one whose brother was bitten by a monkey in the park when we were on a family picnic?"

"Yes, I'm the one. I'm here at the airport."

After that bit of unorthodox introduction, the good doctor picked Juanita up and drove her to his home where his wife prepared a good meal. She had a good night's sleep and with $200 which the doctor advanced her, she was taken to the Darwin Sailing Club where a water taxi brought her back to CILIN II.

With her thirst for adventure on the high sea fully satisfied, Juanita Finnegan was soon on her way back to her home in Perth and back to the classroom as a schoolteacher. Meanwhile, there was a festive air about the Darwin Sailing Club as sailboat crews from around the world renewed acquaintances and prepared for the race to Ambon. I wanted very much to join in the race, but there was much repair work to be done on the boat before she could go to sea again.

With the help of some new friends, I moved from the sailing club to a new luxury marina at Cullen Bay where extensive repairs from the fire cost more than $1500.

HENRY BYRON WILLIAMS

ON THE WAY BACK TO THE BOAT from my home in Indiana to Cairns, Australia, I saw a fellow at Hickam Air Force Base terminal typing on a laptop computer. Sometime later I met this fellow and learned that he was Henry Byron Williams, a retired Air Force Major from Dallas, Texas. He was a curious, serious-minded little fellow, five feet eight inches tall and about 160 pounds and slightly bald headed. He was also on his way to Australia to visit his nephew who was there on an education exchange student program. When I told him that I was on a sailboat, he indicated he might stop by and see me.

Henry "Hank" Byron Williams & his Bicycle

Over the following months, I tried without success to buy a bicycle to take on the boat. I had put notices on the bulletin board at Cairns and later at Darwin, but with no success. At Travis Air Force Base, California, on the way to Australia, I bought a bicycle helmet, knowing they were mandatory in Australia or you pay a $50 fine. With a helmet and no bicycle I felt like a cowboy with a saddle but no horse to ride. My frustrations at not having a bicycle came to an end one day in July when Henry "Hank" Byron Williams, after a barrage of fax messages to me, appeared at the Cullen Bay Marina in Darwin, smiling as he unwrapped a big package containing a new Dahan collapsible bicycle which he had brought from Hawaii at a cost of $400 to me. During the ensuing weeks it proved invaluable as a means of transportation to the many shops for parts and supplies for the boat.

Major Williams, in addition to the bicycle, bought and installed a new Trimble Galaxy INMARSAT-C satellite radio together with a new Toshiba computer. With the radio, it was possible to send fax messages anywhere in the world from my boat. Also he bought a full set of equipment necessary to rewire the electrical circuit box and various instruments on the boat. Most important of his tools was a Swiss Army knife with blade, saw, screwdriver, file and a myriad of other useful things. For Williams, CILIN II became his toy workshop as he drilled many a hole through the panels and strung wires about the boat until I had to ask which switch to turn to do what I wanted it to do. There were soldering irons, 12 volt and 240 volt, new electric fans, 12 volt and 240 volt battery charger, and so on. For the first time in nine years, CILIN II had adequate compass and G.P.S. lights with proper switches, if I could find which one to turn.

In the process of getting the boat in shape for the Indian Ocean, it was determined that four of the cables holding the mast needed to be replaced. I also discovered that the VHF radio antenna at the top of the mast 37 feet above the deck had somehow broken off and fallen into the sea.

A neighbor on a nearby boat turned out to be a Good Samaritan. A. B. Atkinson and his charming wife, Adrienne, a New Zealand couple, headed out on a world cruise, first invited us over to their boat for a home cooked meal. Then, little by little, they became an important part of our lives for several weeks. I had a feeling that A.B. and Williams were collaborating in an effort to get me to do what they considered important repairs to CILIN II. Anyway, it resulted in many trips up the 37 foot mast for each of them, in the process of removing the old antenna mount, installing a new one, replacing four of the cables holding the mast and replacing lights on the mast.

In the interim, there were more delicious home cooked meals on their boat, DAWN TREADER, dinners at the marina restaurant and dinners at the fabulous Sizzler Restaurant salad bar in Darwin.

While the work was being performed on CILIN II, Major Williams made remarks from time to time about me letting him come along sailing with me. I had let it be known that I was a confirmed solo sailor but knew he was well aware that Dr. Purdie and Miss Finnegan had sailed from Cairns to Darwin with me. There was no question, after all he had done for me, that I was at least morally obligated to take him with me when I sailed. So, we provisioned the boat and sailed from Darwin on the way to the Cocos Keeling Atoll 2000 miles to the West.

Hank had worked diligently, hour after hour and day after day, installing the Trimble Galaxy INMARSAT-C satellite radio. He actually worked all night on two different nights in getting the thing functional. He was certain that the salesman from whom he had purchased the equipment had misrepresented his capabilities to him. He was upset when he learned that the mailbox feature did not function unless the radio was turned on at the time a message was sent. If not, the message was lost. He also learned that all the messages to the radio had to be sent via TELEX. In addition, the radio made so much interference that the accompanying Sony radio could not receive weather fax information from satellites as he had expected it to.

In the process of working out the details, there were many phone calls by Hank and radio messages to the earth stations in California, Perth, Australia, Maryland and the Netherlands. In the end, it was determined that the radio was in order. The messages were simply typed on the accompanying Toshiba computer, the address punched in and the message was on its way. It turned out to be invaluable in the months ahead. Now with the new satellite radio that Hank had installed, I had a worldwide communications capability. Up to that time, I had no shortwave transmitter and only the VHF radio, with a range of about 18 miles.

The Cullen Bay Marina was developed on tidal land that was actually higher than the normal sea level; therefore, it was necessary to traverse a set of locks between the marina and the sea. Our time to go through the locks was set at 8:00 a.m. on August 29. A.B. and Adrian were dutifully waiting there to assist us with our lines and deliver a large chocolate cake as a going away present. We thanked them and sailed away, not expecting to see them again.

The wind was good and the sky clear as we sailed out past the buoy marking an offshore sandbar. To our right we could see dozens of boats anchored in the sea off the Darwin Sailing Club where CILIN II had been anchored during the first two weeks after the fire, before moving to Cullen Bay. The wind remained good and gave us an excellent day of sailing. Hank spent most of the time in the bunk the first day. He was not sick, but motion caused a drowsy feeling.

Though the wind remained remarkably good that first day at sea, we learned that it carried us far south of our desired course. On the second and third days the wind was miserably light. When the Australian customs plane flew over, we were doing more drifting than sailing. On the sixth day out, the map showed that we had traveled only 96 miles for an average of 16 miles a day. Again, we were able to contact the customs plane only to learn that the weather was the same 200 miles to the north and 200 miles to the west.

We were surprised at the sight of sea snakes between four and five feet long nearly 100 miles off shore. I was more surprised on the morning of the seventh day when I pulled in the fish line to see that I had hooked a four-foot long shark. I made quick work of getting him off the hook and back into the water. I had better luck the next day in pulling in a 14-inch fish which provided a good meal for the crew. On the ninth day a report came over the radio warning that a seismograph ship in our water was towing two-two-and-a-half mile long cables and it would soon be to our starboard. The captain instructed that we should turn starboard and give him a wide berth. The radio operator told us it was a Danish ship and that it spent its time traveling in circles, exploring for oil in the Timor Sea. When I called the ship again at 2:00 in the morning, a cheerful female voice answered and assured me that they were well away from us.

We decided on the 13th day out that we should determine whether to proceed toward Cocos Keeling or turn back to Darwin. Three hundred sixty-eight miles in 13 days averaged 28 miles per day. At that rate it would take almost two months to travel the 2000 miles to Cocos Keeling. The wind decided for us. A good wind at 45° made it possible to make a good heading on a 270° course. Again, the customs plane passed over and told us two yachts were moored at Ashmore Reef about a day ahead of us, so we decided to stop at the reef to rest and take on fresh drinking water.

As we were headed toward the reef, we came upon the beautiful TABASCO V, a yacht that had been our neighbor at the Cullen Bay marina for a couple of days. An Australian couple, Philip Welsh and his wife, delivered the boat to various resorts around the world for entertaining the owner's friends.

I personally did not look forward to seeing Captain Philip Welsh again because of an incident that had taken place back at Cullen Bay. I had noticed an old fellow aboard who I considered to be very unfriendly. I thought the old fellow was the owner of the yacht and I had told Welsh that I thought he was a real grouch.

"That is my father. He is 67 years old and he has had a stroke," was Welsh's reply. I was, of course, deeply embarrassed and apologized, but that did not take anything away from my embarrassment.

Captain Welsh had obviously forgiven me because he turned his big yacht around and told us to follow him. He would lead us to the entrance to the channel to the reef where a ranger from the park service was waiting in a powerboat to guide us past the coral heads to our mooring place at Ashmore Reef.

After we arrived ashore, the Australian park ranger told us fresh water was available from a well about a mile away across a lagoon. I took out empty jerry cans in the dinghy and paddled for a long distance to reach the other shore, but there was no well to be seen. I wandered aimlessly, more consumed by the beauty of the place than in my search for water. The place was so unspoiled and natural that it looked as if no other human being had ever been there. The foliage and great variety of birds made it a joy to behold.

At one place I saw what I took to be a dune of white sand but as I drew closer, hundreds of white birds filled the air, screeching at me for disturbing them. On the ground were dozens and dozens of white eggs. At last, I came to realize that I should be looking for the water well and found it very easily as I returned to my dinghy. Then I paddled back to my boat where Hank was waiting.

In a visit with the park ranger later, I related my experience with the birds. Then he said, "Those were Turns. If you want fresh eggs, you could destroy all of them they left on the ground and go back the next day for your fresh eggs." Then he added, "But you can't do it here because this is a National Park."

The following day we left Ashmore Reef as we had arrived, being guided out through the coral reefs by the Ranger in his little powerboat. It was mid-afternoon when I became alarmed at the depth of the water under the boat and felt certain that we were in very shallow water. It was clear and clean and the bottom was clearly visible. I grabbed the sea chart and was able to tell that we had safe depths all about us.

Then Hank shouted, "There is a big manta ray right behind us!" I rushed to the stern to see a gigantic fish as wide as the boat following us and then went in search of the movie camera. When I returned, it had disappeared under the boat. Hank determined that it was not a manta ray because he saw that it had fins. Upon later consulting with some fishermen, we were convinced that the huge monster had been a whale shark, a mammoth but harmless fish.

At 2:00 a.m. we saw the glow of a band of lights across the side of an island ahead of us. We later learned that the lights we saw were from the casino, one of the island's major attractions. Then, just as dawn was breaking, we made our way around the north end of Christmas Island into Flying Fish Cove. What we saw was not very impressive as a tourist attraction or anything that would remotely have anything to do with Christmas. There was a giant conveyer system leading down from high on a hill to the sea. The mining and shipping of phosphate is a substantial industry on this paradise of the Indian Ocean, with much dust blowing around a large area of the cove.

In spite of our first impression, the island proved to be one of our delightful stops along the way. We found a suitable place to moor the boat away from the dust and then were warmly greeted at the local yacht club where we enjoyed freshwater showers. Then we learned that, like Ashmore Reef, Christmas Island, though it is 1500 miles from the mainland, is another National Park where a large area is devoted to a wildlife preserve.

Near the shore is a village of Muslims who work in the phosphate industry. From a mosque, prayers are broadcast by a P.A. system five times a day. Young girls in long dresses and boys in religious uniforms were seen along the streets. The social relations between the Australians and Muslims are wholesome but separate. We enjoyed Indonesian food in a restaurant and good Chinese cuisine in another later in the day.

An attractive young lady, Christiana Dinse, stopped by near the yacht club for a rest from her jogging. She was an employee of the casino and looked very much like the All-American girl, but she was Australian. She acted as a guide for VIP visitors to the casino and told me that during the past week the casino had seen its largest wagers ever. In one evening, one person bet $1,000,000 on one play and lost. Another bet $750,000 on one play and won. I asked her if I would get a VIP tour if I came by the casino, feeling that being an American tourist qualified me for such distinction. She said she would be glad to show me around if I would stop by at 8:00 to 8:30 on Friday evening.

Hank and I were happy, a couple of mornings later, when we saw our good friends A.B. and Adrienne Atkinson. After they moored on a buoy nearby and got settled, we decided that we should have dinner and visit the casino on Friday night. One of the good features of the casino is that it provides bus service in fairly luxurious, air-conditioned buses for their patrons. Since we were on the way to the casino, we considered ourselves patrons and boarded their bus to ride to the other side of the island to the casino complex, which included the casino and several restaurants, a hotel with cottages and, on the front, three large circular swimming pools. The front side of the hotel with the bright lights had been our first view of Christmas Island at 2:00 a.m. a few mornings before.

The foyer was ornate and in exquisite taste. We passed through a long hall, passed a restaurant and a large casino room to the front of the casino, which faced the swimming pools and Indian Ocean. It was all magnificent.

At a little after 8:00 I went to the business office and asked for Ms. Christiana Dinse. In a few moments she appeared, not as I had seen her in her jogging apparel, but in a maroon jacket and skirt, appropriate for meeting VIP's from Indonesia. I introduced the Atkinson's before she escorted us into the gaming room. It was not what we had expected to see at all. There may have been a couple dozen gambling games of various kinds, but the whole place seemed subdued. The gamblers sat or stood at their tables, all very serious and thoughtful. The place did not have the glitz, glamour or excitement of a Las Vegas or Atlantic City casino. I did not notice at first but soon it became apparent that all of the gamblers were Oriental from Indonesia and Singapore. There was not a single Australian person at any of the gambling tables, other than the people working for the casino. Our guide had explained to me at our first meeting on the beach that many of them fly in by jet from Java, arriving at 10:30 or 11:00 at night, gamble until 2:00 or 3:00 in the morning and then fly home. The casino maintains a fleet of long, white limousines to transport them from their jet planes at the airport to the casino. After the tour, our guide excused herself and we moved to one of the restaurants to enjoy our evening meal. After that we boarded the casino bus back to the other side of the island.

The next day Hank and I bade our friend's goodbye and set out for the Cocos Keeling Atoll. With the matter of getting our provisions taken care of and the formalities – getting our invoice for the $50 mooring fee, walking it to the office of the collector of public monies and paying $50, then walking about a mile to the police station where the police, who are also the customs officers, furnished a "port clearance" to be shown to the next port – it was 10:00 before we set sail.

The night was spectacular! Whether it was from the phosphate or whatever, the water had an effervescent glow. Upon the bow, while trimming the sails, I saw numerous porpoises darting about the boat and leaving florescent trails in their wake. It was a spectacular sight. We then watched the lights of Christmas Island and the Flying Fish Cove fade in to the night as we sailed to the north on our way to Cocos Keeling, 500 miles to the west.

Without adequate sea charts, I was worried about the approach to the atoll. At last we were able to find a marker for the entrance to the channel. Then with the use of the G.P.S., I was able to make a course directly to a red marker. From there we headed 145° to a point where we saw a number of boats moored and learned later that except for the high tide, we could have been in trouble on the course we had followed from the red marker.

People on other yachts told us where to anchor and wait for the customs officials. When the officer did arrive, he placed a dozen and a half eggs and a half dozen papaya under seal and ordered us not to break the seal until our departure. Having no refrigeration, the whole lot spoiled and had to be thrown overboard at the time we departed.

Decorations by various yachts at Cocos Keeling

We were at Direction Island, one of several which made up the Cocos Keeling Atoll. It was primitive and preserved in its natural beauty, again by the Australian Parks Service. There was a small shelter house and picnic area with two long tables under the palm trees on the sandy shore. In the evenings yachters congregated for pitch-in meals and visits.

Shelter House at Cocos Keeling

Modern ecologically correct WC at Cocos Keeling

Signs of various yachts that had visited there were tacked around posts in the shelter house with interesting and unique designs. I recognized only one from the year before. MORNING WIND had been in Port Villa with us a year before. There were yachts from France, Germany, Australia and the United States, all making their way around the world. The passengers were an interesting lot because many of us had stopped at the same places on our way around the world, including Gibraltar, the Canary Islands, Panama, Tahiti and many other places. We had much to talk about.

We were not surprised this time when, a couple of days later, DAWN TREADER, with A. B. and Adrienne dropped anchor near us. There being nothing but nature's wonders on Direction Island to Home Island and back, it was necessary to charter a boat to take us to Home Island, where we could catch a ferry to the West Island to do our provisioning and make preparations for our departure.

Hank needed to get back to his home and his sick and aging father in Dallas, and I needed to sail on. A couple of days later, he took the ferryboat to West Island to catch his plane, and I headed back out the channel to the open sea on the road to Malé in the Republic of Maldives. This time I was being lead out of the channel between the coral heads by A.B. Atkinson in his dinghy, but before departure Adrienne had presented me with another delicious rum cake, all for myself.

A.B.'s last words before we parted were, "Be sure to take care of that auto helm because if something happens to your Atoms System, you will be in real trouble." They were my self-guidance systems and I knew that it was good advice. So I sailed away, leaving A.B. and Adrienne, Hank Williams and all of my new sailor friends and headed out alone for the Maldives, far to the north of the equator.

COCOS KEELING TO THE MALDIVES

A. B. TOLD ME TO TAKE CARE of my electronic auto helm because something might happen to the newly repaired Atoms Wind Vane guidance system. It had been my faithful servant through nine sailing seasons and I had confidence in it. I had not gotten far out to sea when calamity struck. As I was sailing along, the excruciating sound of metal grinding against metal told me that I was in trouble. In fear of doing great harm to it, I disengaged it and installed the auto helm as my backup. It worked like a charm and as A. B. had suggested, I would take good care of it. The trip ahead was some 1500 miles to the Maldives. I would be crossing the equator and be facing light and variable winds. It was on the fifth day out that the little auto helm locked up and refused to budge, leaving me without any self-steering device. That meant that I would have to be at the tiller whenever the boat was moving. It would cut my progress down to 25 to 50 miles per day instead of the 100 miles that I had expected to average. I would be heading into the inter-equatorial conversancy zone where the winds were expected to be variable. It was then I decided to change course and head for Diego Garcia, a British Naval and air base in the Indian Ocean. In my mind, I reasoned that on that course I could expect constant winds and would make better time.

By that time Hank Williams was back in Dallas, running a daily position report on CILIN II by the satellite radio he had installed on

CILIN II. I notified him about the change of my destination and that I did not have adequate sea charts for the area about Diego Garcia. He then contacted the commander of the Navy support organization in Diego Garcia to get permission for me to land. Then Hank came back with word that since Diego Garcia was a restricted area, I could not land there but might have to leave the boat there and return for it after the navy repaired the auto helm.

That left me in a quandary. I wondered where I might go while I left the boat in Diego Garcia for repairs to the auto helm. What was I to do? At best it seemed like a dismal prospect.

Then another message from Hank giving me the latitude and longitude of a point near Diego Garcia where I should wait to be intercepted by a Navy launch.

It turned out that the decision to not cross the equator was right because I had good winds all the way to Diego Garcia. But upon reaching the rendezvous point a couple of days later, I called Navy Support on the VHF and was informed that I would be met in about 30 minutes by a Navy launch. I kept wondering if this rendezvous point was where I was supposed to anchor while the auto helm was being repaired.

In less than half an hour, a sizeable launch made its way toward me. Once alongside, a Navy chief by the name of Bryan Gilvey and two Filipino crewmen came aboard the CILIN II. Still wondering where I was supposed to anchor, I was much relieved when Chief Gilvey told me we were going to shore. We motored for a couple of miles to reach the small boat area and dock. There I was met by uniformed British Customs Police and executed the usual paperwork for clearing into a port. I was then told I was restricted to the small boat basin area during the time I was in Diego Garcia unless accompanied by a British Customs Security Officer. The officers and Chief Gilvey departed, saying Gilvey would be back in a couple of hours.

In the meantime, an electronics expert came to examine the auto helm. When he took it away, I felt certain that he would be unable to put it back in working order. At the time, I was completely worn out, mentally and physically, with three weeks' growth of beard and hair long overdue for the barber. I climbed off the boat and walked across the street to an office where I was told I could get a drink of cool water.

There a Filipino lady by the name of Angela not only gave me a drink of water, but also spread out a lunch of rice, chicken and salad, apples and oranges. I did not realize until that time that I had not eaten since early morning. When I offered to pay, I learned that there would be no charge. The personnel in the office were Filipinos from Bataan and Subic Bay in the Philippines, where I had spent much time in World War II.

Back at the boat I was glad that Chief Gilvey did not return as he had promised because I was ready for a good sleep in the peace and quiet of the small boat area. When I awoke a couple of hours later, I was surprised that the Chief had still not returned. I took a shower, put on clean clothes and waited, but he did not return to the boat that evening.

While I was waiting, a young Englishman by the name of Anthony Medicott approached the boat. He was a civilian, employed by the Cable Wireless company Communications Center on the island. What prompted him to do it, I have no idea, but he presented me with a cold six-pack of beer, which I deeply appreciated. At the end of a long cruise, when you are all wrung out, when the boat is at rest and not rocking under your feet, there is nothing as soothing and relaxing as a cold beer. Anthony Medicott had no way of knowing that as he is a skydiver, not a sailor. A handsome young man in his 30's, he was on an extended tour with the cable company, but his first love was to fly to different countries of the world and jump out of airplanes with a parachute, floating to the ground. That was his hobby, but in my book, he rated very highly as a humanitarian.

The British Security Police had sent a message that an escort would meet me at 9:00 the next morning for whatever I needed. What they did not tell me was that my escort would be a pretty English girl by the name of Sally Hodgson. She arrived at 9:00 and asked what I wanted to do. I told her I needed to find a barber; a laundry and then I needed to buy some supplies. She obligingly drove me to her quarters where there was a battery of electric washer-dryers and an adequate supply of soap. While the clothes were in the machines, we walked a short distance to a barbershop, then to the store where I was able to replenish my dwindling supply of cookies and take home some provisions for the next leg of the journey. We also stopped by a ship store where I bought a new cap, a razor and a good supply of Christmas cards. I felt sure that Christmas cards would not be available at my next stop, the Muslim Republic of Maldives, a hunch that turned out to be one hundred percent correct.

After my shopping trip, my escort took me back to the boat where Chief Gilvey was waiting with the repaired auto helm. He then accompanied CILIN II back out to sea to the point where he had first met me. On the way out I decided to test the auto helm. I quickly learned that its controls had been wired improperly. On pushing the button to turn to the right, the auto helm turned the boat to the left and vice versa. I considered that it was a matter that I could handle and get used to by pushing the right button to go left and then left button to go right. I thanked the Chief and they left me at mid-afternoon.

After the Chief had gone, I soon learned that I had an impossible situation. I had considered that I could handle the difficulty but the computer inside the mechanism would also get the wrong signal and turn the boat in the wrong direction. It was useless, but I sailed on. I was in no better position than when I had first stopped in Diego Garcia. Then I thought of the 1000 miles ahead of me, sailing across the equator and the Intertropical Conversancy Zone. I knew that the technician could correct the problem in five minutes by hooking up the wires correctly if I could get the auto helm back to him. My problem was that it was Friday evening and I was about ten miles out at sea. All of the shops would be closed and the technician would be difficult to locate. After thinking it over, I called on the VHF to report the problem. The radio operator was able to contact Chief Gilvey, who instructed me to return to the original rendezvous point where a boat would meet me, take the auto helm to be corrected and return it to me. With unfavorable winds it became necessary to motor for a couple of hours. It was unpleasant but would be well worth it if the auto helm would function properly. When I reached the rendezvous point I was told by VHF that a boat would meet me in half an hour, which it did. It was well after dark when a big boat pulled up beside me and took the auto helm. For a couple of hours I sailed back and forth in the dark until I finally received the good news that the auto helm was repaired and would be back to me in half an hour. I was much relieved when, through the darkness, I could see the boat coming my way. Instead of coming alongside, he squared off and backed up to CILIN II. The

Filipino crewman handed me the precious package. Then he handed me a second package that contained half a dozen apples and a friendly note saying, "We were glad to help you." There in the dark, two miles out to sea, I felt a warm glow of appreciation for the people of Diego Garcia and all they had done for me.

With the auto helm working perfectly I set the course, ate an apple, and took a nap. I was on the way to the Republic of Maldives. I would be passing the Solomon Islands. I had given some thought to stopping for a rest to break up the trip, but gave up the idea when I studied the map and saw that it would take two or three miles of motoring to reach the anchorage inside the atoll.

Before leaving Diego Garcia, a couple of big British security police had asked me to deliver a message to a couple named Peter and Tina Lickford on a sailboat moored in Solomon Island. They had been there for months repairing their boat and enjoying the tropical paradise. On the third day out I was close enough to the Solomon Islands to reach the yachters on the VHF. After a couple of tries, a man's voice came on identifying himself as Peter. I delivered the message from the British Security officers that the water was foul and they should not be drinking it. It was contaminated. I learned that there were four other yachts anchored there. Peter reported that they were enjoying life in the tropical paradise and invited me to stop over for a while. The invitation was tempting but I wanted to get to the Maldives where I could rest for a while before heading for the Red Sea. I had been at sea almost continuously for two months.

Jimmy Cornell's "Royal Cruising Yachts" explained that the northwest monsoons would set in toward the end of November. That was perfect for me. I should reach the Maldives before the monsoons set in. Having departed Diego Garcia on November 10, it would take one week to reach the Maldives. But came November 17, when CILIN II should have been moving toward the Maldives, the wind was directly out of the northwest, the direction I needed to travel. In addition to that, the equatorial current from the west remained strong until I was four degrees north of the equator. With this combination of circumstances, CILIN II was pushed to within 120 miles of Galle at the southern tip of India. At that time I was much closer to Sri Lanka than to the Maldives, but I decided to continue to try to reach the Maldives.

Then came the night of November 22 when a tropical storm hit. According to all information, there would be no tropical storms, but with thunder, lightning and winds that tossed CILIN II about I felt that it was one of the worst storms that I had ever encountered. Of course we have to take into consideration that memory fades out some of the past experiences. Anyway, unusual meteorological events are occurring where they never have occurred before. I felt best heaving to and letting the storm blow. That is good in some situations, but not always the correct procedure.

The next morning there was more rain and I had hoped that after the storm there would be a change in the direction of the wind. Not so. It was still out of 270°. It became necessary to tack back and forth between 360 and 240° to make progress toward Malé. To add to my problems, the light at the top of the mast refused to burn, so I brought a fluorescent light on deck at night. By November 27, I was able to make a heading of 250° when 270 was needed. It was getting toward the very end of November when the wind should have begun to change.

On deck the next morning I was applying some black silicon sealant to stop the water leak near the mast. The boat hit a wave, lurched and set me on my bottom side in a puddle of black sealant. It was all the more aggravating for the fact that I was wearing white slacks at the time. But that was not the worst of it. In falling, I hit my head and my hip against the mast causing bruises that lingered for several days.

On the morning of November 30 I could see some white buildings on the distant horizon, telling me that my destination was in sight. I had no idea of the unusual nature of the place or that it would turn out to be one of the most interesting stops on my tour around the world. I was excited as the little row of white buildings took shape. Progress was painfully slow due to the strong current. I was approaching the island from the southeast and steering 60° to make a course of 330° because the current was so strong.

From Dallas, Hank Williams had telexed me a good word picture of the approach to Malé. I was to pass between the east end of the island of Malé and the airport on Huhule Island, then proceed to a latitude and longitude he provided for me, then call the Coast Guard on VHF Channel 16 to get instructions about where to anchor. In my enthusiasm for arriving, I took down the sails and went on motor for about an hour. Then it appeared that I could make better time with the sails, so I put the sails up and cut the engine. I was able to make two more knots per hour with the sails than with the engine. Near the point between Malé and the airport, it was necessary to go back to the engine to get around the coral reefs on the east end of Malé.

By this time I became aware of a fury of activity all about me. There were boats of various descriptions going every which way. There were motorized wooden boats called dhoani, speedboats, and modern fast cruisers. There were helicopters, jet liners, small planes and floatplanes going to and from the airport. What I did not know was that the Republic of Maldives contains some 26 atolls covering 90,000 square miles, with 1190 islands and about 60 resort hotels scattered throughout the archipelago. The vehicles going to and from the airport were taking vacationers from the resorts to the airport and from the airport to the resorts. They came from Europe and Asia, with very few Americans because of the distance. I was in the middle of all of this traffic as I approached the point where I was to call the Coast Guard. There was so much interference on the radio that I could not hear the instructions on where I was to anchor.

Then a clear voice out of the blue, directing me to anchor on the west end of the Isle of Malé between Malé and the island of Willingli. The surprising voice was that of Captain Philip Welsh from TABASCO V, whom I had last seen at Ashmore Reef. His calls bolstered my confidence and I was grateful to him for it. They were familiar with the Maldives because they had been there before and they were waiting there for his ship owner and his party coming to spend Christmas vacation in the Maldives.

I found a spot and dropped the anchor near the island of Willingli, glad to bring CILIN II to a rest after three weeks of sailing from Diego Garcia. I had no time to relax. A few minutes after I dropped the anchor, a small boat pulled alongside. It was the customs officials and the security police. Then the familiar routine of filling out forms for the bureaucracy. How many times, over and over, I had to write that CILIN II grossed eight tons, had seven tons net, my passport number was 022184669, the length of the boat was 30 feet, etc., etc., etc. I have never been able to understand why there is not a standardized form with all of the pertinent information. In return for my efforts to receive a

"Certificate of Pratique" from the health officer, a card setting out the rules of emigration properly stamped, a "Security Check Clearance Form" from the National Security Service, and a copy of the "Entry-Exit Declaration" happily signed and stamped by the officials. The officials were young men in clean, neat uniforms.

But there was one person in civilian clothes who turned out to be my agent from a shipping agency called FIFO. He was there to take care of my documents. I had taken care of them myself but I got a bill from him for $28 for "work" he had done. Agents are handy in foreign ports to help with communication, handling of the cumbersome problems of getting shipments of parts and equipment through customs and for various other services. They can also take advantage of a lone sailor.

In spite of all of that, I felt fortunate that Philip Welch had recommended the FIFO Shipping Agency to me when I learned of the experience of a Danish yacht that had been turned away by the Coast Guard at 4:00 in the morning because he had not made arrangements for a shipping agent. A Norwegian ship's captain had come to his rescue to work out his problem for him.

After the officials departed I noticed that the anchor was dragging. CILIN II was drifting dangerously toward a reef along the Willingli Isle to the west. After some difficulty in pulling the heavy anchor and 80 feet of chain, I motored to a point closer to Malé Island where I found a fine, firm anchorage.

About sundown, two Spanish sailors anchored 50 yards to the north of me and came to invite me to have dinner with them onshore. I really did not want to go because I was very weary, but later I was glad I did. We rode into the new ship harbor in their dinghy and walked three or four blocks to find a restaurant called the "Goodness Café".

Eating

I learned that the Goodness Café was a standard teahouse for local people. The small rooms were usually crowded. Foods of various kinds were set out in little dishes. Some dishes had one item, others two or three. There were forks and spoons and a pitcher of water, but most people ate with their hands. A waiter appeared to take your drink order for coffee, tea, fruit juice or even Coca Cola. He poured a glass of water, leaving the pitcher nearby. I was glad for that when I learned that almost every dish is hot and spicy. There were fish, salad, eggs, bananas, all done up in special sauces. You see what you think was a cookie and you grab it because you think it would bring some relief for your burning throat. It was not a cookie but fish, and hotter than the last bite you had. After the meal, you learn that there is a faucet and washbasin where you could have washed your hands before you ate, but now you really need it. The mystery to me was how the waiters knew how to figure the bill. I had taken some things where there were three items on a plate. Someone else took the other two. Then the plates were being replenished constantly. How did the waiter know, keep count or calculate what I had taken? It was really inconsequential at the end of the meal when the waiter hands you a small slip of white paper with a number on it. The number is in rufiyaa. It may be 33, which is less than three U.S. dollars, at the rate of 11.72 rufiyaa per one U.S. dollar. It was a satisfying meal and I enjoyed many more of them at different teahouses around the city.

Malé

The streets of Malé were narrow and crowded. Many of them were packed coral sand and unimproved, and after a rain big puddles of water remained. There were ongoing efforts to improve the streets and widen them to accommodate the ever-increasing automobile traffic. It seemed an injustice that people in cars bulldozed their way through the crowds of people as if the people had no right of way. They honked their horns and sped along with pedestrians and bicycles ducking to get out of the way. With all of this, I had yet to see an accident or collision. That had a lot to do with the agility of the people on foot and on the bicycles.

Bicycles

They were everywhere! There were so many that parking spaces were at a premium in the business area of the city. A jay-walker may have had to walk half a block out of his way to get around the bicycles packed closely together along the curb. Many bicycles were left unattended with no locks. Penalty for thievery was so serious that few people take the chance.

School Children

Seeing the young people going to and from school was a real delight. All schools had standardized dress. Across from the post office was an all girls' school. A short distance away was an all boys' school. The girls wore white dresses with pleated skirts, green ties, short white stockings and white canvas shoes. They were all very clean and neat with dark brown eyes and long black hair braided in back. They seemed cheerful and happy.

It was a surprise to see the young schoolboys in short pants. Almost all of the adult men wore long trousers. The only men wearing shorts were foreigners. Like the girls, the boys are cheerful and orderly.

The only playgrounds for the schools were cement and the playgrounds were small. The school term ended at the end of the calendar year, followed by a two month vacation. Malé is the capital of the archipelago and is a very unique city. Sixty thousand souls are packed onto an island of only one and eight tenths square miles in size.

The day after I dropped anchor, I paddled the dinghy into the New Ship Wharf and walked the full distance around the island. It was Friday, the holy day for the Muslims, so there was less activity than there would have been otherwise. With its gray stone buildings and narrow streets, it reminded me of cities in North Africa. I would not have been surprised to see Humphrey Bogart somewhere along the street. The main difference between Malé and cities I visited in Morocco and Algeria some 50 years earlier was that Malé was clean. I was surprised to find so many unimproved streets. On my walk I observed a complex of red brick buildings, which was a departure from the gray stone color of most structures. It was a hospital with a big sign across the front of the main building, announcing that it was a memorial to Indira Gandhi, the former Prime Minister of India who was assassinated in 1984. The hospital, I was told, was a gift to the Maldives from the people of India.

Walking along the north side of the island I saw many little machine shops that kept the hundreds of diesel engines of the dhoanis in operation. On the waterfront, in harbors, space was provided for small vessels bringing cargo from the many ships at anchor in the sea.

Fishing

Fishing is one of the main activities of the Maldives and the surrounding areas. In the early days Maldivian fishermen plied their trade in sailing dhoanis. The single sail of a dhoani is a thing of beauty when it is before the wind. Fishing from a sailboat is slow and cumbersome. Japanese fish canneries took an interest in the Maldives fishing industry because it is a rich fishing ground. The Japanese in turn sold thousands of dollars worth of diesel engines to the Maldives fishermen to enhance their catch and make more fish available to the Japanese canneries. With their new engines, the fishermen continued the ancient practice of catching tuna fish. First they catch a large number of tiny fish. To keep them alive, they store them in the bilge of their dhoani where new, fresh saltwater is constantly in circulation. The dhoani cruises the waters to locate a school of tuna. A congregation of birds on the sea frequently indicates the presence of a school of tuna. When the fishermen get near this spot where the school of tuna is located, they release a large number of the tiny fish to attract the tuna.

As the local fishermen describe it, "The tuna go crazy going after the small fish." Five or six fishermen aboard each dhoani throw in their lines with empty hooks. The tuna are in such a state of frenzy that they bite the empty hooks and are hauled into the boat. One fisherman told me that he and two other fishermen hauled in 600 tuna in one afternoon.

In the afternoon, the dhoani make their way to the fish market on the north shore and display their catch to be purchased by the highest bidder, or to be taken by canneries that have a contract for fish. It is estimated that one half of the work force of the Maldives is engaged in the fishing industry.

Marriage and Divorce

The report on the status of women in the Maldives would be enough to cause cold chills to run up and down the spine of an avowed American "women's libber". It is unbelievable! In the past, the women's place had been in the home, but with increased educational opportunities, their horizons have broadened.

Women marry very young, at about 15 or 16. The ceremony is completely unlike an American wedding. It may take place in the groom's home or in the island official's office. The bride may or may not be present for the ceremony. The wedding party may include the husband-to-be, his father, the uncle of the bride and two witnesses. A man may have as many as four wives; however, it has become more common for men to have one wife. If he has more than one, they live in different houses. If he divorces one, he is required to support her for the rest of her life.

Divorce is easy for the man. All he needs to do is to point to his wife and repeat, "I divorce you" three times, and then report the fact to the judge, a "ganzi" in the Maldives language. For the women, it is more difficult. She must take her case before the ganzi and prove cruelty, desertion or adultery. Adultery may be punishable by beating. It is not uncommon for people of the Maldives to marry ten times, but the average is about four times. Eight out of ten married people divorce at least once.

Few women were seen on the streets during the daylight hours. Some women worked in shops, in the schools and in the post offices, but other than that, few Maldivian women were seen about the city except around their homes. The homes are for the most part ground level residences facing the street. People walk from the streets into their homes and it appeared that they may have been very crowded. In some places, there were courts with an entrance off of the street and then a number of houses or quarters inside the court. They were very primitive. Many parts of the city apparently did not have drinking water piped into the residences. Women were seen going to watering places that were ordinarily located not more than two or three blocks from any residence. Great progress was being made in Malé with new water lines being installed about the city and streets being hard surfaced by generous grants from nations around the world. The Germans, Indians (Hindus), the Japanese and other countries were very generous in giving large grants of money to Maldives. One local person told me it was because of tourism. These countries feel it would help their economy by getting tourists, booking agents, airline travel and all, to have the Maldives with better facilities. He said other countries wanted to help the Maldives because, as a third world country they were doing things right, and great improvements were being made.

There was a rumor that the president, who was serving his fifth term in office, took $30,000,000 of a $100,000,000 grant from Germany and bought himself a castle in England. In the Maldives he lives in expensive grandeur. On the outside of his Maldives home was a sign that says, "The President's Palace". It was nothing more than that. It was in the business district of the town and had a high wall and big steel gates and fence around it. From the outside you could see no activity on the inside. The word was that the president reported that his new palace cost $16,000,000, but rumors said that it cost $64,000,000. Enough to say that it would make the Governor's Mansion in Indiana look like a low cost rental house.

MALDIVES

THE RESORT HOTELS IN THE MALDIVES HAVE a reputation for not welcoming sailboats. Captain Philip Welch suggested that the big lagoon at the Club Med would be a good place to anchor. He was sure I would be welcome there. I wanted desperately to get away from the moorage where passing speed boats and dhoanis kept CILIN II rocking and rolling, night and day. I particularly wanted to find a quiet location where I could write and address my Christmas cards and pen little messages with them. The Club Med lagoon looked like the ideal place for that, so I motored the five miles to the north and anchored in 30 feet of water, just to the right of the entrance as Welch had recommended. It was quiet and peaceful, and a lot better than the place I had been before at the west end of Malé Island.

I wrote cards and messages for a couple of days, telling of the paradise I had found in the Maldives, with white sandy beaches, palm trees and beautiful weather. It was December 5 and if cards were to get back to the States they needed to be in the mail. Well satisfied with my work, I took my cards and paddled across the lagoon less than a quarter of a mile to the beautiful Club Med. There in the gift shop I purchased the proper number of big, colorful stamps and I dropped them in the postal box. Then I thought it only proper to introduce myself to the manager of the Club Med. One of the employees pointed him out to me and told me his name was Jon Pierre. He was a little round man dressed casually. He stared at me with buggy eyes as I approached him.

I introduced myself. "I'm Ed Whitcomb on the little sailboat out there," I said, pointing to the boat.

He exploded, throwing his hands high above his head. "No sailboats," he shouted, as his beady eyes snapped. "The Club Med is a private club and this lagoon belongs to the Club Med." I thanked him and told him I just wanted to mail my cards.

He said, "Alright, you can stay here a couple of days, get fresh water if you want, but you'll have to leave." There were all of those Christmas cards, 50 of them, with notes telling of the paradise lagoon with its white sand and clear water. I had dropped them in the mail and they were on their way to my family and friends in America.

I stayed a couple of days and then, with a feeling of rejection, sailed back and dropped anchor in the busy channel at the west end of Malé where I had been before. Again CILIN II was being bounced around by passing vessels.

That was not the worst part of it. In order to get to shore it was necessary to paddle the inflatable dinghy to the New Ship Harbor about a quarter of a mile away. From there I could walk or take a taxi to the other end of the island where the shipping agent, FIFO, was located. There were also various shops, a supermarket and post office. FIFO became something of a social center where I could pick up my mail, fax messages and have a cup of coffee while visiting with the staff members and others that happened to be in the area.

At FIFO a day or two later I met Hussain Abdullah, a 29-year old diving instructor at Bolifushi Island Resort, 10 miles southwest of Malé. He was a Maldivian. He told me that he was sure I would be welcome by the manager of the Bolifushi Island Resort. So on December 22, just two days before Christmas Eve, he and I sailed to my new island paradise. It turned out to be just that. With white sandy beaches, a clubhouse where we could watch CNN TV every evening at 7:00 while visiting and enjoying refreshments.

Hussain turned out to be a real friend. On numerous occasions he invited me to the dining room at the resort. For an outsider, not booked in at the resort, the cost for food and drink were high by my standards. At the Club Med I learned that lunch would have cost $35 and at

Bolifushi a cup of coffee cost $3.00. Hussain arranged with the head waiter that I would be his guest and I had many fine meals, including Christmas dinner, and coffee at breakfast time in the clubhouse at low cost. I appreciated that very much, but more than that, I appreciated being with the people.

Within 100 feet of the place where CILIN II was anchored, I found snorkeling to be better than anyplace I had experienced in the world. It is like the most beautiful underwater garden a person could imagine. There are many varieties of coral in pastel colors and multi-colored fish by the zillions. It is like an aquarium that goes on and on. Sometimes colorful little fish feed on a particular kind of coral. Other schools of fish seem almost transparent. Then there is a ledge where a person could look deep down into the sea where larger fish move about more slowly. None of the fish are disturbed by the presence of snorkelers. They swim all about but if the snorkeler stops moving, they will nip at his body. This stimulates quick movement by the snorkeler.

I was glad for the snorkeling equipment, complete with wet suit, that I had bought in Panama, and every day was a real delight to go back and view the wonderful sights under the sea.

TROUBLE AT SEA

AFTER TWO GLORIOUS WEEKS OF HOLIDAY FROM sailing the seas, I decided to head back to Malé to prepare for the next leg of my journey, purchase provisions and get the boat in shape for the 1450 mile trip to Salalah, Oman. It would take some time and I wanted to be on the way by January 15.

Bolifushi Island Resort had been an ideal place to vacation. Since Hussain Abdullah was a diving instructor, I spent most of the time with him and his fellow instructors during their off hours. We spent evenings at the clubhouse where entertainment was provided for the resort guests, after watching a TV show and dinner. Sometimes we had dinner in the clubhouse and sometimes in the main dining room. Entertainment consisted of music programs, a magician from Sri Lanka, and local dancers. The local dancing was different than I had observed in any other part of the world where frequently it is very boring. In this case it was a boisterous affair and people on the floor were moving with great gyrations. I even observed Abdullah, who was a very quiet, retiring person, out dancing and doing his thing. Later he told me that he tried to work himself into a trance, but he said he had been unable to get into a trance.

Guests at the island resort were from Europe and Asia. There were large groups of Chinese, Japanese, German, Italian, French and some British, but I was the only American present.

As all good things must end, the vacation was over. Christmas had come and gone and I was on the way back to Malé after bidding my friends goodbye. It would be a ten-mile sailing trip but I would not be able to sail. The prevailing wind was from the northeast and that was the direction I had to travel. On my first trip from Malé to Bolifushi, Hussain had guided me through the coral into the lagoon to the club resort, but on the way back I would take a different route out of the lagoon. I was worried about it and asked Hussain and others the direction of the pass through the coral.

"Are there any shallow places near the passage?" I asked, several times.

"No. No. All clear", was the answer. I asked the same question of Mohammed Heleem. He ran the diving school and knew the waters well. "No shallows," he said. This was the second time I had asked him.

It was about noon when I pulled anchor from the 60 foot depth. Having no windlass, it is always a struggle with an 18 pound anchor and 80 foot of chain and 125 feet of rope rode. I would motor east a couple of hundred yards past the resort, then north until I could see the reef and then follow it in a westerly direction until I could see the opening to pass through into the channel. All went well. I was through the reef and headed for Malé. Though it was now less than 10 miles, sometimes Malé was not visible because of the haze.

Motoring was very slow. I hated it and am always glad when I can cut the engine and catch the wind tug at the sails. The afternoon winds became strong and more and more whitecaps appeared. I finally realized that I was making very little progress and decided to try sailing. I could tack and make better headway than running with the engine.

The wind was very strong and directly against me. In addition, there was a very strong sea current against me. How strong I did not know. There does not seem to be a schedule for current in the Maldives. They are unpredictable and can be very strong at times.

With all of these obstacles I cut the engine and hoisted the sails. With the good wind and the boat moving fast through the water, I did not know how far north I could tack before coming to a reef, because I had no detailed sea chart of the area. The water was clear ahead until I was ready to make my turn. Then I noticed the G.P.S. showed 330º.

I was losing ground because the wind and the current were pushing me back. Then on the other tack, I found the same thing. I was being moved backwards and making no forward progress whatsoever.

There was only one thing to do. I would return to Bolifushi and wait for more favorable wind conditions. I downed the sail and started back to the pass that I had come through about an hour and a half earlier. Then I thought about the reefs near the resort and I became fearful that I might run aground. I knew the area back at the west end of Malé where I had been anchored for several days earlier. There were lights along the shore and lights from ships and I felt comfortable about going there after dark. After mulling it over and over, I decided to turn back and head to Malé again, even if it took all night. I had been in situations before where it was necessary to sail all night rather than to try to enter an unfamiliar port in the dark. Once again I turned and headed for my original destination. I gave the engine more throttle than usual and the little 24-horse power engine chugged along bravely, but the G.P.S. told me what I did not want to know. I was still being pushed backwards and making no forward progress. All the time I was aware of the predicament that would result if the little Volvo engine decided to call it quits. Then there would be no place I could go safely. The sea to the west contained more and more reefs and I did not have a sea chart. At that time I made a resolution that I would never go to sea again without adequate sea charts to show me where I was going. Even though this was a little ten-mile trip, I knew that it was necessary to have sea charts.

There was only one thing to do. By then it was almost 5:00 p.m. I needed to head back to Bolifushi while there was still time to see the passage through the coral reef. I found it and was looking ahead for the route back to the resort. There was coral ahead to avoid. As I was looking toward Bolifushi, about a mile away, there came the most excruciating crash. I knew it well. It's the kind of sensation that goes through your entire nervous system. You know you have run aground.

But I did not stop. Maybe it was just a boomie coral head and I had run over it. But no. There were more crunches and thuds with the metal of the keel scraping and grinding against the rocks. Then the boat stopped dead in the water. I cut the engine, put on my snorkeling gear and went over the side to assess the damages. There it was. The huge

235

boulders and coral and the beautiful fish I had enjoyed so much over the past couple of weeks. But they did not look so beautiful now. CILIN II was locked in. There seemed no way out. It was growing dark. I could see the lights of the resort and wondered if anyone saw me. I was alone and knew exactly what I was faced with.

There were three anchors aboard, a fisherman's, a danforth and a plow. I put a rope on the fisherman's anchor and hauled it in the rubber dinghy about 50 feet and dropped it. It took hold and gave me a feeling of some stability. Then I put out the other anchors in different directions. The purpose was to pull CILIN II off the boulder it was bouncing on and avoid pounding the boat to pieces. It was completely dark by the time I finished the work, but I felt the boat was secure. I would wait until morning to see if there was any chance to save the boat. There was nothing more to be done, so being totally exhausted, I lie down and fell asleep. I may have slept a minute or ten minutes, but I was jarred out of my sleep by another crash. The swells lifted the little boat and then bounced it on the rock. I was dejected and realized the danger I faced. During the past week, strong winds had come up at night, screaming through the rigging and bouncing the little boat around while I lay at anchor at the resort. If we had that kind of wind again, the boat was certain to be badly damaged and possibly destroyed. I thought of the ridiculous situation. I had sailed the Atlantic, Pacific and the Indian Oceans successfully, but had gotten caught up in a little ten-mile side trip from the Bolifushi Resort to Malé. The wonderful vacation had turned into a disaster.

I wondered about what I would do if the boat were destroyed. What could I do? For ten years CILIN II had been my home. There had been problems before like when the propeller came off in the Mediterranean and I had sailed all night and called on the radio for help. I had paid $1500 to be towed 13 miles to port. After that I had gone to sleep and ran aground in Sicily. And there was a second time the propeller came off and I was able to repair it myself. Later all electrical power had been lost and a Spanish tuna fishing boat came to the rescue. All of those problems had been resolved successfully, but this was different. I was alone and in despair. If the boat sank, I felt sure I could make it back to the resort in the rubber dinghy. It would take all of my endurance to paddle the mile against the wind and the current. I was well acquainted with it from paddling from the anchorage to the dock at the resort each morning and evening. It was a strong current and took a lot of paddling to make headway against it.

It would be embarrassing to face my friends in the lodge and admit that I had lost the boat. A dhoani would take me from the lodge to the airport where I would fly to Singapore, Paris and back to the U.S. Life on the sea would be finished. My dream of circumnavigating the globe would end.

But it didn't happen that way. At dawn I was able to extricate CILIN II from the coral and sail back to the resort.

SALALAH

THE MOST INTERESTING THING ABOUT CIRCUMNAVIGATING IS that every port and marina is different from the last. Salalah was no exception. It was 19 days since I had departed the Maldives and I was eager to find the marina and drop the anchor.

Twilight was coming on when I sighted a promontory on the Oman coast which told me I was very near the destination. The cruising guide gave perfect directions and the G.P.S. was working properly. For some unexplainable reason I sailed on past the marina. By the time I realized the mistake it had grown dark. Then to add to the confusion of finding my way into the marina, a maze of colored lights made it impossible for me to see the navigational markers.

At last I called harbor control on the VHF radio, gave my location and asked for directions. His answer was that he could not see me. I should sail north for one half hour and call him again. I followed his instructions but when I called him, I was unable to get any response whatsoever. What was I to do? I was in the sea with multicolored lights all about the area but nothing to show the way into the marina.

One alternative was to sail back to sea and heave to for the night. After 19 days I did not want to spend another night at sea, so I called on the VHF radio, "anyone monitoring channel 16, please answer and give me direction on how to enter the port."

Luck was with me. The voice of a man came on in clear English, advising that he would come out in his dinghy and lead me into the marina. The approach was simple and soon CILIN II was anchored in 16 feet of water where numerous other yachts were moored, with the crews enjoying their evening meal.

After dinner and a good night's sleep aboard the boat, I decided to explore Salalah. It was then that I learned that CILIN II was in a harbor by the name of Mina Raysut, 12 miles from the city of Salalah. Before departing the boat it was necessary to wait for the customs boat to arrive and clear me into the country.

For that I had to wait until noon with the yellow quarantine flag displayed on the shroud. I could see the customs boat making its way from one yacht to another, until with a crew of five, it pulled alongside CILIN II. One very dignified looking fellow sat in the cab while the crewmembers, including a couple of women, sat on deck. I was invited to come aboard.

Then the usual questions, the name and length of my boat, the last port visited, the next destination, any guns aboard, etc. It was all conducted in a friendly, businesslike way, and after all the papers were signed and stamped I was free to travel to the city.

The highway to Salalah was up the hill about a quarter of a mile, but before departing the port it was necessary to stop at the police security station near the gate. There a dozen uniformed officers milled about as if they were not certain of what they were supposed to be doing. What they were supposed to be doing was to return my passport, which the customs officer had taken when I was clearing into the port.

Finding the passport turned out to be a major operation, as they shuffled papers and asked questions. Then I was free to go, with the admonition that I return before midnight. The officer's friendliness somehow made up for the apparent inefficiency of the operation. Getting a ride into the city was a simple matter. The officers advised that the first car that came along would stop for me, if it had room, and transport me to anywhere I wanted to go. It happened just that way. The first automobile that came along stopped to pick me up. The driver was not only happy to have me as a passenger, but was glad to deliver me to the post office, bank, and market or wherever I wanted to go at no charge. It was the same on subsequent days when I went to the city to buy provisions or to go sightseeing.

Returning to the port from the city was a different matter. Eager taxi drivers were happy to haul you, but the fare was the equivalent of 12 U.S. dollars. The harbor police explained to me a couple of days later that the going fare for a ride from the city to the port was three Rials. With the rate of exchange being one dollar for 1.35 Rial, the charge for the taxi should have been $4.05 U.S. instead of the $12 they had been charging. We quickly learned that the taxi drivers in the Muslim world were not much different from taxi drivers elsewhere.

In visiting with shop clerks and other people I met, I learned that many of them lived in high hopes of coming to America. When I asked them why, the answer was always the same, "You have so much freedom." This came from people living in one of the finest places in the world, the southern coastal area of the Arabian Peninsula. To them, the freedoms we enjoy in America are more important than living in a land with a perfect climate.

After spending five wonderful days in Salalah, I checked the cruising guide for instructions on clearing out of the port. It said there were six steps. First, collect four copies of the clearance application form at the police gate. The police could provide you only one copy. It is carried down the street to a new, well-landscaped building where you are directed to the second floor. At the end of a long hall, a secretary stamps the application. Then the paper is to be taken back to the custom office, which is next to the police station. After getting another stamp on the application, it is to be carried to the top of the hill for the harbormaster's stamp. From there the clearance application is taken to the harbor office at the bottom of the hill where you exchange it for your ship's papers. In my case, my ship's papers consisted of a flimsy paper about one fourth the size of a sheet of typewriter paper entitled "Validation of Registration and Excise Payment for the State of Indiana."

With it in hand, I went back to the police station to collect my passport. I was ready to sail. The procedure can take two to three hours. Goodbye Salalah.

CILIN II headed out of the harbor of Mina Raysut at 6:00 p.m. on February 11, 1996, headed for Aden, Yemen. This would be the last stop before entering the Red Sea. I expected the trip to Aden to take about

8 days. Winds were favorable the first night out and I stayed awake all night long. The following morning the wind died, the boat rolled with the swells and the sails flapped back and forth. This can be very aggravating to a sailor and there is little that can be done about it other than starting the engine. On that first day out we covered 11 miles, the second day 18 and the third day 25 miles.

Sailing was discouraging but my morale got a boost when I hooked a Dorado, but the line slacked when the fish flipped off the line just as he reached the boat. After that the wind picked up and I soon landed a three foot long Dorado. I hung him in the fish dryer, a wire contraption that hung from the boom close to the mast. The fish was clamped in a vertical position to be dried by the hot, tropical sun and sprayed by ocean waves from time to time.

My interest in using the drier was stimulated when I landed another Dorado about three feet long. This called for a replaying of "Victory at Sea" by Richard Rodgers. It was my victory song that sounded out from the Sony tape recorder on the occasion of landing a big fish.

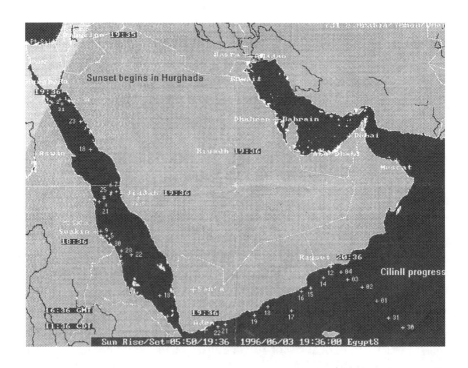

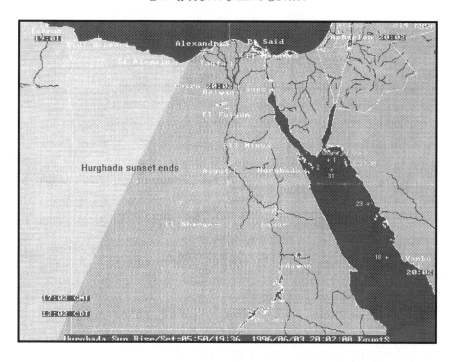

On the 11th day, I arrived at the head of the three-mile long fairway leading to the port of Aden, Yemen. I made a mistake by lowering the sails at the marker buoy. By the time I had secured the sails, CILIN II had drifted far away from the fairway. It took a long time to motor back to get the boat into the marked channel and a much longer time on the engine to reach Aden.

There were about a dozen yachts at anchor preparing to enter the Red Sea. Among them were Eric and Robin Lambert from Marina Del Ray, California. We had previously spent a pleasant afternoon eating popcorn and visiting while anchored off Malé in the Maldives. Also waiting were Tony Evans and his wife, who I had met and visited with over a pitch-in dinner at Cocos Keeling; Eric, a Danish airline pilot and Brian, a retired school teacher from Oregon who was also solo.

Clearing into the port was a simple proposition, but I was taken back a bit by the customs and immigration official's request for a Christmas present for their services. That seemed odd since it was then the month of February. My Christmas spirit had long since departed. I thanked them and wished them a Merry Christmas.

The first order of business after clearing in was to find a bank to exchange U.S. currency for Rials, the local money, and then to make a trip to the Egyptian Embassy to obtain a visa for entering Egypt later. It would be much later for some of us.

The Sailor's Cruising Guide recommended Omer Hamza as a taxi driver and we found him waiting on the street when we cleared into the port. He turned out to be a very resourceful man who served us well.

Upon returning to the boat I discovered that the anchor was hopelessly hooked onto something about 30 feet deep so I could not pull it up, as much as I tried. Finally a little fellow named Ali Abdullah Mohamed saw my difficulty and offered to help me. I rejected his offer because he did not look like a person capable of doing the job.

Finally, I gave up for the evening and waited until morning to start working on it .again. The little fellow appeared again and offered to help me. Finally, I told him frankly, "I do not want you to try it. You don't have an oxygen tank and the anchor is in 30 feet of water."

He said, "Give me a try."

"How much would you charge?" I asked.

"Oh, it is up to you," was his answer.

So I said, "I don't do business that way. If you want to help, tell me how much you would charge."

Without hesitation he said, "Ten dollars."

I was surprised because the usual price for a diver is more like $50.00. He borrowed my facemask and dove down 30 feet without an oxygen mask and tied a rope around a pipe holding the anchor. By pulling up the pipe and giving slack to the anchor rode, he was able to free the anchor. CILIN II was moved to another position where she was anchored well. Once again I was saved by the grace of a stranger.

Yemen, being a Muslim country, has no drinking, no alcohol and no taverns, except for some reason or another, there is a Sailor's Club where beer is sold. Some local people frequent it but it was not crowded, possibly for the reason that a beer costs 350 Rials. That is $2.45 in U.S. money, and a lot of money in poverty-ridden Aden. But any taxi driver can provide Scotch, Vodka or Bourbon at the black market price of $15.00 for a fifth for those who are really thirsty.

Aden to the Red Sea

CLEARING THE PORT AT ADEN WAS A simple process compared to Salalah. It was a matter of crossing the street from the Prince of Wales Pier to procure a paper from the immigration office to take to the harbormaster for his signature and clearance form. These were returned to the immigration office in order to retrieve my passport. Then I was ready to set sail.

I planned to leave on Thursday at the same time as my friends, Eric and Robin Lambert, but it turned out that the harbormaster's office was a long distance down the coast, up a very steep hill and up three flights of stairs. There the harbormaster enjoys a panoramic view of the gigantic harbor of Aden.

He was very friendly and spoke good English. He signed my clearance and I was on my way. Aden had been a very interesting stop but I was happy to be on my way. Then an accident occurred which could have delayed my departure for a long time.

I was wearing open-toed sandals and while making my way back to the immigration office, I stubbed my big toe on a pipe sticking out of the ground, suffering a half-inch split at the front of the big toe on my right foot. It worried me greatly because I was afraid of an infection. I cleaned it well and got some medication and bandages from a drug store.

The "HEATHER" with Eric & Robin - Aden 1996

The next morning, as Eric and Robin were clearing out, I asked them to ask the harbormaster to give me a few more days in port to make sure that I did not get an infection. I knew that when I left Aden it might be weeks before I would be able to get help if I needed it. He gladly agreed to give me an extension saying, "Yes, let him stay until he is ready to sail."

Yacht Heather 1964 - 1997. Heather at the bottom of the sea.

That was not a happy situation because Eric and Robin were sailing that day for the Red Sea and I had hopes of making part of the journey with them.

CILIN II was an absolute mess and looking more like a derelict as each day went by. Aden, being a port that exports petroleum, was the dirtiest I had ever encountered. The dinghy and deck of CILIN II and even the sails were smeared with grease, oil and tar. There was no sense in trying to keep the deck clean because it would be necessary to do it again whenever the dinghy was brought aboard.

In preparation for my departure, Omer Hamza, the friendly taxi driver, took me to the produce market, the drug store, the food market and post office. I had not received any mail for a long time and did not expect any, but stopped by just in case. Much to my surprise, there was a long letter from my daughter, Shelley.

It was a lonesome feeling when I finally pulled anchor and headed out to sea. All of the friends who had made life so enjoyable at Aden had already departed, but I knew that I had done the right thing in making sure there was no infection.

The weather was clear, as it had been for days, with a light breeze. I decided to put up the sails for the three-mile buoy-marked channel to the sea. I had been instructed to call the harbormaster on the VHF radio, channel 16, upon departure. I tried and got no response, but as I was leaving the harbor, a police patrol boat came alongside.

"Why did you maneuver about the harbor?" he asked.

I answered, "I wanted to put up the sails."

He said, "You call the harbormaster."

"I have been trying to call him on channel 16," I replied.

He said, "Call him on channel 13."

I called on channel 13 and that nice harbormaster that had been so friendly earlier turned out to be a true villain.

"Why are you maneuvering around the harbor? You have broken the rules. You will return to mooring and pay a fifty dollar fine." He shouted.

Oh, this nice man took me aback. He surely did not know that I was the fellow who had the busted toe. I could not believe that he was the harbormaster who had been so kind.

I was aghast. I knew that if I went back into the harbor, I would be delayed at least another day, not to mention the $50.00 and all of the inconveniences involved.

"I do not hear well," I replied. "Let me repeat this, sir. I am supposed to return back to the mooring from where I came and pay a $50.00 fine for maneuvering in the harbor?"

Then, to my surprise and delight, he said, "No, you tell that patrol boat to come back in. You may go."

I could not believe it. It was a great relief. I felt as if I had been freed at last.

I was sailing out of the dirty harbor, back into the clean water of the Gulf of Aden, leaving the war-ravaged city and the gruff port captain in our wake. The people we had met there were friendly and helpful at every turn, except the port captain, who had gotten upset because I maneuvered CILIN II in the shipping harbor when putting up the sails. The good news was that 20 miles up the coast was Raz Iran, where it would be possible to get rid of the oil and tar that had accumulated on CILIN II during the two weeks in Aden.

The scenery along the coast of Yemen was spectacular, with high jagged peaks in the distance, reminiscent of the beauty of Moorea near Tahiti in the Pacific Ocean. Off the port beam I saw a small fishing boat approaching me and I could see three young fishermen waving at me. They held up a string of fish and then, as they drew closer, they threw a couple onto my deck. In return, I tossed them a package of Marlboro cigarettes. They were happy with the cigarettes, but then they made signs that they wanted something to drink which, of course, meant alcohol. They were good Muslim boys, out away from their families, wanting to do something they could not do at home. I let them know by sign language that I had nothing to offer them, so they waved goodbye and sailed away.

After a short time they returned and headed back toward CILIN II. "What now?" I thought. What were they up to? Then it became very clear. One was holding a cigarette in his lips, making signs that he had no way to light it. When they drew closer, I threw them a book of matches and they sailed away, happy with their smokes.

A couple of cartons of Marlboro cigarettes had been purchased in Aden to be used for gratuities for the pilots when I reached the Suez

Canal. It is well known to cruising sailors in that area of the world that the pilots through the Suez Canal expect to receive tips of "baksheesh" for their services. Word is that whatever is offered is never enough. If one pack of cigarettes is offered, they want two. If five dollars is offered, they want ten. It is a little game, so wise sailors make their first offer in small amounts.

With the G.P.S. operating, I headed directly for Raz Iran; but I could not see the anchorage. I was too far from shore. A fishing boat came by and with sign language, I asked directions. The fisherman pointed down the shoreline and led me in that direction. It was getting dark and I realized much too late that he was leading me away from Raz Iran instead of toward it. I knew that if I turned back, I would be trying to locate it in the dark.

There was no way to satisfactorily communicate with my guide. I wanted desperately to find Raz Iran because I knew that there would be other sailors there visiting and eating during the evening, but it was getting too dark to try to find them.

I parted from my guide and sailed on all night long to reach the next anchorage after a hectic day in departing Aden. During the night I could see many ships in the shipping lane coming out of the Red Sea. They were far to the south and created no problem.

At dawn I observed that there was an anchorage at Raz Al Arah, 31 miles from the Red Sea. It would be an ideal place to rest and clean up the boat before entering the Red Sea. A good breeze carried me the two miles to the shore at Reaz Al Arah, where I anchored in 15 feet of water, 300 yards from a village. The boat was at rest and I enjoyed a cup of coffee and a bowl of cornflakes with bananas and slept from 9:00 in the morning until 1:00 in the afternoon. Then I cooked a couple of eggs with the fish and drank a glass of orange juice and a second cup of coffee. Then I was ready to start cleaning the boat.

The town on shore at Raz Al Arah looked like it might be a fishing village, with many dilapidated buildings and a lot of poverty-ridden people. I expected the immigration officials to appear, but none came to the boat. Being weary from the sleepless overnight sailing trip, I did very little on the first day at anchor. On the second day, I scraped the oil-saturated moss along the waterline and was able to make the hull look more respectable. On deck it was a different story. The sails and lines were so soiled with oil that it appeared that they needed to be replaced.

On the third day I decided to replace the zinc on the propeller shaft. I had learned that when the boat moves through the water while sailing, it creates electrical current and electrolysis causes metal to disintegrate. I had first learned of it in Costa Rica when the handle to a seacock broke off in my hand when I tried to turn it. In order to avoid having vital metal parts deteriorating, the little pieces of zinc attached to the propeller shaft absorbed the current. It needs to be replaced from time to time when it is eaten up by the electrolysis process.

I put on my facemask, took a wrench and went over the side into the water. Under the boat I was able to release the bolt that held the zinc in place. Then I went up on deck to rest for a moment. A little boat appeared with a couple of young boys. I explained by sign language what I was trying to do. One of the boys was eager to help me. He took my facemask, went under the boat and very quickly exchanged a new piece of zinc for the old one.

He was very much pleased when I handed him a package of Marlboro cigarettes for his assistance. I had no other company during the three days I was anchored at Raz Al Arah and the immigration official never made an appearance.

At two o'clock in the morning of March 11, 1996, I weighed anchor and headed for Bab Al Mandab, which according to the great sailor, Triston Jones, means "The Gate of Tears". That title could have been more meaningful to me had I known what lay ahead for CILIN II and me. I knew that by starting at that early hour I would reach the entrance to the Red Sea sometime before noon.

The wind was out of the south and I was making good time for about an hour. Then I noticed that CILIN II was being pulled to the port side. I pushed the tiller over but it had no effect. Then I found the trouble. I had run into another fish net. At three o'clock in the morning, one hour after my early morning departure for the Red Sea, I was hopelessly entangled.

A glance at the sea chart told me that just across the Bay of Aden was a shark feeding ground. That ended any thought I might have had about going under the boat to untangle the net. I probed with the gaff hook, an eight foot long aluminum pipe with a hook on the end. Soon it became so entangled that it became necessary to cut the net to release the hook. It was then that I observed a long, slim boat in the dark of the night about 50 feet off my stern. No sound came from it until I shouted. At first there was no response, but after a while the boat drew closer. It was the fisherman, and he started talking to me in a language I could not understand.

I shouted, "I am sorry but I do not understand."

He kept on talking and became violent. He raged on and on. After a while he paused. I assumed he was waiting for me to respond, so I repeated, "I am sorry but I do not understand." Then I shined the flashlight on my face to show great sympathy, great agony and every expression I could muster to show my deep sorrow that I had sailed into his fishing net.

It did not work. It stimulated him to rage like a mad man, on and on. Then he started to babble. I did not know what he was saying, but thought it might be very uncomplimentary. He could not know if I were American, Russian or whatever, but rich people running into fishnets at night are no good.

Soon he started to sing and I thought that he was surely out of his mind. I was glad that he was on his boat and I was on mine. If he could get his hands on me, he would surely do me great bodily harm.

At last he stopped and I did the only thing I could do. I told him again that I was sorry.

After he became quiet, I launched the inflatable dinghy and started paddling my way around CILIN II to see if I might tug on the fishnet and free it. The waves knocked me against the boat time and again but I had no inclination to get into the shark-infested waters there in the night.

At last I was able to free one of the big bobbers from the net. It was a large one, and I thought that it might be attached to the end of the net. All was silent on the fisherman's boat, so I paddled over to present the bobber to the fisherman. There was not a sound, but as I drew closer, I could see that he was asleep in the bottom of the boat.

There being nothing more important to do, I paddled back to CILIN II and slept until dawn. I dreaded the dawn for what it might bring, but when I looked out across the water expecting to see a wild man, I was surprised at what I saw. The fisherman was a nice-looking fellow about 25 years of age. His fury had disappeared. He dove into the water, swam over the CILIN II and without a word motioned that he wanted my facemask. After one inspection trip under the boat, he returned to ask for a knife. There was no way that I would have provided him with a knife in the dark of the night before, but things had changed. After cutting the net under the boat, he returned the knife to me and swam away toward his boat with my facemask. I shouted, "Hey, my face mask," but he paid no attention. I sat on deck and watched him as he reeled in his net, pulled up his anchor and sailed away. The loss of the facemask was a serious matter for me, first because it was a fine piece of equipment that I had purchased in Panama a long time before and second, because I needed it to go under the boat from time to time. It is an important piece of equipment for a cruising sailor. It was gone and I did not have another one.

By that time it was mid-morning. There was no wind stirring and I had to decide whether to head for the Red Sea or wait for another day. I wanted to be certain to arrive at Bal-Al Mandab in broad daylight, because of the heavy ship traffic entering and leaving the Red Sea.

I thought at first that I would heave to and wait until the next day, but after a short time, a good wind came up. I decided to pull up the anchor and give it a go. The wind stayed strong so that after a couple of hours I could see the hills around Bab-Al Mandab.

It seemed a good time to throw out the line to see if I might catch a fish. As we were approaching the entrance to the Red Sea, there was a strong tug on the line. It looked like a very large tuna. It was, in fact, so large that I felt that it would be difficult getting him into the boat, so I was not disappointed when he slapped against the side of the boat and escaped. Ships were near at hand, entering and leaving the Red Sea, and it was necessary to position CILIN II into the right channel to avoid the restricted military zones and steer clear of the busy shipping lane. It was a busy time and things were working fine as I sailed through "The Gate of Tears" into the big Red Sea.

It was mid-afternoon, with plenty of daylight left for getting far into the sea and away from the shipping lane. Again I stayed awake all night, but had no problem with ship traffic. Other sailors I knew were sailing along the western shore and pulling into anchorages at night, which requires some careful navigating to avoid the coral reefs. Having an assistant on the bow to watch for coral reefs is a much safer way to travel than sailing solo. I had decided that I would stay well out from shore until I reached Port Sudan. Entering the Red Sea was as interesting and exciting as the trip through the Strait of Gibraltar on the way to cross the Atlantic so many months before.

I knew very little about the Red Sea except what I had read in the Bible. I had long thought that when I reached it I would be almost home and back in Tel Aviv, Israel where I had started. It was something of a shock to learn that it was 1700 miles to the Suez Canal. Added to this aggravation is the fact that the shorelines of the sea are laced with coral reefs from one end to the other. Ninety percent of the eastern shores of the sea are occupied by Saudi Arabia, where sailors are not welcome except in an emergency situation. In addition to other problems, Malaria fever is prevalent in some areas. The Sailors Cruising Guide reports that chloroquine resistant malaria is epidemic in both rural and urban areas of Sudan.

The most terrorizing news came from a passing ship, warning me of piracy in the Hanish Islands ahead of me. For a lone sailor that is the worst kind of news. In areas where piracy is threatened, the imagination can run wild. Each boat that heads in your direction seems to be a cause for alarm. I remembered well the trauma caused by boats approaching and following CILIN II in the night off the coast of Morocco in the Atlantic.

Things were going well until I noticed a local boat crossing my course about half a mile away. It was traveling at a good speed, suggesting that in addition to the sail, an engine was powering it. I was interested because I was not acquainted with that type of boat, but I became more interested when it turned and headed in my direction. Pirates! I was sure of it. Why would it turn and head back toward me?

I was terrified. Then I thought of the emergency distress signal on the satellite radio which Hank Williams had installed for me back in Australia. I was nervous as I plugged in the radio and booted up the computer. The boat was drawing closer to me as I studied the display on the monitor. There were the buttons to indicate the emergency distress options. They were:

1 – Fire/explosion; 2 – Flooding; 3 – Collision; 4 – Grounding; 5 – Listing; 6 – Sinking; 7 – Disabled and adrift; 8 – Abandoning ship;

9 – Require assistance; 10 – Piracy/armed attack. That was it: Piracy/ Armed attack. I pushed number 10. Then before I could understand how to activate the signal, I observed that there were a lot of people on the approaching boat. Quickly I could tell that it was a group out for a joy ride, possibly from the military base nearby.

My first but not my last piracy scare was over. I became alarmed a couple of times during the next few days when boats appeared to be heading in my direction at night, but in each case it was a false alarm. After passing the Hanish group of islands, where there were rumors of pirate activities, I stopped worrying about pirates and turned my worries to navigating the boat.

I had been sailing in the Red Sea for almost two weeks and was still far from Port Sudan. The wind from the north and northwest had me trapped so that I could not make progress toward my destination. On a compass heading of 280°, the G.P.S. would indicate that I was making 240°, meaning that I was being pushed backward from the desired course. On a compass heading of 100°, the G.P.S. indicated a course of 110°. The little 24-horse power Volvo engine was of little help in moving north. On some days, I would find that I was further south than the day before. I was losing ground and wondered if there was something I should know that I did not know about sailing. I felt trapped and embarrassed. I wondered if I had made a mistake in trying to sail the Red Sea. I was there for several days, very depressed and concerned that I might be there for an extended period of time and not be able to get to an anchorage.

I studied the sea charts and found that there was an anchorage that would be easy to approach if I could get to it. At last the wind changed so that I was able to make a heading of 280°. That took me in the direction I wanted to sail toward the anchorage of Khor Nawarat.

The Shady Lady

After 20 hard days at sea, the anchorage of Khor Nawarat was in sight in the late afternoon. Soon I would be at anchor and get some rest. There might even be some other sailboats there. As I scanned the horizon to see if there were any masts in view, I was thrilled when I was able to make out the figure of a sailboat mast above a point of land at the anchorage. I was even more thrilled when I saw another and then another. There would be people to talk to and discuss the storms we had been through and the winds that would not allow me to move northwest.

As I was glorying in the prospects of having people to talk to, possibly people I had met before, my heart sank when I realized that all three boats were pulling away from the anchorage. "Hey, wait a minute!" I wanted to shout, but they were moving out of the bay.

But the wind was favorable so that I was able to reach the anchorage well before dark. There were no other boats. There were no buildings and no sign of life, other than the birds in the air. I found a well-protected area and CILIN II came to rest after a hectic two weeks in the Red Sea. I had my evening meal and slept.

The following morning, I was rested and felt like giving it another try. After about half an hour of sailing I realized that I was faced with the same strong, northerly wind. I could make no headway, so I returned to the lonely anchorage to spend another day and night.

It was certain to happen and I thought it happened on March 31. In sailing solo in the tropical climates, there are times when the weather is very warm and clothes are not necessary. I frequently wore only a T-shirt to keep the sun off the body and feel comfortable. The cruising guide says that the Red Sea has the hottest average temperature of any place in the world, and I believed it. Wearing only a T-shirt cuts down on the laundry bill. On long trips, it helps conserve clean clothes for arrival at the next marina. It's comfortable, but sometimes when I step up into the cockpit from the cabin I take a quick look about to make sure a boat hasn't pulled up alongside with people viewing my semi-nude body. It's always a relief when I find there are no other boats in sight.

Not so on March 31. I started to step up into the cockpit when out of the corner of my eye I caught the sight of a beautiful white boat drawing up beside CILIN II. As luck would have it, I saw it in time to get back into the cabin and dress properly before making my appearance on deck. It was a special moment for me, because I had not talked to anyone since that nasty fisherman had stolen my facemask and he had been no fun to talk to. That had all been more than two weeks ago. I needed to talk to someone about whether I was doing the right thing in trying to sail up the Red Sea, and this appeared to be an opportunity to do it. Thus begins the saga of THE SHADY LADY.

It was two wonderful weeks, as great as any two weeks I spent on my entire trip around the world. The occupants of the white boat beside me were Tom and Laurie Shade from the State of Washington. Tom was a veteran of the U.S. Navy who, during his Navy career, became an expert in electronics. He was married to Laurie, and they took an assignment in Saudi Arabia to raise money to purchase a sailboat. After three and a half years, they went to Hong Kong, purchased a boat which they named THE SHADY LADY, and started sailing. They sailed the Pacific from Hong Kong to the Philippines, Hawaii, Washington State, Alaska and then back to many of the Pacific Islands until they finally ended in Australia, where they started their trip around the world.

They invited me for dinner aboard their boat in the evening and we had a good visit. Then after a couple of days, we headed out to the north to the island of Dar Ah Teras. That was their destination and I decided that I would give it a try and spent ten hours on the engine, which was not the way I liked to travel, but I wanted to stay with my new friends.

There was, of course, a great uncertainty about how things would hold together. The propeller shaft rattled and groaned from time to time as I revved up the engine to make four and five knots. Finally, just before dark that evening, I found them moored at the island and sailed in to anchor nearby. They did not need me, but I needed them. After the months of sailing alone, I took great delight in their company. Laurie was an excellent cook and prepared better meals than I had enjoyed for a long time, and Tom had every kind of snorkeling gear including a spear gun and underwater camera. After Dar Ah Teras Island, we stopped at Tella Allah Kelur. The islands were all unspoiled as if no human had ever set foot on them. Each island was more beautiful than the last and each a snorkeler's paradise. We spent our days in the water and in the evening visited and talked about sailing.

From the last island we would sail to Suakin, Sudan on the mainland of Africa. As I was pulling anchor, I noticed that Tom was racing his dinghy to a point behind CILIN II. He called to tell me that I was drifting onto a coral reef and then pushed CILIN II until I was able to haul the anchor and get the engine running. If not for his help, I would have been in deep trouble.

From our sea charts, it appeared that the entry to Suakin was lined with coral reefs for a distance of four or five miles. It was decided that I should follow very closely behind THE SHADY LADY to make certain that I stayed away from the reefs.

After sailing in the channel for a long time I observed an unbelievable sight up ahead. It was a magnificent city with towers and ancient architecture like something out of Arabian Nights. I had no idea of seeing such grandeur on the African Coast. It was like a dream; but as we drew closer, it appeared there was no activity about the city.

We were to learn later that it was the ancient city of Suakin, which had been ruled over by King Solomon a couple of thousand years before. In 1910, a new port had been built 35 miles to the north. It became the principal port of Sudan. Most of the people abandoned Suakin and moved to Port Sudan, but some remained. Suakin continued to grow from the few that remained into a city of 16,000 in population. It is a phenomenal place with the many people living in a city with no door-to-door mail delivery, no sewer system, no electricity and no city water system. Water is hauled on carts made of two 50-gallon drums welded together on wheels and pulled by donkeys. Taxi service is convenient and economical and consists of flat bed carts pulled by donkeys.

Trade supports the community and life appears to have changed little since the days of King Solomon. The city has simply moved from old Suakin with its magnificent ancient buildings to the south, with old Suakin's magnificent ancient structures being fenced off as a tourist attraction.

We moored in what appeared to be a well-protected area in eight feet of water. I dropped the anchor and felt reassured by letting out ten or 12 feet of chain. It should have been several times that to be secure, but the area seemed well protected.

On the second night, just after dark, Tom called on the VHF radio. "Ed, I think your anchor is dragging."

I checked the G.P.S. and it did not indicate any change of location, so I called back that I thought the anchor was holding.

A little later, he called again, "Ed, you are dragging. You'd better check your anchor."

The wind was picking up and Tom was right. I was drifting toward the other side of the bay. With Tom in his dinghy alongside, I started the engine and was moving back into position. Then Tom took over while I tried desperately to dig a second anchor out of the anchor well. Tom pushed the wrong button and killed the engine as I was tugging at the heavy anchor. Try as we would, we could not restart the engine.

"We're 30 feet from the beach!" Tom called. That meant that we were about to go on the rocks. Tom jumped back into his dinghy and was able to hold the boat off the rocky shore until I finally dropped the second anchor. That stopped our drifting.

All the while the wind was blowing violently. We could move ahead only by taking an anchor in the dinghy 40 or 50 feet ahead, dropping it and then pulling ourselves forward with that rode. Then we took the second anchor and repeated the process several times. Finally, with two anchors out and with a proper amount of scope, we felt she was secure for the night.

We knew that we had been battling the wind and the waves for a long time there in the dark, but we were surprised when Laurie said, "You may not believe it, but I timed you. You have been at it for two hours." The boat was secure and we did not have to move it again until we were ready to depart Suakin several days later.

It became necessary for us to employ an agent for clearing in and later out of the port. It was known among yachters that agents charged more in Port Sudan 35 miles to the north than in Suakin; consequently, many chose to stop in Suakin. In some ports the officials can be difficult in taking an unnecessary amount of time or by making the job of clearing very difficult. This can all be avoided by hiring an agent.

We were fortunate to get a good agent by the name of Mohammed. The company had two agents both by the name of Mohammed. In addition to our agent, there was a 13-year-old boy by the name of Taj who was very helpful. He was very bright and capable. Since we were anchored out from shore, it was always necessary to go ashore in our dinghy. Taj would always be there to help secure the dinghy and guard it while we were absent. He would also accompany us on shopping trips to make sure that we did not pay too much for our various items.

During the time we were in Suakin we had the opportunity to go by bus to Port Sudan on the coast 30 miles to the north. I was particularly interested in purchasing a straw hat. The last one I owned had joined a long list of hats and caps that had left a trail across the seas around the world where I had sailed. A sudden gust of wind or a line raking across your head can quickly put a piece of headgear out of reach.

The bus station was crowded and we found the bus does not run on schedule. It runs when there is a busload of passengers. The route to Port Sudan is along the sea for a long distance and then through desert country where tents of nomad tribes and their camels can be seen in the distance.

Mohammed accompanied us on our trip and explained that members of the various nomad tribes are identified by the kind of clothes they wear, mostly flowing robes. He told of the Rashayda Tribe that migrates two times each year between Suakin and Kassala, a distance of 365 miles, to find good grazing for their camels and goats. Apparently this process has been going on for centuries.

The city of Port Sudan was crowded and busy. I spent most of my time there trying to find a straw hat, but in vain. Though Port Sudan is closer to the equator than Mexico City or even Havana, people just do not wear straw hats to protect themselves from the sun.

We returned to Suakin in the evening to prepare for our departure the next day. Provisioning for the trip was very simple due to the many fruit and vegetable stands near at hand.

On April 16, 1996, we were sailing out of the long, coral-studded channel back to the Red Sea. I knew that we would separate when we reached the end of the channel. THE SHADY LADY headed north along the coast and CILIN II headed east toward the middle of the sea. It was a sad moment for me as we parted. Tom and Laurie had been great travelers. His last gesture was to provide me with a recipe for what he labeled "Shady Lady Pancakes". I had let him know that I like pancakes but that pancake mix had not been available at any of the last ports we had visited. I was happy with the recipe and the three cans of baking soda he provided. From that time on, there was never a shortage of good pancakes on CILIN II.

As THE SHADY LADY disappeared in the distance, I could imagine Tom and Laurie's relief in getting away from the old man in the little white boat who seemed to somehow survive from one calamity to another.

Suakin to Jeddah

THE FIRST NIGHT AT SEA ALONE WAS dismal after leaving THE SHADY LADY and the good company of Tom and Laurie Shade. It was also frustrating as CILIN II jibbed several times in the dark because I was trying to sail too close to the wind in order to make progress toward the north.

Being alone on a long passage can be a very enjoyable experience after you get settled in and occupied with the many problems of navigating, cooking, cleaning and repairing little things that need fixing. The loneliest time of all is the first couple of days out after having been ashore or after having had someone aboard for a period of time.

In this case, the loneliness was short-lived because of the difficulties involved. At about one o'clock in the morning, the wind came up strong and CILIN II sailed north past Sha Anbar Reef. Shortly thereafter the wind died down leaving the boat north of a large area indicated on the sea chart as "un-surveyed reefs and coral heads", making it necessary to sail westward to avoid the danger of being blown into that area in the event there would be another strong blow out of the north.

The second morning out was beautiful. Porpoises came alongside the boat to keep me company. Then I discovered that pilot fish, which I had observed days earlier, were still with me. They are about 16 inches long and look much like a baby shark, but they are harmless. They have what looks like suction cups along the lower side of their body with which they are able to attach themselves to the hull of the boat as it moves through the water.

I first became aware of the pilot fish when I threw a scrap of fish overboard. Three of them darted out from under the boat, devoured the food and then returned to the underside of the boat. I then learned that they would go after a baited hook. That was easy. I caught one with the first attempt but it darted back under the boat. I was unable to reel him in. I thought at first that the line was wrapped around the propeller shaft but then realized that the fish had attached itself to the hull. After some tugging, I was able to pull it free from the boat and pull it into the boat. Then I felt sorry for him and gave him his freedom. After that only two would come out whenever I threw food scraps into the water.

The pilot fish became my friends and stayed with me for a couple of weeks, over a few hundred miles of travel. Then for no reason they were gone. I was alone again.

The fourth day brought on strong winds with a rough sea. At night there were several ships in the area. One seemed to be heading in my direction, which I took to be a ferryboat taking Muslim Pilgrims to Mecca. I quickly called on the VHF radio on channel 16 and got an immediate response.

"Did you just pass Wingate reef?" he asked. I answered that I did not know the name of the reefs. Then he said that he could not see me.

"You're coming straight toward me" I shouted. His lights were looming brighter there in the black of the night. He was getting dangerously close and did not appear to be changing course. In changing my course to avoid being hit, it was necessary that I cross in front of the oncoming boat, but it was a chance I had to take. I was uncertain of the distance between us. After a few breathless seconds, I was away from him and relieved to be out of danger.

After it was over, I considered the possibility that the ship I had been communicating with was not the ship that had come so close to me. There were other ships in the area and I had probably been talking to another one. If it had been the ship that nearly hit me, he could have seen me clearly because he was so very close.

The wind was very light for the next couple of days. Then in the morning of April 21, 1996, the satellite radio came on with a warning of gale force winds from ten o'clock in the morning until eleven at night. I was amused by the report because the sky was clear all day with winds less than ten knots. I was sure that the announcement concerned some other area of the world. Then just before midnight the wind came up very strong out of the north. During the night the wind caused a rip along the edge of the storm jib. When it was calm enough the next morning I exchanged the working jib for the storm jib so I could repair the rip. It was then that I discovered that the sail thread was nowhere to be found. Being in a plastic bag, I had apparently thrown it out with the trash. I looked everywhere and finally ended up mending the sail with dental floss, of which I had a good supply. It worked very well.

The next day I took a nap after dinner. When I awoke a little before midnight, I realized that I had slept too long. CILIN II was in the midst of a shipping lane. That was one thing I had studiously avoided, always keeping in mind the admonition of the great Trestan Jones when he said, "If you can see another ship, you are too close."

There were several ships to be seen. Two in the distance off the starboard bow attracted my attention. An instrument which I used to tell the direction a ship was traveling at night was out of order. With it I could tell in a few seconds whether a ship was moving to the right or left. If the reading on the instrument told me the ship was going neither to the right or left, look out! It meant that the ship was approaching or going away from CILIN II. In that case it was necessary to watch the ship for a long time in case it was coming toward me.

I had been intently absorbed in watching those two ships when I turned to step into the cabin. Then out of the corner of my eye, I caught a sight high above me that shocked my entire system. I could not believe what I saw. It was the fantail of a very large ship high above me. I hardly had time to react when there was a crash, with CILIN II lurching wildly.

I grabbed the radio microphone. "Sailboat to ship! Sailboat to ship!" I called.

An answer came back quickly. "Sailboat, your lights were so dim that I could not see you until I was upon you. I had to divert my course to avoid hitting you."

"I was hit by something. There was a heavy crash," I insisted.

"No, I did not hit you," he replied.

Then I realized the jolt CILIN II received had come from the wave made by the ship when it diverted its course to avoid hitting me. I was so shaken that I could think of nothing to say except what I usually said when contacting a ship far at sea. "Can you give me any weather information?" I asked.

"Stand by on channel 16," he requested. I waited and waited until finally a crackling sound came on channel 16, but he had moved so far out of my range that I could not understand his message. I was unable to get the identity of the vessel or to thank the captain for avoiding what could have been a disastrous collision.

The weather continued rough and during the night the mainsail and the working jib suffered rips. I needed a sail mender badly. Fortunately, I had a spare mainsail aboard. So I installed it when the weather was calm enough to be on deck. Mending the sail with dental floss was tedious work but it worked satisfactorily.

In the afternoon of the next day I heard a persistent thumping against the hull. I had heard it one time before and found that the plow anchor had slipped off the bow with a couple of feet of chain attached and was beating against the hull. Upon examination I found the anchors securely stored in the anchor well.

At last it became apparent that the thumping was coming from the stern. There to my surprise I found that one of the two propane gas tanks had been knocked off from its platform and was dangling from a U-bolt and beating against the side of the boat with each wave that hit the boat. It contained the reserve supply of gas for cooking. Fortunately I was able to rescue it from the sea and restore it to its mount.

With a couple of sails ripped, a propeller shaft threatening to go out at any time and lights so dim as to not be visible to ships, it became apparent to me that I should get off the sea for some repairs at the first opportunity.

I did not want to go back to Port Sudan because of the coral reefs and because I would be moving farther south instead of north. The next best option appeared to be the port at Jeddah, Saudi Arabia. I had been warned against going there and understood that only yachts in distress were permitted to stop there. I felt that I was in distress and needed to make the stop.

In the evening of April 26, 1996 I positioned CILIN II about 30 miles northwest of Jeddah, planning to approach the harbor and pass through the triple lines of coral reefs at noon the next day when the light would be most favorable for seeing the reefs. The wind had carried me at five knots all afternoon and I estimated approaching the harbor at that speed. At 8:00 a.m. the wind had dropped off until our speed was slightly over three knots. The course was straight at 90°, but because of my reduced speed, it was 2:00 p.m. before I reached the reefs. Nevertheless, I was able to see the three rows of coral reefs clearly as I passed them by.

I was somewhat apprehensive about entering the Jeddah Harbor. It just happened to be the time of the four-day Hajj pilgrimage to Mecca for people of the Muslim faith all over the world. It was estimated that a million people would be arriving by plane and by ships. Efforts to call port control on the VHF radio 15 miles out were unrewarding. Finally a voice came on, telling me that my signal was garbled and that I should try again when I was closer in.

As I drew closer in, I could see a very tall tower with a huge dome at the top, unlike anything I had ever seen. I was to learn later that it was a place used, in addition to other things, for receptions for dignitaries. Transport ships were parked along the road to the west of the port for as far as the eye could see.

I called the port control again to tell him of my problems with the mast light, the torn sails and the propeller shaft bearing. Without hesitation, he authorized CILIN II to enter the port.

It was a good feeling, as I drew near to the tall dome, to see two large arrows, one red and one green. That was the gateway to the harbor. CILIN II was in the right position.

"CILIN II, where are you?" the controller inquired. I replied that I was at the gateway near the marker.

"I do not see you," he said. Then he suggested that I might be somewhere else. That was confusing and disturbing. Was I lost in the big harbor?

Repeatedly he asked for my position and I repeated over and over that I was at the gateway. I did not know what else to say. There were these two big arrows that told me I was in the right place.

Later when I was safely on shore I had the opportunity to talk to that same controller, he said that his office was used to looking for big ships and that he could not see the little 30-foot CILIN II.

At last the controller told me that a pilot boat would lead me to my mooring. Soon a pilot boat did appear and lead me around to the port side behind the tall domed tower that I had seen from far at sea. CILIN II was moored beside a wide cement pier, which turned out to be an area where pilot boats waited for a message to escort a ship into or out of the big Jeddah harbor.

It was a good feeling being at rest where the water was calm after a hectic 12 days at sea since leaving THE SHADY LADY and the peaceful village of Suakin, but there was no rest. First one automobile would drive up on the pier alongside CILIN II, then another, with an officer from immigration, port police or customs. Some wore uniforms and others were in civilian clothes, all with the usual questions. Where had I been? Where was I going? Did I have any pets or firearms aboard? But there was one question I had never been asked before, "Do you have any magazines aboard?" The answer was negative, but apparently foreign magazines are taboo in Saudi Arabia because they contain uncensored materials.

The officers never introduced or identified themselves. They were businesslike and a bit abrupt but never rude. One took my passport, but I had no idea which office he represented.

I was told that there was no place on the pier to get food, but I assured the officer that I had an adequate supply on board. I was also told that I could get drinking water and take a fresh water shower at the Coast Guard Headquarters 100 yards across the cement pier.

Then one of the officials pointed to a sleepy-eyed guard at the end of the pier hugging his automatic rifle and said, "He will tell you when you can leave the port."

I sensed that if I tried to talk to the guard he would not understand a word I said, and if he could understand, his answer was certain to be "no" to whatever I asked him. We got along well. I never asked any questions and he never spoke to me.

What I wanted more than anything else was to get some rest and sleep. I did not cross over to the Coast Guard building that first day.

I slept until just about dusk, and then I climbed off the boat onto the quay.

The pilot boats raced in and out of the harbor throughout the evening while boat crews stood by their boats or mingled with other crewmembers. Several of the crewmembers stopped by to visit and ask questions. They represented a number of nationalities including Pakistan, the Philippines, Bangladesh and India. Almost everyone I talked to expressed a burning desire to come to America. They were captains, pilots, electronic technicians and mechanics. Some were retirees from naval services in their respective countries and many displayed credentials to show that they had completed technical schools. The problem the crewmembers had was that they wanted a better life than they were getting. Some reported that they were receiving a salary of $200 per month. They were housed in barracks where they ate, slept and showered. No TV or other entertainment was provided. Most of them smoked cigarettes but none ever asked for one. What they did ask for was magazines. I wondered if they wanted to read or look at the pictures but since few of them could read English, I assumed that their interest was in girlie pictures in magazines, which are censored by the Saudis.

One after another they approached me, pleading for assistance. Some saw no reason I could not take them along on my boat to America. One fellow, tall and thin with dark circles under his eyes, looked across the quay and said, "I'm not supposed to be talking to you. They are watching me. They have all of the latest equipment and they keep watching." He told me that the Coast Guard was also the secret police.

"It is all the same." He said. "I don't know why they have to be so mean."

My first thought was that the fellow must be mentally deranged. Why would he be talking to me if he knew they were watching him? I never knew the answer and he never came by the boat again.

At other times, when one or two crewmembers were visiting, a pick-up truck or jeep driver would speak to them. They would then walk away without saying anything. It seemed strange that at other times three or four crewmembers would visit with me at length without being interrupted.

On the second day, I crossed the quay to the Coast Guard building for some cold drinking water and a shower. The officers and men I saw did not look or act mean. They were informal and very friendly. One officer wore three oversized stars on each shoulder of his uniform that would do any Lieutenant General in the U.S. Army proud. Upon inquiry, I learned that he was the lieutenant in charge.

I observed camaraderie and fraternization between the officers and men, which is not common in the U.S. military. On one occasion the lieutenant in charge grabbed the cap from the head of one of the men and placed it on the head of another man. He then repeated that with other men and everyone seemed to enjoy the horseplay.

I was taken back a little when I observed the greeting extended to visiting officers. The men would render a snappy salute but the officer in charge would kiss the visitor on the left cheek and twice on the right cheek. It looked as if he smacked his lips between the two kisses on the right cheek, as if it tasted good.

On the second floor I found the toilets and a shower in a filthy, stinking room. One toilet was conventional like in the U.S. but no paper was available. Instead, a water hose provided water for washing. The other two toilets were mere holes in the floor with the image of large footprints on either side like some we had previously observed in Greece and Turkey. Again a water hose took the place of toilet paper.

The bathroom was about 20 feet square with a door on each toilet and a door for the shower. In American military facilities I had experienced, most of the showers were open with no doors for privacy while showering. I thought nothing of leaving the door opened as the low-pressure water of the shower trickled over my body. That is, I thought nothing of it until a member of the Coast Guard entered the door. When his eyes caught sight of my nude body, he screamed a scream that could have been heard back at my boat across the quay. "CRMTZ! GRMTZ!" he shouted. With his eyes ablaze, he ran over to slam the door violently. The latch did not catch the first time, so he slammed it again.

The sight of my nude body surely terrorized him. I took a long time in the shower until I felt certain that my assailant had departed. From that time on, I kept the shower door firmly closed when I took my shower.

That evening the lieutenant invited me to join the Coast Guard members for their social hour. The affair took place on the second floor of the Coast Guard's building near a large open window where I could look out across the quay to see CILIN II peacefully at rest at the pier.

Before finding a place to sit with the men on a large carpet, each person removed his sandals or shoes. A teapot was kept hot over a little burner and everyone sipped tea as we visited. The lieutenant provided an interpreter and asked me to tell something about my sailing experiences. Few of the two dozen men could understand or speak English.

They listened attentively and were duly impressed when they learned that their guest was a retired U.S. Air Force Colonel. As I looked over my audience, I wondered which one of these nice fellows had slammed the shower door in my face. I also wondered how these people could be as cruel as my hollow-eyed visitor to the boat had described them the evening earlier.

After my little talk and refreshing of their teacups, the lieutenant prepared for a little game they would play. He tore small pieces of paper, wrote a number on each one, then wadded each one into a little ball and put them into a pile. Each member drew a little wad of paper to see if he got the lucky number, which was announced by the lieutenant. The winner showed great delight even though there was no prize or no reward. The prize seemed to be in the glory of getting the lucky number. I had not been invited to participate in the game and was glad because I knew I would have had a hard time expressing my joy, had I drawn the lucky number.

I sat through several games until everyone retired to the TV room. I thought it would be hard to visualize a group of American Coast Guard officers and men sipping tea and enjoying the camaraderie those fellows enjoyed. For me it was an evening of hospitality, but back at the boat I was perplexed, trying to reconcile the idea that those fellows could be mean policemen. I had met only one mean one, and that was only for a brief moment in the shower.

Different officials continued coming by the boat on the third day. One introduced himself as Captain Mohammad A Al-Tweijri and was particularly friendly. He told me to come by his office on the second floor of the building next to the Coast Guard building if I needed anything. The lieutenant had previously told me the same thing when

269

he said, "If you need anything, tell me or one of my officers and they will bring it for you."

Later I decided to make a call on Captain Mohammad A Al-Twierjri. I found him in a large L-shaped office from which I could see the channel to the west where I had sailed into the port. In the other direction was the skyline of the city of Jeddah, three miles across the big harbor.

It turned out that Muhammad A. Al-Tweijri was the Marine Department Director. He was an affable, easy-going person with an open door policy to his office. "Come in any time," he said. "If the door is closed, come in through my secretary's office. At that moment there were half a dozen men in civilian clothes making themselves comfortable on the plush furniture of the office.

I discussed my problems with CILIN II with the Captain. He suggested that I should employ a shipping agent to handle my affairs. He also suggested that it would not be a good idea to try to have the propeller shaft bearing repaired in Jeddah. They were not prepared for or interested in doing repair and maintenance for foreign yachts. He told me that one couple on a yacht spent three months and $10,000 getting repairs for their sailboat. That left me with only the mast, light, and sails to be repaired.

Then the Captain changed his mind about my needing an agent. He decided that I could get along without one. The real surprise came when the Captain changed his mind again. He requested the Arabian Establishment for Trade and Shipping Agency to represent me, and he graciously let me know that there would be no charge for their services. I later learned that the AET was owned by Captain H.R.H. Prince Abdullah Al Faisal Al Saud, and a more prosperous agency was not to be found. It is the largest and most prestigious shipping agency in Saudi Arabia. Having a prince as owner was no detriment to the agency. It was really more than an agency. It was a conglomerate with a modern container repair and storage depot. It is also an agency for several aircraft companies and Lloyds of London Insurance Company. That is not to mention that upon Captain Muhammad A. Al-Tweirjri's request they were also the shipping agents for CILIN II. I felt that I was in good hands.

Jeddah to Hurghada

WHILE PERUSING THE SEA CHART OF THE navigators in Jeddah, I came to realize than on the next leg of my sailing journey I would cross the 35th meridian. That would be the moment when CILIN II circumnavigated the globe. That was the meridian passing through Tel Aviv, which I crossed June 8, 1987. There would be no friends or relatives to greet. I would be alone at sea as I had been for most of the past 35,000 miles.

I would sail on to Hurghada on the eastern coast of Egypt; pass through the Suez Canal into the Mediterranean Sea and then what next? At that point, I had no future plans. In the past I had been so excited about the peace plan of Yitzhak Rabin that I had dreamed I would like to sail back to Tel Aviv to see if I could possibly get to meet him and congratulate him. I was of the impression he had come closer to bringing peace to the Middle East between the Israelis and Palestinians than anyone in history. But tragically, his plan had fallen apart when he was struck dead at the hands of a Jewish student. I had carried a newspaper clipping of his death in the Bible aboard the boat since that time.

Other than that failed mission, I had no future plans about what to do with my boat. It had done what I wanted it to do and it could not have served me better. One option which had crossed my mind was to sail CILIN II back across the Mediterranean, the Atlantic, into the Gulf of Mexico and up the Mississippi and Ohio Rivers to put her on display in the museum in my hometown in Hayden, Indiana. There I would have it to remind me of some of the happiest and hectic days of my life.

I had even joked with some of my sailor friends along the way that upon reaching the Mediterranean Sea I would take her to the middle, scuttle her and send her to the bottom to rest for eternity. She deserved that kind of rest after the treatment she had suffered at the hands of this novice seaman. But that was not to be. Her ultimate fate was worse than I could have imagined on that peaceful day in May of 1996 when I sailed out of the Jeddah harbor.

The bearing on the drive shaft growled angrily when the engine was engaged as I prepared to motor out of the Jeddah harbor to the sea channel. The sun was bright, and with a brisk wind out of the northwest, it appeared to be ideal for sailing west along the channel. I cut the engine and upped the sails, but soon learned it was necessary to go back on the engine to stay in the channel. But when I fired up the engine, it balked and refused to run.

I called the port controller to report my problem. "You have permission to return to port," he volunteered. I thought for a moment. I did not want to go back to the confinement the Saudis had imposed upon me. They had been courteous and helpful at every turn. I had no idea what to expect when I first sailed into Jeddah harbor 14 days before. I could not have expected any better treatment but I had no freedom.

I called to the controller, "Everything will be all right," and sailed on, knowing I would not have an engine for the approach to Hurghada.

CILIN II stayed on a heading of 260° for ten miles and then 30° to get past shipping traffic traveling in different directions, approaching and departing Jeddah. As darkness descended over the sea, the lights of the city brightly illuminated the eastern sky. Due to heavy traffic, I was unable to sleep during the night.

The Atoms and Autohelp self-steering devices were both non-functional, so it became necessary to fall back on the elastic cord tied across the cockpit with a loop over the tiller. It had served well on the Indian Ocean and had worked well as a last resort, freeing me from the tiller for long periods of time.

On the sixth day out I tried to start the engine again, thinking that what it needed was a good rest, but the blue light came on, telling me there was inadequate oil pressure. That made certain I would have to approach Hurghada without an engine to guide me through the coral reefs.

The wind was very contrary from 6:00 a.m. to 9:00 a.m. Swells caused the sails to flap back and forth and there was very little to do about that. It was very annoying. At 9:00 a.m. the wind came up, making it possible to make five knots on a heading of 320°. That was very welcome, considering I had traveled only ten miles the day before.

Diary entries were as bleak as the weather.

Seventh day – no sun. Sprinkle of rain, first for months. Heading mostly 270°, need 300°.

Twelfth day – saw no ships. Bright sun. Light north wind all day. Very peaceful. Dark clouds across the sky at 9:00 a.m. brought good wind. Set sails for 300° and slept. By 2:45 a.m. wind was dead. Had moved 12 miles.

Thirteenth day – May have broken bone in left foot. Swollen and sore.

Fourteenth day – reached 27° north and 35° and 43° east on westward heading. Was 13 miles south at 2:45 on Sunday morning. Took new heading and gained back lost ground by 7:45 p.m.

Fifteenth day – Sun is beautiful and bright. A new day, a new beginning. Short wave radio fell on deck and broke, leaving me with no radio for world news. Working jib ripped eight inches at bottom. Attempted to patch it with two-part epoxy. Left foot is feeling better.

Seventeenth day – Radioed Hank Williams in Dallas on satellite radio asking him to radio Hurghada, Egypt for a dinghy to guide me into port past the coral reefs.

Hank Williams reported that a Captain Sobby was listed in the Red Sea Cruising Guide for boating services. He would call him. That was good news. Then Hank radioed back that he got no response from Captain Sobby. He then radioed Fantasia Shipping Agency. Hisham Ahmed, the manager of Fantasia, volunteered that he would take the job and he would do it cheaper than the Egyptian Navy.

Twenty-first day – Able to make VHF radio contact with Fantasia manager, Hisham Ahmed and reported my position as ten miles east of Careless Reef. He told me he would soon be on the way.

I waited four hours. When there was no sign of a boat, I called Fantasia again. This time Hisham reported that the sea was too rough, that no boats could come out. (The sea was not rough. I knew it. I was there.) Then he promised that a boat would meet me at four o'clock the following morning. I asked him what I was supposed to do in the meantime. His answer was simple. "Just throw out an anchor."

When I asked how he expected me to anchor in 400 feet of water, there was no reply. The VHF radio clicked off.

I hove to and slept. It was still dark when I awoke, but I was startled to see that I had drifted into the shipping lane. Ships were everywhere as they poured out of the Gulf of Suez into the Red Sea. At first I was uncertain which way I should go to avoid a collision. I headed back toward Careless Reef. Had I not awakened when I did, there could have been a disaster.

As I neared Careless Reef, there was no boat to be seen coming from the direction of Hurghada at four o'clock in the morning. Efforts to arouse anyone on the radio at Fantasia were fruitless until nearly nine o'clock in the morning. Then the Fantasia Shipping Agency reported that it had been unable to get a vessel to come out to meet me. They would find one and come for me soon.

Weeks later I was much embarrassed to learn how easy it would have been for me to sail into the port at Hurghada, even though the engine was not working. My failure to try it was a mind-set that I could appear near Careless Reef and a boat would lead me in.

I had been told that a boat was on the way and I foolishly waited for it. Also I was intimidated by the very heavy storms I had previously endured in the Red Sea. Lastly, I was a victim of poor judgment resulting from those long, lonely days and nights at sea.

It was during this time, while I was floundering around near Careless Reef, that I crossed the 35th Meridian. I, a sailor who had endured untold hardships and survived in the oceans around the world, was waiting for a boat to tow me into harbor because I had a dead engine and was unfamiliar with the area. I would have been embarrassed except for my frustration. What had seemed a simple operation had become quite complicated.

At one time I saw a boat in the distance that I thought was the Fantasia boat coming my way, but it continued on a course away from me. It was about 3:00 p.m. when I sighted a boat which I thought was surely the Fantasia boat. As it drew closer, I observed that there were 10 to 12 people on deck enjoying themselves as if on a holiday. It turned out that they were friends and relatives enjoying a boat ride on the Fantasia boat.

As the boat drew near, we had trouble getting the towline on to CILIN II. The Captain, obviously not an experienced seaman, drew too close to CILIN II, crashing into and damaging the bowsprit. Someone I took to be the boat owner called out, "We can fix that back at the shop." It was bent badly out of shape. When the line was finally secured, we headed toward land, but very quickly the line snapped. Then we substituted a line from CILIN II.

If the boat had arrived when he first promised, I could have sailed into Hurghada, following him in. During the delay for more than 24 hours I had drifted far to the south and had to be towed in to port. At one point we pulled in to shore on a small island because of some mechanical problem on his boat. At that time Hisham Ahmed, the Fantasia manager, boarded CILIN II and rode the rest of the way in to port with me.

Hisham was so very polite, calling me Captain in a tone that you would expect to see honey dripping from his lips. We had a good visit and arrived at Hurghada at 6:30 p.m. Representatives from Fantasia Shipping Agency took my passport and crew list in order to take care of the formalities of clearing in. I was glad when the boat was tied up. Everybody was gone so I could rest from the ordeal of the past 25 days.

I had hardly closed my eyes when there was a knock on the hull. It was Hisham Ahmed. He came aboard. "About how much did you expect you would have to pay to be towed in?" he asked.

"Oh, I would not be surprised at anything," I replied, as my mind went back to the experience in the Greek Islands.

I was wrong. I was shocked when he said, "They want $3,500." I could not believe it.

"Thirty-five hundred dollars!" I repeated. "That is ridiculous." He did not think it was ridiculous. He was serious. He had a receipt book ready to sign. It appeared that he had come to collect the money even before I had gotten settled in. He had a paper that he insisted that I sign. I refused and that infuriated him. Our relations were never the same after that until the time I departed Hurghada more than two months later. I was no longer the "dear captain". I was made to feel like a deadbeat, a fellow who would not pay his bills. I prevailed upon him to go back to his boss and come back with a more reasonable figure.

The Fantasia office was about one city block from the dock. On the left side of the street was a thriving boat yard, where dozens of big deep-sea diving boats were under construction. Numerous derelict dive boats were strewn along the shore. It was a junky looking layout, but the boats in the yard were adequate for the ever-growing charter boat business for deep-sea divers.

On the right side of the street stood a white, conical structure about 40 feet tall with many small holes from top to bottom. I learned it was the pigeon house at the summer home of former Egyptian King Farouk. Remains of the nearby residence had been converted into quarters for Egyptian soldiers.

The waiting room at the Fantasia Shipping Agency headquarters was spacious, with the usual divan and chairs. Adjacent to the waiting room was the well-appointed office of Samir Hares, the apparent boss of the Fantasia operation. He had the demeanor of a cunning weasel and his accomplice, Hisham Ahmed, resembled the late John Dillinger, a world-renowned bank robber.

Hisham talked to his boss and informed me that he had agreed to reduce his charge for towing me to $2,700. This was all a part of sailing the seas that I could never have imagined when I first started cruising. There was no one to talk to about it, no place to turn. Our negotiations went on for several days, with Hisham becoming more irascible each time I talked to him. I finally agreed to pay $2100 to get the matter settled, but even after I paid the $2100, Hisham continued his hostility toward me. He was my agent to whom I would be paying a fee in addition to the towing fee.

LIFE IN HURGHADA

ON THE BRIGHTER SIDE, I FOUND MYSELF moored at the dock alongside two French yachts, one a monohull and the other a catamaran. Passengers on the two boats were 15 French school children, ranging in ages from 13 to 17 years. They were finishing a nine month tour of the Mediterranean Sea, learning all about sailing, including navigation, meteorology, cooking, repairing and trimming of sails, writing and underwater photography. Each boat had two adults, a man and a woman, as counselors to provide instructions and maintain discipline. On their trip they had visited many ports in the Mediterranean where they met with children of their age groups to exchange information about their various cultures.

Since they were nearing the end of their cruise, the young people were busy writing a report of their various experiences to be embellished with photographs they had accumulated.

The children were friendly and courteous, but few of them spoke English. Those who did acted as interpreters. When I returned to CILIN II, overburdened with provisions, they were quick to assist me in transferring supplies from the dock to my boat.

I was invited for dinner on each of the boats, first on the monohull and a few nights later on the catamaran. There I learned that from the beginning, each child had the responsibility of preparing a meal. I was glad that I had met them at the end of their tour, as I wondered what kind of a meal a 13 year old who had never been in a kitchen before would prepare on his first attempt. Now after nine months at sea, each child performed his responsibility as competently as an adult.

On the night before they sailed away I hosted a party with cookies and ice cream, which was well received by all. The day before their departure, they all came aboard CILIN II for a group picture, which they assured me would be included in their yearbook.

Needless to say, the dock was a lonesome place for a few days after their departure, but as some boats sail away, others come along to take their place, bringing new and interesting friends.

I learned of a place three miles down the coast where I could anchor to get away from the dirt and noise of Old Harbor. With a brisk wind I made the trip very quickly to anchor in 18 feet of clear, clean water. I soon discovered I was anchored near a new Marriott Hotel. The next day I paddled the dinghy to the hotel dock and introduced myself to the manager, an American by the name of Peter Giacomini. I told him where I was anchored and a bit about my travels.

"Please feel free to use our swimming pool while you are here," he offered. That opened a whole new world for me. Each afternoon found me basking in the sun at the pool of the luxurious Marriott Hotel, along with people who were spending lots of dollars to enjoy the Egyptian sun, watching the entertainment provided for the tourists, enjoying sandwiches and refreshments from the pool bar and, best of all, taking a freshwater shower daily. Otherwise I would have been bathing in salt water.

In addition to the benefits of the hotel, Mr. Giacomini's secretary, Farida Faud, a widow lady from Sudan, assisted me in a variety of ways including:

- Shopping for a cartouche for each of my four daughters;
- Locating a dentist who removed two crowns from my molar teeth and replaced one;
- Introducing me to a doctor to examine a blemish on my hand, which I feared might be melanoma. At Farida's suggestion, he made no charge for the professional visit.
- Obtained a release of a G.P.S. from the customs office in Cairo. Hank Williams had forwarded it by Federal Express and I had been notified that it had been delivered to Cairo

in four days, but it had not reached Hurghada. The Federal Express agent in Hurghada, being a friend of Farida, told her that the Cairo Customs had received the shipment and notified the Fantasia Shipping Agency to send a document establishing that it was a bona fide shipping agent. Hisham Ahmed, the manager, had let the request lay in his files for nine days when Mrs. Farida Faud arrived at the Fantasia office with two six shooters ablaze. I could not understand a word she was saying, but was sure it was emphatic. I could not but feel sorry for the scoundrel, Hisham Ahmed, for the barrage she unloaded on him.

She told me later that at first he said the accountant was not there that day and he did not know the whereabouts of the document that was sent from customs in Cairo. She then said, "You are the manager here and you do not know what is going on?"

Finally Hisham wilted under the pressure of her haranguing, walked across the room to a file cabinet, picked up the document and faxed it to customs in Cairo. The G.P.S. was on its way from Cairo to me the following day.

Hank Williams, on the other end of the line, was harassing Federal Express for failure to deliver the G.P.S. to the point that they refunded my $68 shipping cost and awarded me a check for $200 for damages. Knowing that the delivery of the G.P.S. was not the fault of Federal Express, I promptly returned the $200 to them.

For days I looked for a diesel mechanic to find why the Volvo engine had no oil pressure. At last I was directed to the top mechanic at the boatyard near the Fantasia Shipping Agency. I felt good about having the top mechanic on the job. He came aboard, turned the flywheel a few times by hand and then concluded that there was no compression in the cylinder. He suggested that the engine would have to be taken out of the boat and to a machine shop, parts would have to be ordered from Sweden and I could be tied up for two or three months. To me that was the worst of all worlds. Hurghada was a very fine place, but the idea of being tied up two or three months was too much.

I took the trouble to check with a couple of other mechanics. When I told them what the top mechanic at the boatyard had said, their response was, "Nonsense". I was able to find a Dutch sea captain who took the engine apart and then reassembled it so that it ran fine. The help given by fellow sailors with no thought of compensation was heartwarming and, of course, deeply appreciated.

With the engine operating smoothly, I said goodbye to the luxury of the Marriott Hotel and the friendly assistance provided by Farida Faud and motored back to the Old Harbor in preparation to set sail for the Suez Canal.

CLEARING OUT

ON AUGUST 6, 1996, CILIN II CLEARED out of Old Harbor at Hurghada, Egypt, on the last leg of the around the world journey. The engine had been repaired, the sails mended and there were adequate provisions to reach the Suez Canal, a distance of about 180 miles. If all went well, I expected to arrive there in about 22 days. The sea was rough and a strong headwind made it necessary to go on the engine from the start. CILIN II was making good progress as we moved north along the Egyptian coast for a couple of hours under a clear sky. My spirits were high because I knew that I was on the last leg of my long journey. Then suddenly the unexpected happened. The engine stopped dead. It happened abruptly with no warning. It refused to restart in spite of my best efforts. I was very discouraged because I thought the engine was in good shape and we would have smooth sailing for the remainder of the trip.

There was only one thing to do. I had to return to Hurghada where I had spent the last couple of months getting the engine repaired and getting ready for the trip. I turned back and raised the sails. It was then that I came to realize how easy it would have been for me to have sailed to Hurghada when I had first approached the place two months earlier, even with a dead engine. Had I made the effort, I could have saved a lot of money and avoided the controversy with the manager of Fantasia

Shipping Company. Now I was embarrassed at the idea of facing them again.

When I finally moored the boat two hours later, back at Old Harbor, I was pleasantly surprised to find the people at Fantasia friendly and helpful. They summoned an engineer for me. He examined the fuel line and filters and determined that the fuel pump needed to be repaired. He would remove it from the boat, take it to his shop and return at 7:00 the next morning.

I learned that if I could depart the port before 8:00 a.m. the next day, it would not be necessary to clear in and clear out again, because I was still within 24 hours of my original departure time.

The next morning I waited impatiently for the mechanic to appear. He did not show up at 7:00 a.m. or even at 8:00 a.m., or 9:00 a.m. I waited nervously, expecting a hostile port official to descend upon me at any moment, demanding that I clear in to the port and pay the usual fees. Finally, the mechanic appeared at a little after 10:00 a.m. with the repaired fuel pump in hand. It was now two hours past my time for departure, but he quickly installed the pump and had me on my way.

The engine ran smoothly, but now the propeller shaft bearing continued to grate and rattle as before. I was able to turn off the engine after a couple of miles and proceed under sail for the remainder of the day, on a heading of 45°.

During the night, while crossing a shipping lane, I observed a ship that appeared to heading in my direction. When he was so close that I was fearful that I could not get out of his way, I called on the VHF radio to ask if he saw me. An operator answered promptly.

"Are you a small fishing boat?" he inquired.

"No, I am a sailboat and you are headed directly toward me," I answered excitedly.

"I'll alter course to port," he stated calmly.

I could see his change of direction and breathed more easily as he passed within 100 yards.

At dawn on the second day out, CILIN II was directly south of the Sinai Peninsula. If the wind had remained as it was the day before, we would have been in a perfect position to travel under sail to Bluff Point, out next destination, but the wind shifted at dawn. It became necessary to take down the sails and proceed on the engine. The noise of the propeller shaft seemed louder, but we proceeded for ten hours on the engine to reach Bluff Point in the late evening.

As I dropped anchor, I saw a sight so unreal that I could not believe it. A flight of hundreds of large birds with very wide wing-spans, like storks or maybe flamingos, flew over. They covered the sky from horizon to horizon in such numbers that for an instant the evening sky darkened a few shades. It seemed a fitting salute to CILIN II for a successful day of travel on the engine.

After a short time, a chartered dive boat full of happy vacationers anchored a couple of hundred yards to the south of CILIN II. It made me feel very much alone and wishing I had someone to talk to other than my temperamental engine. As I prepared my evening meal I was sure they were having something better than spaghetti. As I watched the evening sun sink below the distant horizon, I wondered what excitement tomorrow would bring.

Before pulling anchor at 8:00 a.m. the next morning, I discovered that the rubber hose feeding sea water to the propeller shaft gland had ruptured, leaking water into the bilge so that it was necessary to pump the bilge every five minutes. That was a situation I could not live with. To solve this new problem, I wrapped a small sheet of dinghy patching material, like tire patch material, around the hose and secured it with hose clamps. I spent the remainder of the day tidying up the boat and resting at the peaceful anchorage.

In the late afternoon I observed a small fishing boat headed in my direction. There were two people aboard, which gave me cause for apprehension. What could be their purpose? As the boat drew closer, I could see that a man was rowing and his passenger was a young boy. He pulled alongside my boat and let me know by sign language that he wanted some food. I gave him a can of beans and a half of a loaf of bread. They both seemed pleased. Then again, by sign language, I asked how far he had to paddle his boat to reach his home. He indicated that it was six kilometers. Then he and the little boy disappeared into the evening setting sun.

The wind came up strong at 8:00 a.m. on the fourth day out of Hurghada. It was against me again, so again it was necessary to run the engine. When I turned the key, the blue light came on, warning that there was no oil pressure. I could not proceed without the engine working properly, but efforts to find the problem were fruitless for a couple of hours. Then miraculously at 10:00 a.m., the blue light went out and the engine started working perfectly.

My next destination was Marsa Zettya. It would be necessary to sail on a heading of 30° until noon and then back across the shipping lane to the western shore of the Gulf of Suez. I was nervous when two ships approached on either side of me in the shipping lane, but they turned out to be at a safe distance.

The wind slowed until I was uncertain whether I could reach the anchorage before dark. CILIN II passed a huge oil well platform and arrived in the vicinity of Marsa Zettya at dusk, but I could not see the harbor. I sailed on until I could make out a basin at an oil terminal. There being no ships present, I sailed in and dropped the anchor, preparing to spend a peaceful night. A short time later I noticed that the wind was picking up. Then I noticed that the anchor was dragging, but fortunately there was a mooring buoy nearby. If I could get a line to it CILIN II would be secure for the night. I moved quickly because the wind was blowing stronger, but I missed my chance. We drifted away from the buoy before I could get a line to it. CILIN II was moving out of the entrance to the basin and on a collision course with a big ship anchored dead ahead of us outside the basin.

Then, to my surprise and delight, the anchor slowed our forward motion and we stopped in the mouth of the basin. I quickly hoisted the mainsail so that if the anchor did not hold I could sail past the ship and out into the gulf. It did not work that way. A strong gust of wind caused a six-foot rip in the sail. There was nothing else to do but lower it.

Fortunately, the wind abated some so that I felt secure for the night unless the wind should come up again or a ship should appear heading into the mouth of the basin. At about 10:00 p.m., I was preparing to settle in for an uneasy night of rest when I discovered that a copper tube that carried sea water to cool the engine had rubbed against the propeller shaft and ruptured, causing water to leak into the bilge. Water was coming into the bilge faster than I could pump it out with the bilge pump. I would not be able to run the engine until it was repaired. At that point it was necessary to uncouple the copper tube from the engine, cut out the damaged section of about three inches and then re-couple the cut tube by inserting the ends into a rubber hose and clamping them with hose clamps.

Finally, with the job completed, I slept from 1:00 a.m. until dawn. CILIN II had not moved from the point where the anchor had finally taken hold in the entrance to the oil terminal basin. After my breakfast of oatmeal, orange juice and coffee, I pulled anchor, hoisted the spare mainsail and headed out to sea. Again the wind was fierce during the morning but abated somewhat by noon. My new destination was an anchorage at Sheikh Riyan. I sailed all day, but when it became apparent that I could not reach the anchorage before dark, I started the engine. Then to my dismay another problem cropped up. The water hose to the propeller shaft gland, which I had repaired three days earlier, failed. Water was pouring into the bilge until I cut off the engine. At that juncture, I hove to and prepared to spend the night making the repair at my leisure.

A rough sea greeted me the following morning when I set out. The boat had drifted during the night and I found myself dangerously close to a rocky area. There were warnings in the cruising guide of the coral reefs along the shore of the Sinai Peninsula, so I headed out to sea for what seemed a safe distance.

In the six days since I had left Hurghada, CILIN II had traveled only 60 miles. I should have been discouraged at that kind of progress, but instead I felt elated. On the second day out of Hurghada, my trusty craft had left the Red Sea in her wake as she moved into the Gulf of Suez. Another 180 miles and she would reach the Suez Canal leading us back into the Mediterranean Sea.

The Red Sea had been a challenge to my seamanship ability, such as it was. Until the time I had first entered at Bab el Mandeb, I had given little thought to it. I had always considered that it would be an easy run, but the more I read about it and the more I learned about it, I came to realize that it could be very difficult. I was surprised when I learned that it was 1700 miles to the Suez Canal and was more surprised to learn that I would be facing head winds more than two thirds of the way. With all the problems I had faced, I treasured memories of snorkeling, along with THE SHADY LADY; the visit to ancient Suakin once ruled over by King Solomon, the visit to exotic Jeddah and the happy times in Hurghada, Egypt.

The excitement of happenings in the Red Sea crowded out memories of things that had happened so long ago in the Greek Islands, the Atlantic Crossing, Panama, the crossing of the Pacific and the Indian Ocean. The Red Sea had been an ordeal. Now it was in the past, like all of those other wonderful places. I had already passed the 32nd degree east meridian where I had started my sailing journey nine years earlier. I had sailed around the world. At 9:00 a.m., August 16, 1996 we were within five miles of our destination. I could not see Sheikh Riyadh Harbor but thought that I could see the coral reef about a mile off the starboard beam. I thought CILIN II was making good headway as I steered 270° to get farther away from the reef. I had set the coordinates for Sheikh Riyadh Harbor into the G.P.S. and it showed the heading for the harbor to be 360°. Just before I turned to head north I observed a ripple across the water and assumed it to be caused by a gust of wind, but shortly after I turned north there was a terrifying, crunching sound that I knew so well. The keel of the boat was scraping on rocks and coral! Instead of trying to alter course or throw out the anchor to stop forward motion, I sailed on, thinking I would pass over the coral and rocks. It was a fatal error though I did not realize it at the time. Instead of passing over the reef, I was getting deeper into it.

Finally the keel wedged between two boulders and CILIN II came to a rumbling, shuddering halt. Water was racing across the coral. I did the only thing I knew to do. I went overboard to see if I could possibly move the boat, but the current was so strong that I had to grab the gunwale to keep from being washed away. I pulled myself back into the boat and sat for a while, pondering the situation. At no time did I consider that the situation was hopeless. I had run aground before and had gotten out of many difficult situations. I felt that I could somehow get the boat afloat again.

A little after noon, I realized that I was not going to get CILIN II afloat without help, so I called for assistance on the VHF radio. There was no response for a long time. Then came an answer, but it was so garbled that I could not understand. I told the speaker that I could not understand. He may have become disgusted with me because there was no further response. Finally, at 2:00 p.m. came another response from someone who said that he would help me. He said that he would send a boat. Later, a helicopter passed over, obviously to evaluate my situation.

It was late in the evening when a small boat showed up in the distance. I assumed that it was a fishing boat but could not see it because of the darkness. They offered to take me off my boat but I refused. Then they said they would send a larger boat. I waited and waited but heard nothing further from them.

By this time I was becoming very discouraged. I was well aware that I could not get the boat moving without help, and help did not seem to be available. I sat for a long time looking out across the sea and wondering what to do next. With nothing more important to do, I prepared a meal and tried to sleep. The night was not restful because the boat sat at such an angle that I could only lay wedged between the bunk and the bulkhead.

My VHF radio, with a range of only 18 miles, got no response the next day until 4:00 p.m. when a radio message from a ship identified as MALDIVES V reported that it

was on the way. It did not arrive until after dark. It then withdrew and announced that they had good news. GULF FLEET 33, a ship with professional deep-sea divers that serviced the oil well platforms, was on its way to help me and would arrive at 2:00 a.m., the time for high tide in the area. The ship arrived but the captain reported that it was too dark to attempt a rescue and that he would return at dawn.

As dawn broke the next morning, I saw GULF FLEET 33 approaching, but it stood off several hundred yards. Then I saw a very large inflatable dinghy with five Egyptian divers approaching me. They examined CILIN II and determined that she was so deep into the coral reef that they could not move her. They then asked me to accompany them back to their ship for a conference with the Captain.

For security reasons, I gathered everything that I could store in a duffle bag, including such navigational instruments as were detachable, and boarded the dinghy for the ride to GULF FLEET 33. I had expected that we would be discussing means of getting CILIN II afloat again, but was bewildered when the Captain, after consulting with members of the dive team, announced that CILIN II could not be saved. He explained that she was too far into the reef. Their lines were not long enough to reach her and if they could, she would be destroyed by any effort to pull her through the coral reef. I was bewildered, but finally came to realize that CILIN II was gone. My journey had ended.

The Captain provided me with dry clothing and a cup of hot coffee before I climbed to the top deck of GULF FLEET 33 to see my boat as we sailed away. Soon she was just a tiny speck on the distant horizon.

My boat, which had carried me completely around the world, my boat, on which I had spent the better part of the past ten years, my boat, which had provided me with more joy and frustrations than a person would expect in a lifetime.

She had protected me through many fierce storms at sea.

She was the vehicle by which I realized my dream.

She carried me safely over 30,000 miles of ocean.

She introduced me to new people, new places, and new ideas.

She carried me through an unreal world of hallucinations and finally delivered me to a safe haven.

Slowly the reality began to sink in. She was gone and I would never see her again. In my sadness I recalled an ancient Buddhist saying:

"All things come to pass

Nothing comes to stay."

On shore at Ras Shukhein, Egypt, I was escorted to the customs office where stern-faced Egyptian officials cleared me in. The clearance form read as follows:

CLEARING OF SHIPS OR YACHTS

Name of Vessel	CILIN II
Last port	Hurghada, Egypt
Next port	Hayden, Indiana
Nationality	American
Gross weight	8 tons
Net weight	7 tons
Length	30 feet
Depth	4 ½ feet
Type of engine	Volvo Diesel
Total HP	24
Crew	Edgar D. Whitcomb
Passport	U.S.A. No. 022 184 669

It was not a clearing paper. It was an epitaph to a lady. She would never sail again. I had navigated her on an uncertain odyssey around the world. At 78 years of age, I was clearing out of a world of fantastic adventures that I could never have imagined. There remained nothing to do but take a bus for a 180-mile ride to Cairo. From there a plane would deliver me to my Indiana home.

Good-bye CILIN II

On an ancient wall in China where a brooding Buddha blinks
Deeply graven is this message, "It is later than you think".
The clock of life is wound but once and no man has the power
To tell just when the hands will stop, at late or early hour.
Now is all the time you own, the past a golden link.
Go cruising now, my brother. It is later than you think.

(Author unknown)

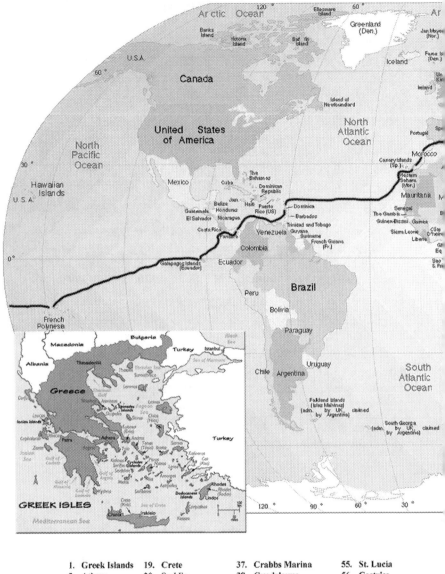

1. Greek Islands	19. Crete	37. Crabbs Marina	55. St. Lucia
2. Athens	20. Sesklia	38. Guadeloupe	56. Castries
3. Delphi	21. Navpaktos	39. Deshaies	57. Granada
4. Rhodes	22. Illini	40. Isles Des Saintes	58. St. Georges
5. Turkey	23. Catania	41. Terre de Haut	59. Los Testigos
6. Marmaris	24. Malta	42. Bassa Terre	60. Isla Margarita
7. Lindos	25. Cape Passero	43. Deep Bay	61. Pampatar
8. Panormitis	26. Gozo Malta	44. Gustarea Bay	62. Isla Cubagua
9. Symi (Simi)	27. Barcelona	45. French St. Barts	63. Puerta La Cruz
10. Kemur	28. Port Empedocles	46. St. Maarten	64. Tortuga
11. Cyprus	29. Costa de Sol	47. Great Bay Philipburg	65. Conte de Mar
12. Antalya	30. Cartagena	48. St. Eustatius	66. Venezuela
13. Izmer	31. Marbella	49. St. Kitts	67. Caracas
14. Ephesus	32. Gibraltar	50. Isle of Souls	68. Carabelle
15. Paphos	33. Gran Canaria	51. Riviere Sans Marina	69. Puerta Calera
16. Lanarca	34. Fuerteventura	52. Dominica	70. Bonaire
17. Tel Aviv	35. Mogan Marina	53. Scotts Head	71. Curacao
18. Bethlehem	36. Antigua	54. Anse Mitan	72. Sarafundy Marina

Circumnavigation Route 1

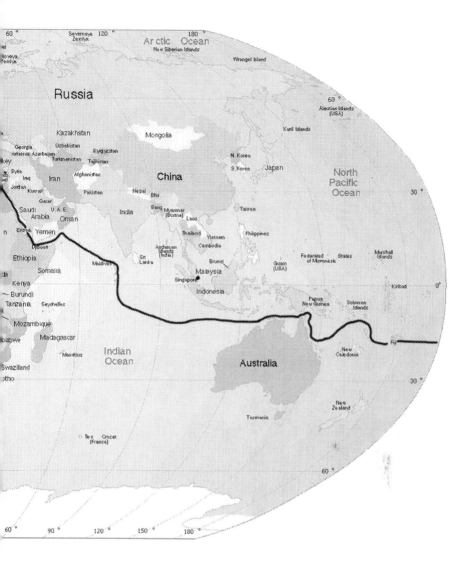

Circumnavigation Route 2

About the Author

Men and women dream of serving their country with distinction, living a life of adventure and facing danger with courage. Few accomplish so much as Edgar Whitcomb who escaped from a Japanese prison camp in World War II. Upon his return to Indiana, he became an attorney and later was elected as Indiana's 43rd Governor. In his retirement, after the age of 68, he made a life decision to circumnavigate the globe on a 30 foot sailboat. This is his solo sailing odyssey; a tale of adventure and danger.

Ed settled in the small Ohio River town of Rome, Indiana – Population 36 –

**Former Governor
Edgar D. Whitcomb**

where he enjoys a quiet life outside the limelight and far away from the tall buildings and boardrooms that define many former governors. His is a story about a thirst for excitement and world exploration; a tale of danger and adventure that both begins and ends in the hills of southern Indiana.

Ed retired from a very active political career as State Senator, Indiana's Secretary of State and as Indiana's 43rd Governor to write books about his military experiences in the Pacific during WW II. His works are *Escape from Corregidor, On Celestial Wings* and his latest autobiography *A Solo Sailing Odyssey: The Closest Point to Heaven.*